The Crimson Beret

Who Else but Us?

Revelations by a Special Forces Officer

By Gennadii Ternovskii

Strategic Book Publishing and Rights Co.

Strategic Book Publishing and Rights Co., LLC
USA | Singapore
www.sbpra.com

For information about special discounts for bulk purchases, please contact Strategic Book Publishing and Rights Co., LLC Special Sales, at bookorder@sbpra.net.

ISBN: 978-1-62857-526-2

Author's Note

The Crimson Beret is about the 6th SWAT detachment, otherwise known as Vityaz, of the Internal Troops of Russia's Ministry of Internal Affairs. It is Vityaz where the Internal Troops' Special Forces proper originated, and it is Vityaz that gave birth to the legendary crimson berets.

This story featuring Russia's Special Forces is close to life, as it is based on the recollections of Vityaz veterans and was written by one of them. This book is meant to destroy the stereotypes that popular films and books gave rise to.

It was in 2004 when the work was started, and it took eight years to finish. Since that time, we have studied numerous episodes from the twenty-five-year experience of the detachment, using both short dialogues and detailed stories that reflect the authentic spirit of Vityaz. We decided to unite those into one big plot, placing it within a certain time and giving it a certain artistic form. All the events described (dialogues, situations, battles) are true. Only their timing and actual participants are different.

The story mostly focuses on the daily routine and unique lifestyle of the detachment. Readers have an opportunity to watch its officers and soldiers develop special brotherly relations, experience the unique traditions never seen in any other army of the world, and witness the way their soldierly spirit and their commitment are nurtured, and how their unrivalled professionalism, admired by all their foreign colleagues, is achieved.

The second part comprises some of Vityaz's warfare experiences.

The final part of the story features the battle that took place on April 18, 1995, at the settlement of Bamut. There, fifty Vityaz soldiers, trying to help their fellows from Rosich SWAT detachment, faced a gang of several hundred well-trained daredevils, led by Basayev, the ill-famed international terrorist. The details of the battle are based on what the participants remembered of the events. There are abundant examples of outstanding courage and heroism.

There is numerous historical evidence (including statements by Russian and foreign specialists, various stories about competitions among SWAT detachments, and reports on special missions and other assignments) to support the facts contained here. From about 1985 till 1994, when the detachment was headed by Sergey Lysuik, a legendary SWAT soldier and Hero of Russia, Vityaz was considered the world's best SWAT detachment.

Currently (and this is an unbiased opinion), the Internal Troops' Special Forces comprise Russia's best-trained and most mission-capable units, thanks to Vityaz-inspired traditions.

This book features these traditions and how they were formed.

G.V. Ternovskii

CHAPTER 1

Moscow
July 1994

It was a beautiful summer day, but its beauty could neither hide nor suppress the anxiety and tension hanging in the air. Howling and rumbling, some APC[1] vehicles were rushing down the street, accompanied by the traffic police and clouds of black smoke. An ambulance followed them closely, its alarm sounding loud. Crouching, heavily armed SWAT soldiers were scurrying from building to building, while shooters were taking up positions, settling down to search for their targets through the optics.

The hectic scene was caused by terrorist bastards who had taken hostage some people on the third floor of one of the buildings. One of the terrorists, wearing a black mask and holding a machine gun, was dictating their conditions, his voice thick with aggression. Right in front of him, hands held high and eyes filled with terror, was a young man whom the terrorist was using as a human shield.

"I don't give a shit about anything of that!" the terrorist was shouting, hiding behind the hostage. "You'd better take care of it, or I'll shoot his brains out. How about that, huh?"

To seem more convincing, he put the gun to the hostage's head.

The square in front of the building was dominated by the figure of Lieutenant Colonel Nenashev, the commander of the 6th SWAT Detachment — Vityaz[2]. A megaphone in his hands, his voice quiet

1

and confident, he was trying to calm the terrorists down while negotiating.

"Just stay calm! We are doing our best," Nenashev tried to persuade the terrorists, playing for time. "We're preparing a plane right now. The bus is on the way. It's only the money that causes the delay as the sum is pretty big, and you can't but account for that."

Meantime, assault teams were quietly approaching the building from the other side. Each SWAT soldier was wearing an armour vest and a metal helmet, their faces hidden behind black masks. Three of them were carrying climbing equipment (that was the "spidermen group"). As they came close to the building, they started to climb up the fire escape ladder, one of them carrying a ZABOR device (a large metal shield) on his back. The man was climbing last to spare some space for the others. At the third floor level, the team split, the "spidermen" going higher up to the roof, while the ZABOR team entered the floor.

The hostage release mission was headed by the commander of the 3rd SWAT team, Lieutenant Yegor Menshikov[3]. The young officer's masculine face looked extremely tense; hostages' lives depended on how his soldiers would do their job.

He sounded calm and cold as he ordered around the assault teams and the shooters, revealing the real professional he was, who always knew all the whats and whens. One of the radio sets he held in his hands spoke up in the voice of a shooter, whose nickname was Lis.

"Nine zero three, it's Lis calling."

"Listening to you, Lis," Yegor answered.

Lis, looking through the SWD[4] optics, reported, "I can see the second terrorist through the side wall window. He's holding a hostage."

"Got you," Yegor answered and lowered his hand with the radio.

"I give you another half hour!" the terrorist cried out loud. "Then the first hostage is to fly down!"

Right then, the spidermen group, having secured their ropes, started going down. Two of the spidermen, carrying AK–74s[5], descended along the window line, coming to a halt between the fifth and the fourth floors, while the third spiderman, with an APS[6], his head upside down, climbed down to look over the edge of the window where the terrorist was standing, and now hovered at the height, controlling him.

One of the furthermost spiderman reported, "Number two ready."

In the meantime, an assault team entered the floor, approaching the room where the terrorists were hiding. They had a field engineer install blast charges at the door, while the soldiers, nestling close to each other, covered themselves with a ZABOR.

The soldier closest to the ZABOR reported, "Number one ready."

Done with the reports, Yegor connected to the shooter once again.

"Lis, it's nine zero three calling."

"Listening to you," the shooter responded.

"The second one at two," Yegor ordered. "Did you get me?"

"Got you. The second one at two."

Holding the second radio set close to his mouth, Yegor reported to the detachment's commander, "We are ready."

"Got you," Nenashev responded. "Go ahead," he concluded and went back to negotiating with the terrorist. "We've just been informed that the money problem is solved. So, as soon as the bus is here, you can just make your way to the airport."

Just then the bus came, accompanied by a traffic police vehicle.

Having psyched himself up, Yegor announced the launch of the hostage release mission, his voice filled with an inescapable power, which made each and every soldier wind up to the maximum, like a spring.

"Attention! Countdown started!" Inhaling, he mentally put a

cross over himself, and then exhaling, pronounced, "Five!"

And the spidermen clenched their arms.

"Four!"

And the shooter put his finger on the trigger.

"Three!"

And the assaulters near the door to the room came still closer to each other.

"Two!"

The shooter pressed the trigger lightly, his body flung a little back by the recoil.

"One!"

Near the buildings, light and noise charges exploded as the spidermen pushed themselves off the wall.

"Attack!"

And the spring went off!

A field engineer hit the blaster and the charge exploded. The door swung open to let the assault team in.

The spidermen landed on the windowsills, firing unceasingly at the terrorists to make them take cover.

The assaulters entered the room just a second later. The ZABOR soldier, acting like a crazy loco, attacked the one terrorist who remained alive, pressing him against the wall with his shield.

The spidermen, having pushed themselves off the windowsill, rushed down to the ground while the assault team escorted the terrorist and the hostage to the exit.

The spidermen were already firmly on the ground when the terrorist and hostage appeared at the building exit. Both were then pushed against the wall and searched, in case they happened to be accomplices. While the assaulters were busy with the search, the spidermen were managing the situation.

Then all the detainees were escorted into the bus, and, once all the SWAT soldiers got on it, the bus started off.

"Stop!" Nenashev commanded. "Yegor, line the team up."

This all was only practise at Vityaz training center.

Yegor, holding the radio set at his mouth, ordered, "Attention! Nine zero three; everyone, assemble!"

Getting off the bus, the soldiers began lining up in the square in front of Yegor. The shooter was also there.

"Hey, Lis!" Yegor called out to him.

"Here!" he made a swift turn toward the commander.

"Go find the target. You have thirty seconds."

Lis started off, heading for the building.

When he came back, holding the target in his hands, the 3rd SWAT team was already lined up by combat units.

"May I fall in, comrade lieutenant?" Lis asked the commander.

"Bring it here," the commander ordered.

Lis ran up to Yegor and showed him the terrorist–hostage situation target.

The bullet hole was right where the hostage was supposed to be!

Yegor, his face changing expression, turned his head toward Lis. His gaze was cold as ice. "There you go, brother; nice job!"

It was easy to tell by Lis's expression that he was completely aware of his result, being exactly the *opposite* of what his fans expected.

"Go join the line!" Yegor ordered harshly.

Lis turned on his heels and out of the boss's uncomfortable stare, while Yegor said to his back quietly, "A shit of a shooter," and, sighing, he turned to face the team. "Team, dress!"

Pausing to make sure the soldiers did as ordered, Yegor went on. "Ready, front! Dress middle!" and, saluting, he turned toward Nenashev, who was approaching the team.

"Comrade lieutenant colonel, the 3rd SWAT team is lined up and ready to sum up the training results. Commander of the team, Lieutenant Menshikov, reporting!"

"Stand easy," Nenashev commanded, turning to face the team.

"Stand easy!" Yegor repeated the command and put his hand down.

Nenashev, slowly pacing in front of the team, started the analysis. "On the whole, the hostage release mission was carried out in an orderly manner. Soldiers acted concisely and in coordination. However, let me mention some faults. Firstly," and he doubled his finger in, "team camouflage security as they were approaching the attacked object was rather weak. You failed to use the ground folds. Secondly," and another finger was doubled in, "the ZABOR team was causing too much noise on the floor," and, holding up his hand, he looked over the line of soldiers. "Field engineers, did any charges fail?"

"None!" the field engineer responded.

"Good," Nenashev said, content with the answer. "Shooter!" he called out to Lis. "What was your observation scope?"

"One terrorist in the right window, and another one at the side wall."

"Good. What were the results?"

On hearing the question, Yegor, who had been staring blankly at the space in front of him, shifted his gaze toward Lis and, sullen, responded, instead of the shooter, "Nothing you could call results."

"No target hit at all?" Nenashev specified.

"I wish," Yegor's answer came, still gloomier.

Nenashev looked at Yegor, and, having caught exactly what he meant to say, just nodded.

"Okay." After a short pause, he continued. "Well, have I ever told you that foreigners consider a special mission a success provided they lose not more than twenty-five percent of the hostages? However, our main task is to have *all* hostages alive; otherwise a mission can be called a failure." He paused again to look at the soldiers. "Thus, as you have it, my dear brothers, your grade is bad." He made a helpless gesture. "You are like my children, you know, but as they say, the truth is more important than relations."

Then Lis heard Kirei appraise his shooting. "Sucker!"

Nenashev continued, speaking to Lis. "And you, brother, you

have to write twelve letters to the 'deceased' hostages' parents. Each should take up two sheets, at least. And then give it to the team's commander for checking."

"Aye!" Lis responded.

Nodding, the commander turned toward Yegor.

"That's it," he concluded. "Get ready, Yegor, to leave for the premises." Looking at the watch to set the time, he added, "One hour twenty will be enough, I think. So, by fourteen sharp, you must report your arrival. Now, give your orders!"

And then Nenashev got in his UAZ and left.

Looking over the team one more time, Yegor dropped a sigh, and, his nerves already settled, added, but without anger, "Well, thank you, Lis, once again." Sighing, he began to deliver orders. "Now, remove the straps and carry all the facilities into the bus. Be ready to leave in ten minutes. Go!"

The soldiers scattered, and Phil, passing Lis on his way, smacked him against the helmet, while Kirei, grabbing Lis by his hand, swung him around, and staring intensely into his eyes, made a harsh enquiry. "Hey, you, brother! Forget how to use the gun?"

Lis was so ashamed he wished the ground would open under him.

In ten minutes, the 3rd SWAT team was all set, armed (everyone wearing an armour vest, a helmet, a discharge vest, and carrying a machine gun), and ready to leave.

"Are all ready to march?" Yegor asked. "Anyone injured?"

Everyone was silent, looking quietly at the commander. Even if anyone were injured, they would prefer to keep it to themselves, thinking, *It's not really worth talking. You can walk, which means you can run. Anyway, that's how this job is.*

"Good," Yegor summed up. "To the right! Double time; march!"

And the soldiers set off marching. It felt so usual, no strain or effort, as they ran farther and farther away.

Notwithstanding all the mistakes, the soldiers were perfectly fit and ready for any mission, though no one expected an opportunity to test their abilities to occur so soon.

Vityaz training center was situated in Novaya village. As a rule, the detachment used it two to three times a week for field firing, the FAC[7] tests, and altitude and special tactics training (releasing hostages in various situations).

The permanent location at the premises of the STD[8], which also comprised Vityaz SWAT Detachment, was twelve kilometres away from the "villie" (this is how SWAT soldiers called the training center among themselves), across country. Usually they simply used their feet to get to the "villie" and back, marching there fully armed. They would leave the division's premises early in the morning and be back by afternoon, except when the detachment was on duty. Then they used APCs.

Half an hour after the 3rd SWAT team set off, machine-gunner Sieden, his nickname Sieda, lagged somewhat behind.

"Hey, Sieda!" Yegor called out to him. "What's your problem?"

"Difficult to keep up, comrade lieutenant," Sieda answered, catching his breath, "because of the machine gun."

He fidgeted to find a convenient position to hold the PK[9].

"Should I carry it for you then?" Yegor enquired.

"Negative!" Sieda responded at once.

"I'll count to three, and by then, you should be right where the rest of the team is!" Yegor commanded harshly. "One!"

And the machine-gunner speeded up, catching up with the team.

---

1. Armoured personnel carriers

2. Special Weapons Attack Detachment

3. Special Weapons Attack Team

4. Dragunov Sniper Rifle

5. Kalashnikov machine gun

6. Automatic Stechkin pistol

7. Firing and assault course

8. Separate Tactical Division of the Internal Troops of the RF Ministry of Internal Affairs; the famous Dzerzhinskiy Division

9. Kalashnikov machine gun

CHAPTER 2

The UAZ stopped in the central alley, beside the detachment's headquarters, and Nenashev got off the vehicle. "So, Sanya, you go fill the tanks, then have your dinner, and, at a quarter to three, wait for me here," Nenashev ordered.

"Yes, comrade lieutenant colonel!"

"Go!" Nenashev said, shutting the door.

The vehicle started off, while Nenashev headed for the headquarters. A soldier appeared at the entrance and was now approaching him. As the soldier came closer, he put his hand to the headgear, saluting.

"Wait a minute!" Nenashev stopped him.

The soldier stopped and turned toward Nenashev.

"Going somewhere?" The detachment's commander had the right to ask such questions.

"Have to do some shopping, comrade lieutenant colonel," responded the soldier impassively. "The political deputy sent me to buy some copybooks."

"How much time do you have?"

"Well," the soldier shrugged his shoulders. "He just said to buy the stuff."

"Okay," resumed Nenashev, and per his usual habit, fished a stopwatch out of his pocket. "You've got fifteen minutes."

And then he started the stopwatch.

"And what about the queue?" the soldier said, bargaining for some extra time.

"Ten," Nenashev cut him short, and the soldier sprinted off and disappeared round the corner.

Nenashev grinned, entering the headquarters.

The soldier gunned into the shop, crying out loud, "Step aside, everyone!" and with no further delay, he made a pass toward the counter.

Everyone turned around to see who was shouting and then moved to the sides to let the soldier to the counter. A moment later, the soldier was putting money on the counter.

"Five copybooks!" he cried out.

The saleswoman, affected by the mood of the crowd, rushed to grab the copybooks and then, in a hurry, handed them over to the soldier, who, snatching them, dashed out of the shop.

Hardly had the detachment's duty attendant reported and Nenashev had a wash when he heard someone knocking on the door. The door to the study room opened, and there came in a soldier, desperately trying to catch his breath, some copybooks in his hands.

"Comrade lieutenant colonel, may I come in?" the soldier asked, panting and saluted.

A quick glance at the soldier, and then Nenashev took his stopwatch from the table. The soldier, still panting, reported, "Comrade lieutenant colonel, your order is fulfilled!"

Having reported, the soldier lowered his hand, waiting for Nenashev to respond. Nenashev stopped the stopwatch, recording the resulting time.

"Good job, brother," he complimented the soldier. "Right on time," and glancing at the soldier, he presented him another "gift." "So now go find the political deputy. I'm waiting for him to call me in a minute." The commander's voice was low and quiet as he started the stopwatch again.

The soldier turned into a "man-meteor" again and "flew" from the cabinet.

* * *

Whatever task was assigned to a Vityaz soldier, it had strict deadlines. The deadlines were minimal, taken that soldiers had to run to cope with the task. This is how the soldiers were taught to be always alert, both physically and psychologically. Besides, it was sort of physical training, too. War, as you know, has little patience for the slow ones.

So, it was usual for the detachment's officers to always carry a stopwatch. And despite the hardship, most guys enjoyed such tasks (well, why not?). Some soldiers were desperate enough to do some reckless things, which was obviously due to their "special" nature. They would enter the orderly room when there were no officers around and would snatch the unprotected device to damage it somehow. It was not difficult, as the mechanism was quite sensitive. A light tap on the table was enough to end the fun. One could see no exterior damage, but the thing was actually out of order. Remember that it was the time when cell phones (with integrated stopwatch functions) were basically science fiction. So the only way out then was to buy a new stopwatch—a luxury, given an officer's salary.

However, when retiring, soldiers usually presented their officers with stopwatches.

* * *

Wet and tired after the march, the 3rd SWAT team approached the headquarters.

"Stop!" Yegor commanded.

The team stopped, while Yegor took out his stopwatch.

"Give you another thirty seconds to climb upstairs," he ordered, adding the action command, "TA!"

Then he started the stopwatch, and the soldiers, one by one, sprinted out toward the barracks.

TA was a universal command, an original invention of Vityaz

soldiers. Short, brisk, and expressive, it was used as an action call, a battle cry, and a slogan. Also, one could say it was the calling card of the Internal Troops' Special Forces.

As soon as Yegor lost sight of the last soldier, he followed his team in.

Once they were all in, the soldiers lined up in front of the orderly post.

"Team three, ready, front!" the orderly cried out as soon as he saw Yegor running in.

"Stand easy!" Yegor commanded calmly, the orderly repeating the same in just a few seconds: "Stand easy!"

Yegor glanced at the stopwatch to take note of the time, looked over the team, and gave some more action orders. "So, now, let's hand over the weapons, clean up, and wash our hands. Fifteen minutes to line up. Sergeants, you are in charge."

Then he left the floor to report their arrival to Nenashev.

While the 3rd SWAT team was handing over its weapons to the AS[1], the orderly, leaning his elbow on the post, was having an enthusiastic conversation. So when Yegor got back, nobody paid attention to him. Yegor chose not to yell at the orderly; he just stood there quietly and watched them talk, thinking of what he was going to do when the man finally noticed him. It was Phil entering the AS who noticed Yegor first and called out to the orderly, "Hey, you, orderly!"

The orderly turned on his heels toward the exit and saw Yegor.

"Team three, ready, front!" he shouted.

Hardly had he managed to finish the order when he heard Yegor commanding calmly, "Rear!"

And the orderly was immediately falling forward.

It was Yegor's first revenge, to begin with the "Rear!" and "Front!" commands (short for "Flash from the rear!" and "Flash from the front!"). On hearing the commands, a soldier is supposed to fall either forward or backward. Another thing is that the commands are shouted faster than a person is able to fulfill them, so in just a few seconds, a soldier's brain stops working and he is driven only by natural instincts. Konstantin Sergeevich Stanislavskiy would be more than happy to watch how the "*Attention, Action, Subconscious*" scheme works. Such an exercise is surely a merit to his system.

It takes only ten to fifteen seconds for a person to come to his senses. Try doing the same for another ten minutes and you are sure to lose your breath, while your body will feel heavy as lead. This time, Yegor had only enough time for the first stage. So, as the orderly regained his consciousness after another rear fall, he announced the next sanction.

"Fifty," which meant that the soldier had to do fifty press-ups.

His hands in fists, the orderly started the workout.

"Lis, come here!" Yegor commanded.

"Lis!" Kirei shouted. "Lieutenant Menshikov wants to see you!"

In just a minute, Lis was there, his expression saying, "Here I am! Any orders, master?"

"Bring me the target," Yegor responded coldly, looking him in the eyes.

Lis was gone, while the orderly, his fists still on the floor, reported he was finished with the press-up workout. "Comrade lieutenant, your order's fulfilled, fifty press-ups done."

"Twenty more in honour of SWAT," Yegor said, his voice as calm as before.

So the soldier had nothing to do but to continue "pushing the ground." When Lis was back, Yegor, taking a pen, wrote on the target, "SHOT BY LIS," for everyone to know the hero of the day.

"Comrade lieutenant, twenty press-ups done," the orderly reported.

"Get up!" Yegor commanded.

The orderly, pink with exercise, got up, looking at Yegor.

"Waiting for me to make up your mug or something?" Yegor's question came as cold as ice. "The AS is open, and you are flapping your mouth here! What the hell is wrong with your eyes?"

"My bad, comrade lieutenant," the orderly whimpered.

"An armour vest and a mask, quick! You have ten seconds," Yegor announced and the orderly set off for the destination.

Three seconds later, he was back from the bay, his armour vest on and his mask halfway over his face. Finally, he made it to the post and froze up, panting, his eyes on Yegor, who was staring intently at the stopwatch.

"Eleven seconds," Yegor reported the results. "Another fifty."

Then, taking the target, he stepped aside while the orderly was back on the floor, sweating himself out. In fact, he thought the punishment for this kind of barney was not bad at all.

Meanwhile, Yegor went to the WC to place the target over a toilet bowl.

If a shooter happens to miss his target, he is put to shame and the target placed over a toilet bowl. And anyone who wishes to speak up can leave a message on the target. In case the shooter has his task completed properly, the target is put up at the headquarters' entrance.

Besides, should a shooter or any other SWAT soldier happen to have "mistaken" a hostage for a terrorist, he had to write twelve identical letters of condolence to the hostage's relatives, and once the commander had checked them, throw them all into the mail box, addressing them "to the relatives of the deceased hostages."

Why twelve, not ten or eleven? S. Lysiuk could not remember exactly. "I don't really remember. It just occurred to me out of the blue — twelve, like the twelve hours on the dial, the twelve disciples, and there was something else memorable with the twelve … ."

Having handed over the arms and brushed up, the 3rd SWAT team would line up at the orderly's post, waiting for Yegor, to proceed to the dining hall. Before going back, Yegor dropped in at the gym and grabbed a grip. As he approached the team, he almost threw it at Sieda.

"Carry this with you till your machine gun loses some weight! Got it?" Yegor was nearly growling.

Sieda, holding close his "new partner," was looking down, aware of his guilt.

"Yes, comrade," he responded humbly.

"Always!" Yegor specified, giving the soldier a level look. "Lining up, training, eating. Even sleeping! Got it?"

Holding his icy stare at the soldier for another few seconds, Yegor reminded Sieda why he was so lucky to have the new partner.

"Remember, soldier, weapons are not fiends, but friends!"

"Yes, comrade lieutenant."

Without looking at anyone, Yegor paced along the line, and, turning toward the soldiers, said, "Enjoy your meals."

The soldiers dropped a sigh of relief, almost all at once breathing out, "You, too, comrade lieutenant."

"Down!" Yegor commanded, and the soldiers sprinted off.

As the team was leaving the floor, a contract soldier, Oyama by nickname, emerged out of the orderly room of the 4th SWAT team, heading for the WC. Teams Three and Four were taking up one floor, just as Teams One and Two.

Already in the WC, opening a cabin, Oyama saw a target in the bowl.

"That's a wow!" Evidently, it was a pleasant surprise. "Well, well, well, look who's here. Lis! Good job, baby!"

Oyama unzipped his pants.

"No mercy for the suckers, right? Hey, you, orderly! Bring me a pen!"

Oyama was "marking" the target at the bottom when the free-shift orderly came back with a pen. Oyama zipped up his pants and took the pen to leave a message: "GOOD TACTICS! No hostage — no problem!"

After dinner, the team was scheduled to clean their weapons. The weapons were lying stripped on the chairs, right in front of the soldiers. The door squeaked and Yegor entered the team's orderly room.

"So, guys, attention!" he spoke up to get the soldiers' attention.

The soldiers put the cleaning aside, looking up at the commander.

"Get ready for checks on targets twelve and thirteen!" Yegor announced. "Sieda, tell us what those are."

"Field strip and post-strip assembly," responded the machine gunner confidently, his "new partner" beside him.

"Good," Yegor, satisfied with the answer, approached another soldier. "Phil!"

"Here!" Phil was all attention.

"Time terms?" Yegor asked. "Take AK, for example."

"Twenty seconds," Phil began his answer, "for field strip is excellent. Thirteen is good, seventeen is satisfactory. For assembly, it's twenty, twenty-three, and thirty seconds."

"Fine," Yegor nodded. "Everything is as usual. If someone's results are lower than 'good,' they are to work on their six-packs, and fifty press-ups to add. The best ones will be riding the worst ones — three laps. Any questions?"

He exchanged glances with the soldiers, their faces calm and composed. There was nothing new to it, as such checks were a regular practise.

"If no, then fine," Yegor said calmly. "Phil, you are the first."

Phil assembled the gun quickly and put it on the chair, waiting for the command.

"Ready?" Yegor asked.

"Yes, I am," Phil responded, looking at the gun.

"TA!" Yegor whiffed the command, pushing the stopwatch button.

It was the start of the traditional, routine check-up where soldiers' knowledge of weapons was tested. Each soldier had to strip and reassemble his gun. The AK–74 was a weapon of choice for riflemen; PK for machine gunners, and SWD for shooters. Yegor switched on and off the stopwatch, recording the time in a copybook. Soldiers' hands were twinkling at quite a speed, though some were definitely slower.

When the soldiers were done with the test, Yegor commanded the team to line up, and having looked at the records in the copybook, announced the results.

"So," he began. "Lisitsyn and Sieden, you have satisfactory."

Yegor put the copybook down, holding those "failures" within his sight.

"Fall out!"

Both soldiers, looking unhappy, took two steps forward.

"Take the attention position!" Yegor commanded.

The soldiers took the position as commanded while Yegor started punching them in the stomach. He seemed really serious about punching, though it's not like soldiers from SWAT teams had never had such punishment. The soldiers just kept their eyes on the commander, breathing out calmly after each punch and waiting for a change of order.

"Now, do the fifty," the order finally sounded.

Lisitsyn and Sieden took the leaning rest position and started the press-ups.

This exercise for "educational matters" was usual, not only for SWAT teams, but it was also widely used in absolutely all of the martial arts clubs to train the fighting spirit and strengthen the physique[2].

As the soldiers finished the press-ups, they reported, still in the leaning rest position, just as they were supposed to.

"Comrade lieutenant, Private Sieden's done with fifty press-ups as ordered."

"Comrade lieutenant, Private Lisitsyn's done with fifty press-ups as ordered."

"Get up!" Yegor commanded. "Fall in!"

The "failures" fell into the line and Yegor continued.

"The best result is by Kireev; the worst by Lisitsyn. Step out!"

The soldiers took two steps forward.

"Saddle up! Go!" The team's commander opened the show.

Kirei, laughing to himself, "saddled up" Lis and, spurring him on, the rest of the team giggling and hooting, rode three circles round the floor. As the task was done away with, the soldiers fell back into line.

"Fall in!" Yegor's voice resounded.

It took just a few moments for the soldiers to take their positions.

"Dress!" Yegor paused and, making sure everyone had done as ordered, commanded, "As you were!"

Gloomy, he looked over all of his soldiers. The results, no doubt, were disappointing, which he immediately communicated to the team. "Guys, I'm really pissed off. Pissed off." He paused so that the soldiers would feel his mood and then went on. "As my battalion's commander at the military school used to say, you can't do bad when your motherland is at stake." His eyes were full of expression as he looked at the line. "That's a first. And, secondly, as for the 'good' grades, you should know the only admissible grade for a SWAT soldier is 'excellent.' And that's how we work. That's a *must*, anyway."

He stared intently into the soldiers' eyes, trying to make out if they were really grasping the essence of what he was saying.

"The standards are just for regular infantry troops, while you are SWAT soldiers. This means you should be better than them."

He could tell that the soldiers were not left unaffected.

"Any questions?"

The soldiers were silent, thinking over the commander's words.

"If you have none, hand over the weapons and get ready for formation. That's it. Now, move."

Yegor headed for the orderly room, while the soldiers marched toward the AS.

---

1. *Arms storage*
2. *My karate coach at school practised the same thing.*

CHAPTER 3

Alexander Kiselev, the commander of an assault section from the 2nd SWAT team, commonly known as Kisel, was just leaving the SWAT Two orderly room.

"There was some fresher from the engineer battalion. Where is he now?" he asked the orderly.

"At the bay." He beckoned toward one of the SWAT Two bays.

Kisel nodded, heading for the bay.

Vityaz barracks were different from regular army barracks with common disposition. In Vityaz barracks, the entire space was divided into small rooms, called bays, where the contingent was allocated by section and platoon. SWAT teams were smaller than those of infantry squadrons, so one floor usually housed two or three teams, except for the Training SWAT Team (TST), which had the entire floor at its disposal.

As opposed to the motorized rifle forces, the Internal Troops' SWAT Detachment was divided, not into squadrons, but teams: SWAT and support teams (supply, technical, and combat). SWAT teams, in turn, were subdivided into SWAT platoons, while the platoons were subdivided into assault sections (assaulters) and combat support sections (comprising shooters, bombers, field engineers, and machine gunners). And the TST stood apart.

The SWAT Two bay, just like the bays of other teams, had a conventional military-style look. On both sides of the bay were bunk beds, armour vests hanging on backrests, bedside tables at the headboard, and chairs, with masks[1] on them, at the foot.

On the wall opposite the door were two posters drawn by some soldiers. The first poster had the SWAT slogan on it: WHO ELSE BUT US?

The second poster was right below the first one.

DO YOU DESERVE TO BE A CRIMSON BERET?

On one of the beds sat Talanych, a fresher who had been transferred from the engineer battalion not long before. Vityaz field
engineers were trained in an engineer battalion, and only those who
were, indeed, willing to join Vityaz could be transferred. Talanych
was one of them.

The door opened and Kisel entered the bay. It was Kisel's section
that Talanych was transferred to. On seeing Kisel at the door,
Talanych sprang to his feet. Slowly approaching Talanych, Kisel was
examining him quietly, almost affectionately, and finally asked him,
his voice also soft and affectionate, "How long have you been serving?"

"It's been five months," Talanych answered quietly.

"Suppose it's a habit with you, at the engineer battalion, that
once you've served for five months you can sit on beds just like
that?"

Kisel didn't sound aggressive. He was perfectly aware that the
soldier had been here, in the detachment's headquarters, for less
than an hour, so he hardly could make things out. Well, and as a
matter of fact, Kisel was a good guy, so he spoke to Talanych
patiently, as if he were a child. However, Talanych knew he had
done something wrong and was a bit nervous.

"Negative!" Talanych responded.

"So, you think it's all right to sit here, then?"

Talanych was silent for a moment, at a loss, but finally murmured: "Sure, my bad."

"So," Kisel went on. "For the first three days, we give freshers a
break. But, just in case, you should remember to watch yourself,
okay?"

"Yes, sure," Talanych replied.

Kisel nodded, as though to sum up this whole "bed" issue, and
enquired, "Ever done any sports?"

"Sure. A little boxing. Karate, too," the fresher responded with
confidence.

"Fine," Kisel nodded again. "Do you know what 'barley-brick' is?"

"Sure."

"Then go ahead," Kisel gave him the first task. "Work it!"

Kisel decided to check the "talents" of his new subordinate, right there and then. Taking up positions, they started the game. "Barley-brick" is an easy sparring. Punches are half-strong, by palm rather than by fist. Such games were used for training purposes.

In half a minute, Kisel stopped, content with the results.

"Well, you seem all right," and he continued with another question: "Any tactical training?"

Talanych, not sure whether he had ever had such training, muttered, "Well, you know—"

"Okay, then!" Kisel cut him short. "Put on the vest, the mask, and take your gun. Waiting for you in five minutes at the orderly post. Got it?"

"Aye!" Talanych responded.

"Go ahead," Kisel said, and Talanych sprinted off for the bay.

While Lebedev, another sergeant from the 2nd SWAT team, was giving weapons out, Talanych, his vest and helmet already on, was studying the posters on the AS walls. Each poster featured a safety rule illustrated by a drawing.

"Sign here," Lebedev told Talanych, and turned the weapons register toward him.

Talanych signed and Lebedev handed him over an AK-74 and a magazine. Taking the gun, Talanych examined it immediately, just as the first poster requested. Holding his finger at the trigger guard, he forced back the bolt carrier assembly and checked if there was a bullet in the breech piece.

SWAT detachments are rather limited in time when it comes to training. It's a common standard that soldiers must be able to carry out any mission in no more than half a year. So, training is always accelerated. Strain is really immense, starting from the first days.

RULE No. 1:
TAKING WEAPONS
DON'T FORGET TO
EXAMINE THEM!
BAD MEMORY —
50 PRESS-UPS!

RULE No. 2:
HOLD YOUR
FINGER AT THE
TRIGGER GUARD!
BAD MEMORY —
50 PRESS-UPS!

RULE No. 3:
NEVER POINT
YOUR GUN
AT PEOPLE!
BAD MEMORY —
50 PRESS-UPS!

RULE No. 4:
NEVER LEAVE
YOUR GUN
UNATTENDED!
BAD MEMORY —
50 PRESS-UPS!

Some people cannot handle the stress. This is where SWAT training resembles that of professional sportsmen. Both sportsmen and soldiers have to suffer some pain, spill some blood, and cry some tears to overcome the "can't do" barrier!

It's only that sportsmen have regular meals, masseuses, enough rest, and all the medical wonders at their disposal (sometimes, even banned ones).

SWAT soldiers, unlike their fellows from motorized rifle forces, are allowed daytime snaps — commander's achievement. He thought through their day schedule so that workouts could be more efficient. However, regular SWAT meals hardly ever included little more than meat, bread, butter, and the like. Meals were pretty much the same as in the rest of the army, whereas training was a hundred times more intensive.

And those were the things every fresher had to go through.

On the ground, in front of the headquarters, Kisel arranged some tactical training for Talanych. The training was about moving across the battlefield. Talanych, still in his vest and helmet, was panting heavily, his face red and covered with sweat. Add some foam at the mouth and he'd look like a blown horse. At least, it seemed he was about to faint. Kisel simply ignored all these symptoms and went on with the barbarian training by flogging the win-no-matter-what philosophy into the soldier's head.

"Get up!" the sergeant cried out over and over again. "Run over! Down! Roll over! Strip for action!"

Heavily panting, Talanych could hardly hold the gun in his hands. His helmet moved down, hindering his sight, but he was too tired to bother to move it back.

"Get up! Run over!" he heard another command.

Talanych struggled some, getting up, and made an attempt to run. It was nothing more than an attempt because his feet actually failed him.

"Move!" Kisel was unwavering. "One, two, three!" he continued, counting the soldier's steps. "Down! Roll over!"

Talanych was again down on the ground and rolled over, but not without difficulty.

"Strip for action!" Kisel didn't move a muscle to stop the torture. "Make the position more precise! Get up! Move, soldier! Run! ONE, TWO, THREE! DOWN! ROLL OVER!"

---

1. A mask here is a metal helmet.

CHAPTER 4

The 3rd SWAT team was up and fully armed on the detachment's training ground, waiting for Yegor to come. The grip Sieda had for his new partner was towering above the soldiers' heads. As soon as Yegor approached the soldier's line, a soldier commanded, "Team, ready, front!"

"Stand easy!" Yegor commanded in response, carefully examining the line to make sure everyone was present.

"Well, and where is Kirei?" asked Yegor when he didn't find the familiar face.

"He's gone to bring the radio sets, lieutenant." Lis was the first to respond.

Right then, Kirei ran out of the headquarters with some radio sets in his hands. The detachment's commander showed up at the door right after him.

"May I fall in, comrade lieutenant?" he asked Yegor.

"Just do it," Yegor answered informally.

Kirei immediately gave one radio set to Yegor, while the rest went to the soldiers.

"Team, dress!" Yegor commanded. "Ready, front! Dress middle!" and, saluting, turned toward the detachment's commander, who was approaching the line. "Comrade lieutenant colonel, SWAT Team Three ready to hear out your order. Team Three commander, Lieutenant Menshikov, reporting."

"Stand easy!" Nenashev commanded and, lowering his hand,

examined the line.

"Stand easy!" Yegor repeated the command, and the soldiers relaxed on one knee.

"And why is that soldier with a grip?" Nenashev beckoned toward Sieda.

"Teaching him to love his weapons." Yegor gave a concise answer.

"Oh, yeah," Nenashev said, sounding like he got it. "I get your point. Team, dress! Ready, front!" and, saluting, the detachment's commander announced his order. "Hear my order out! Take over the duty! Your mission is to be ten minute ready for action in Moscow and Moscow Region. Your commander on duty is Lieutenant Menshikov!"

"Aye!" Yegor's response was clear and concise.

"Duty till takeover! Stand easy!" The detachment's commander finished giving orders. "Give your orders, Yegor."

And Nenashev headed for the barracks while Yegor started verifying combat duty assignments of the on-duty unit, which was another traditional Vityaz rite.

"Who is to take out the ramps?"

Two of the soldiers put their fists up. The thing was that soldiers were not to simply put up their hand, but to make it a tight fist, like the Vityaz emblem.

"Ammunition boxes?" Yegor continued the verification.

A few more people put their fists up, confirming they were ready for service.

All the actions were scheduled, assigned to soldiers, and verified. That way, once the assemble order was given, all the actions could be carried out smoothly, without ruffle, and the soldiers would be armed, vested, equipped, and ready for any (any at all!) battle mission in some ten minutes.

Teams were divided into separate battle groups. An assault team, for instance, would include seizure and cover groups as well as isolation and reserve ones. Also, the commander had to make sure all the soldiers understood their battle group assignments and sequence of action.

"Fine," Yegor summed up. "Now, the schedule is as usual. You are to hand over the weapons and, before dinner, we have a hand-to-hand workout." Then, fishing out his stopwatch, Yegor gave his usual order. "See you upstairs in thirty seconds. TA!"

Yegor started the stopwatch and the team, their munitions with them, sprinted off to the barracks.

CHAPTER 5

"Team, lights out!" the orderly announced, and the lights in all the bays went out.

Only duty lights were left on. All the soldiers from the 2nd SWAT team were in their beds, preparing to get their portion of sweet dreams. There was a squeak, the door opened, and in came Dima Shevchenko (everyone knew him as Chef), the SWAT Two master sergeant. He was naked from the waist up, a towel hanging down from his shoulder and his toiletries in his hands. Chef came up to the bedside table, put his toiletries inside, and, wiping his hands, glanced at Kuznetsov, a fresher. Kuznetsov's bed was right beside his.

"Hey, Kuzya!" he called out harshly.

"Here, comrade sergeant!" Kuznetsov responded in a second.

"You've had a wash?" The sergeant continued in the same harsh manner.

"Yes, I have." Kuzya seemed to mean it.

Shevchenko hung the towel over the bed arch and, taking his pants off, lay down. Stretching pleasantly, he put his arm under his head and called out to Kuznetsov again.

"Kuzya!"

"Here, comrade sergeant!" Kuzya's response was just as quick.

"Go ahead, Kolyan," Chef commanded, giving a stretch across the bed. "Tell me about your first fuck."

"But, comrade sergeant–" Kuzya was evidently embarrassed.

31

"Come on, Kolyan," Chef cut him short. "Don't be a sissy. We are a family here, you know. Just go ahead."

Kuzya sighed and started his tale. "Well, I had this one school-mate of mine, Natashka Morozova."

The bay was suddenly all silent — not a squeak could be heard. Everyone was looking forward to the fairy tale.

"Once there was this disco at the club," Kuzya continued. "So, I was there, and the guys from my class. Well, we had a drink, you know, as usual, then a smoke. And then the girls from our class came, Natashka, too, with them."

This exciting Scheherazade's tale by Kuzya continued for some twenty minutes before he got to the essence.

"So, we are sitting on a sofa, and she's showing me some photos of hers," the soldier went on from his bed. "Well, I'm getting closer, putting my hand round her shoulder. Now I can tell she is all for it." The pauses got longer, while the voice got lower and lower. "Well, so I pull her closer," then again a pause. "I'm kissing her on the neck." Another pause. "Well, she," one more pause, "puts the album aside." Another pause. "And turns around."

There was dead silence. Everyone was waiting for the climax, but it seemed the continuation was not coming. Chef's face was intent, his brain focused on the film going on in his head. As images went bleaker, he was soon fully conscious again, his eyes up.

"Hey, cut that out," Chef called out. "Are you sleeping or something?" and he gave the soldier a kick. "Kuzya!"

A kick and a harsh hollo and Kuzya was up. He jumped off the bed and started putting on clothes. Chef and the other soldiers were watching him, dumbstruck.

"Kolyan!" Chef called out.

Kuzya stopped and turned to face Chef. "Here, comrade sergeant!"

"Going somewhere?"

The soldier, looking blank, shifted his gaze onto the clothes he was holding. "Well. yeah …" he said absently. "It's just—"

"So, just go back to where you started." Chef wasn't in the mood for long explanations.

So the soldier took off his clothes and folded them neatly. A minute later, he was back in his bed, and the bay was silent again.

"Kuzya!" Chef's patience was running out.

"Here, comrade sergeant," Kuzya responded.

"So! What was the end of the story?"

"What story, comrade sergeant?" Kuzya was obviously at a loss.

"Are you kidding me?" Chef started to lose his temper as the conversation was getting really stupid. "The story with your Natashka, I mean!"

"Oh, yeah …" At last, the soldier recovered his senses. "Well, you know, comrade sergeant, that was about it, 'cause her parents came back home and I had to leave."

The bay was dead silent for a moment, and then Kot started laughing quietly.

"Well, you had to at least reach her panties?" Shevchenko couldn't believe that was it for the story.

"No, comrade sergeant. I hadn't."

Having turned it over in his mind, Chef turned toward the laughing Kot.

"Hey, Kot, what the hell was that?" he complained. "He has been selling us some bullshit for some thirty minutes, and it turned out that he wasn't anywhere close to her ass!" He once again asked the soldiers, "Kolyan, you were just making fun of us, or what?"

"No, comrade, no!" Kuzya assured him. "It's just—"

"Go to sleep!" Chef almost growled at the soldier.

"Yes, comrade!" Kuzya responded, and his head was down on the pillow in a second.

Shaking his head in disappointment, Chef commanded in a calmer voice, "Lights out, everyone!"

Then he stood up, took his pants off, and got under the blanket.

Meantime, Artur and Yegor were sitting in the duty attendant's room playing backgammon and sipping tea from military-style iron cups. That day, as Artur was the detachment's duty attendant and Yegor commanded the on-duty unit, the friends amused themselves with dice.

Yegor shook the dice in his hands and nodded, concluding, "Well, something like this."

"Damn it!" Artur sighed, though without any bitterness, stretching his entire body out and, having glanced at his watch, picked up the phone.

"Team Two, assemble, fully armed. Line up on the ground." Hanging up the receiver, he took the stopwatch from the table and started it. "And you, do your moves," he told Yegor, leaving the room.

Hanging up, the orderly repeated Artur's order, "Team Two, assemble! Fully armed! Line up on the ground!"

And the soldiers were up in no time.

"Team Two, Assemble!" Chef's order followed immediately.

The soldiers were putting on their armour, discharge vests, masks, and backpacks while running out of the bays. Dropping in at the AS, they rushed down to the ground where Artur was waiting, with weapons, magazines, and breathers in their hands.

A few minutes later, the 2nd SWAT team was lined up on the ground in front of Artur, fully armed. Artur glanced at his stopwatch and announced, his voice sounding metallic, "Guys! I have asked you to come here as I have two unpleasant announcements to make. First, I lost the game to Lieutenant Menshikov. And, secondly," he paused to look at the line and raised his hand, the stopwatch up, "this result of yours, people ..." his tone made the phrase sound like a sentence. Then Artur put down his hand, staring intently at the soldiers. "Lights out, team!"

The soldiers sprinted out back to the headquarters. The munitions handed over, the soldiers went back to sleep.

Artur returned to Yegor.

"So, how are things?" Yegor asked.

"Don't ask," Artur sounded dissatisfied. "Got to do some extra training."

Artur was evidently upset about the team's results. He took his place on the chair, picking up the dice. "Let's do it," he said, and threw the dice and shifted the chips.

Twenty minutes later, Artur used up his last chips.

"Well, that's better." He was content with the game and, rubbing his hands, picked up the receiver once again. "Team Two, assemble!"

And the training went on till midnight. Once another game was over, Artur would wake the team up to train the assembly signal actions. The soldiers would get up, drop in at the AS, and then rush to the training ground where Artur would be waiting for them, the stopwatch being the usual accessory in his hands. Then Artur would announce the time, and the team would return to bed to be woken up another twenty to thirty minutes later by the orderly, shouting, "Team Two, assemble!"

And another round would start. Artur would check the time and give the "Lights out!" order. However, thirty minutes later, the team would be up again.

"Team Two, assemble!"

Some might think the officer was just goofing on his subordinates. But it was nothing like that. Every Vityaz officer was after *maximum*, rather than required, professionalism and operational readiness of the unit under his command. Consequently, all the training had this purpose. It had to go on till the team (or a certain soldier) was up to its commander's standards!

It was about the eighth round when Artur, holding his hand up, told his soldiers, "Look here, guys!" he started his speech. "Your result has improved by forty-seven seconds compared to your first round. What does it mean? Right! You need to practise more! That's it for now; lights out!" He was about to turn around and go back to the headquarters, but something caught his eye. "Stop!" he said harshly, and the soldiers turned around. Artur examined the soldiers carefully, evidently looking for someone. "And where is Kot?"

At that time, Kot was quietly sleeping in his cosy bed, having concluded that his absence would not be noticed. Some minutes later, Lebed and Kisel were carrying the bed as fast as it was possible, Kot in it, down the stairs.

"Guys," Kot begged them, "let me get up, will you?"

"Face down, you bitch!" Lebed didn't care to be polite, and the sergeants, having accomplished the complicated maneuver between the floors, moved on down.

Artur, already content with the training results, returned to the duty attendant's room.

"So, one more, you think?" He offered Yegor another game.

"No, I'm good," Yegor shook his head. "I'd better do something useful." It was Yegor's turn now to pick up the phone and announce: "Team on duty, assemble!"

And then he started his stopwatch.

A few minutes later, as the team lined up upon the assemble signal, Yegor was checking weapons and munitions. When the check was over, he gave the soldiers some time to rest and communicated the operational situation and the field mission.

"Attention, team!" he started in a serious tone. "A group of terrorists entered the division's premises and seized CP[1] One. Our group was given an order to eliminate the terrorists. The team is to be delivered to the special operation area by helicopter. The airlift delivery complete, we are to march up to the assault area, conduct reconnaissance, and make an assault. After the assault, we are to leave for the evacuation area. Any questions?"

Rarely did SWAT soldiers have questions, so Yegor gave his action order. "To the right! Up to the roof, double time! Sieda, Leave the grip here!"

And the team headed for the detachment's headquarters, running.

"Helicopters?" Phil turned toward Kirei, puzzled.

Kirei had no answer, so he just shrugged his shoulders.

A few minutes later, the 3rd SWAT team was lined up along the edge of the roof, at the side wall of the building. Two ropes were secured and the harness ready.

"Put on your harness!" commanded Yegor. "Get ready for insertion!"

The soldiers started putting on the harness, now perfectly clear on the "helicopter delivery."

"Afterward, don't forget to put the harness back into the rucksacks!" Yegor specified.

Of course, to get a real helicopter for training was next to impossible, so the officers had to use their imagination to make the settings close to real. Naturally, watching films about American SWAT teams, Russians were jealous of how foreign counterparts got whatever they wanted, from simple mechanisms to submarines and airships.

I get a lot of questions like that. "How come I quit the SWAT and went in for creative?"

And that's what I always answer. "I think SWAT is all about being creative!" And I really mean it, you know.

According to Wikipedia, creation is an activity generating something entirely new, which has never existed before.

Regarding SWAT detachments, innovation is an integral element to their life, as they develop new approaches and methods, training and education, new weapons, tactical schemes, and so on. Creativity is connected with imagination. And the above example, which is far from an exception, is a good illustration.

SWAT detachments are in constant search for new opportunities to make themselves more powerful and more efficient. They are always trying to invent new training tricks.

For example, to train bus entry, we had a bunk bed installed in the passage. Then we had a ramp secured in between the arches of the second level. In this way, the assaulters "penetrated" into the bus.

Sometimes, a relay race course was built in the passage. It included a variety of elements: heaving exercises, acrobatics, obstacles of various kinds, shooting, and some elements of hand-to-hand fighting. We made up new shooting sets: shooting in motion, from behind obstacles, and so on.

Vityaz originated many practises now used by the entire armed forces.

The cover of this book depicts Vityaz's flag, a crimson bolt of lightning striking across a black and white background. The Vityaz emblem is also there. Its symbolism can be interpreted like this: black and white, good and evil, terror and peace. And Vityaz is in the center of it all, protecting peace and all the virtues of the world.

This kind of metaphor can be invented only by a creative person with a powerful imagination.

As the Russian Officer's Code of Honour has it, "To be creative, independent both in actions and thoughts, noble in deeds and aspirations … to act reasonably, instead of following the military charter like a blind kitten sticks to a wall … to constantly train one's mind, expanding cultural horizons; to know how to recognize and develop abilities of subordinates."

Having put on their harnesses, the soldiers divided into two groups, getting ready for the insertion.

"Attention!" Yegor announced. "Helicopters are hovering! Ropes down!"

And two soldiers, closest to the edge, threw the ropes down.

"Team, go ahead!" ordered the team's commander.

And the soldiers started jumping down from the "helicopter" in pairs.

Once landed, the soldiers scattered, running toward their

assigned sectors. Down on one knee, tubes up, the soldiers were getting ready to monitor the location and covered their fellows. Yegor was the last to go down. Also on his knee, he examined the team and felt content. He felt proud of his guys. They were all following the right tactical schemes; no one was goofing off. No one thought it was a game; they took it in earnest!

This is a distinguishing characteristic of SWAT detachments. They took regular training routine just as earnestly as if it were a real mission, doing one hundred percent. When at the military school, we had a joint exercise with a SWAT detachment. And I remember being surprised at how they *all* (soldiers and officers alike) were showing remarkable commitment. None of us took it seriously, thinking *I wish it were over.* We were trying to find a place to hide out — something warm and cosy. We were talking loud, singing, etc. However, the SWAT soldiers had other things on their minds. They were determined to find their way into our camp and mark the machines as destroyed. To do this, they had to cross a small river (really a shallow stream). So as not to get caught, they crossed it crawling, their bellies close to the ground (just imagine — a night in early spring in Siberia). All night long, they were working on their assignments *in earnest*, as if it were an actual mission. It's only when we got to serve in Vityaz detachment and grew into the spirit of it that I came to understand *why.* Though it's rather difficult to explain, it's something you feel coursing through your blood, something imprinted in your subconscious. So, now I can answer my *why* question from school times in this way: "*Are there any other options?*"

Once we had a practise where Vityaz soldiers had to divide into groups of two or three and enter an isolated area. One group stopped a tractor that was carrying manure, and they buried themselves in it! At the CP, no one ever imagined that they would be hiding in the pile of shit. Indeed, where have you seen a person who would have a shit bath just for the sake of training? No one is that crazy, except for the SWAT guys.

Perhaps, that's why they are the *best!*

"Phil, Miron; patrol!" Yegor appointed the march security. "Team, move!"

The team set off, changing their order while marching. The patrol was running somewhat ahead, providing for team security.

The soldiers were moving, making almost no noise, sliding across the ground like shadows. Suddenly, Phil and Miron, some fifty metres ahead of the team, made a wide turn, throwing themselves down to the side of the road. In just a second, the whole team was down on the ground. The soldiers scattered away from the road, hiding to get ready for a fight.

The manoeuvring was due to a patrol of one of the regiments moving along the road to take over the duty. However, while SWAT detachments were practising, any person was considered a threat. It would be a mission failure should someone see the team.

The patrol passed them, unaware of what was going on. So as the patrol took a turn, the soldiers were up, arranged in the same marching order, and moved on along the route. Undiscovered, the team successfully reached the assignment area and, surrounding CP1, started monitoring it.

SWAT training is twenty-four hours, as night practise is an integral part of their special routine. It was not every night, of course, but the practise was regular, so to say, extra to the daytime routine. A Vityaz soldier has actually little time for himself to brush up his looks, just about half an hour in the morning and half an hour in the evening. The rest of the day is hard work!

In fact, Vityaz soldiers had their practise while sleeping, too, in both the literal and the figurative sense. Their minds never stopped processing the situation, a side effect of continuous training. When you are practising something till you go crazy, as soon as you close your eyes, the picture is there; you are hanging in between the floors, bursting into a room with an assault team, hitting someone, etc.

Vityaz soldiers never spare themselves, always walking on the edge of their limits.

Once, at a demonstration training, Vityaz was given an assignment to release hostages from a vehicle, that is, to assault a bus. It was planned that while the assault teams were approaching the bus, field engineers would blow up the radio transmission lines, thus smashing the windows. So, just as the chief officer commanded, both assault teams rushed toward the bus. In a moment, they all were at the bus, and the field engineers pushed their buttons. However, something was wrong with the signal (as it turned out, the supply batteries were discharged), and there was no blast to smash the windows, which remained as they were.

The assaulters wavered not a second. They drove the ramps to the windows, smashed them out with their bodies by simply hurling into the passenger compartment—and that's it; the mission was complete.

* * *

Yegor put the binoculars up to his eyes again to check the CP. There was no movement to be seen. Just then, Phil and Kirei emerged noiselessly from the darkness.

"Two people at the control barrier," Kirei said. "The one on the left is sleeping."

"There are three inside," Phil said, reporting his observations. "Two of them are sleeping, and the third one is reading."

Yegor nodded, thinking through an assault plan, and then proceeded to give assignments. "Kirei," he pointed at the sergeant. "You and your group are to seize the room."

Kirei nodded, wordlessly.

"Dima," now his finger was pointing at Phil. "You and Pasha are to deal with the left control barrier."

"Aye!" Phil nodded in response.

"Serega, Sanya," and the team's commander looked at Mironov and Chistyakov. "You go to the right one."

"Got you," the soldiers replied in unison.

"You are to get them all inside the room," Yegor continued. "Start upon radio signal. Once you are at the starting positions, report you are ready."

The soldiers nodded, confirming they understood the assignments.

"Shooter, machine gunners," Yegor gave his instructions to the support group. "You're covering the assault group. Any questions?"

All the soldiers were silent as they were completely clear on the assignments. So, Yegor, watching their reaction, continued. "Leave the iron masks here. Put on the black ones."

The soldiers immediately took off their masks (helmets) and put on the black cloth ones.

"And try to do without bone breaking and concussions," Yegor concluded. "Are we clear on that?"

"Aye!" The soldiers were unanimous.

"Everyone, move!" Yegor commanded, and the assaulters disappeared in the darkness.

Only shooter Lis and machine gunner Sieda stayed behind.

The soldiers approached the CP without making a noise and took their starting positions. One of the guards in the booth at the control barrier was sleeping, his head against the wall. The second one was fighting sleep, almost unconscious, hardly noticing anything around him.

Yegor's observation point was some twenty metres away from the CP room. In just a couple of seconds, he heard Kirei's voice on the radio station: "Kirei is ready."

"Miron is ready."

"Phil is ready."

Yegor sized up the situation and put the radio set up to his lips. "Assault!"

The next moment, the soldiers were off and heading for the CP. One of the groups ran into the room. The other two rushed toward the "terrorists" at the control barriers. And before the "terrorists" could even wake up they were already off their feet and lying on the floor, tied up. Losing no time, the soldiers picked them up and dragged them into the room.

When Yegor entered the room, all the duty shift soldiers were tied up, their mouths stuffed.

"Retreat," Yegor commanded as he saw the soldiers were done with the assignment.

The soldiers, covering each other in pairs, left the room noiselessly and, unnoticed, headed for the assembly point.

The entire operation, from the assemble signal to the retreat, lasted only about a minute.

---

1. CP: checkpoint

Chapter 6

At the morning formation, as all the team commanders were brought before the detachment's commander, the first question was, of course, "Who seized the CP last night?" Nenashev's voice promised no treats.

"Me," Yegor confessed.

Nenashev walked up to Yegor slowly and put his hand on his shoulder. Yegor immediately tightened, waiting for an "educational kick." However, Nenashev, leaning toward Yegor, only whispered softly in his ear, "See you after the formation."

"Aye!" Yegor responded, breathing out, and relaxed.

"Fall in!" Nenashev commanded.

The commanders then returned to their teams.

"Private Drozdov!" Nenashev called out.

"Here!"

"Come here!"

"Yes, comrade lieutenant colonel!" Drozdov reacted and, running out of the line, approached Nenashev.

"Comrade lieutenant colonel, Private Drozdov is here as ordered!"

Nenashev showed the soldier to the spot beside him, while taking from one of the staff officers a sheet of paper, which had the following written on it: "Dear Zinaida Alexandrovna," Nenashev started reading the letter. "I am the commander of Vityaz SWAT Team Six, where your son, Private Nikolay Drozdov, is serving, writing to inform you that your son, Private Nikolay Drozdov, is an exemplary soldier. The commanding officers think he is doing really great, but … You know, he has a strange habit. He likes to hit his head on hard objects: bottles, bricks, boards. The commanding officers are, of course, against it, but he is really stubborn about this habit of his. Officers yell at him all the time, but he would hit things on his head anyway."

Drozdov, as it was obvious from the colour of his face, was now beginning to understand what his mother would think of it.

"We are all worried about Nikolay's health," Nenashev went on, "as the head would be the head, no matter what; a major part of the body, so to say. So, I'm asking you for help. Maybe, you could speak to him about that? Respectfully yours, Lieutenant Colonel Nenashev."

Nenashev finished the letter, folding it.

"Lieutenant Colonel Kriuchkov," he called out to the detachment's political deputy. "Check his records for the address and who sent the letter."

"Aye!" the political deputy answered, taking the letter from Nenashev.

"Fall in!" he ordered, and Drozdov joined the other soldiers.

"I have to remind you all, one more time," the detachment's commander began, "you are SWAT soldiers and you need your head to do some thinking. Leave all these bottle tricks to the pretentious show-offs."

No matter how Yegor wanted it, he still couldn't escape the punishment. Grabbing Yegor by the neck, Nenashev threw some knee kicks. And once the commander thought that was it for the punishment, he sat down at the table[1].

"I have talked to you about that, haven't I?" Nenashev began seriously. "Hardly had I stepped into the headquarters when the division's commander was there on the phone, complaining."

"No one knows we were the ones who did it," Yegor retorted.

"And who else could it be, Yegor?" Nenashev made an inviting gesture as though asking him to bring on his version.

"Well, anyone; say, the regimental SWAT teams or the intelligence."[2]

Nenashev heaved a sigh.

"You know, I've told him the same. However, he somehow doubted my explanations." Uttering another sigh, he turned around to face the window. There was a pause.

"Anyway, Alexander Ivanovich, we had no breaks." Yegor tried to justify his actions. "Well, maybe some bruises. In fact, it might serve them as a warning to be alert while on duty. They'd know better than to sleep at their posts, I think. And what if those were real terrorists?"

"That's it, Yegor!" Nenashev cut him short. "That's my last warning!"

"May I go?" Yegor looked unhappy.

"Yes," Nenashev responded, still avoiding looking at him.

Yegor turned around and headed for the door.

"Hey, Yegor!" Nenashev stopped him.

Yegor turned around. "I'm listening, comrade lieutenant colonel."

Nenashev, still looking through the window, made a short comment. "You are masters, guys," and, turning around to face Yegor, added, "Well done!"

A smile touched Yegor's lips, and he responded in the same quiet, composed manner, "To the honour of the motherland and the SWAT detachment."

For some seconds, they stared into each other's eyes.

"That's it," Nenashev stopped the conversation. "Go!"

As Yegor went out, Nenashev picked up the receiver to report to the division's commander on the investigation.

"Lieutenant Colonel Nenashev speaking!" he introduced himself, taking the lead. "I have talked to everyone. I doubt they would keep it secret, especially from me. Yes, I understand. Yes, sure!"

Hanging up the receiver, he sighed, a smile on his lips.

Of course, the detachment's commander punished for such "practise" (or whatever mistakes his soldiers made) without sparing anyone, soldiers and officers alike. And, of course, his punishments were just as severe as those a father would choose for his naughty sons. However, *never* did he let someone hurt his guys.[3]

There was a knock on the door.

"Come in," Nenashev said, inviting the visitor in.

The door opened, and he saw Drozdov standing behind it.

"Comrade lieutenant colonel, may I come in?"

"Go ahead."

"Comrade lieutenant colonel," Drozdov started at the threshold. "I beg you not to send this letter to my mother, please. I'll never do a stupid thing like this, never again, I promise."

For some seconds, Nenashev kept his eyes on the soldier. "Well, brother, let's do it this way. I'll keep this letter on my table. So, if you ever dare to do something like this, I'll …" and Nenashev beckoned toward the letter. "You got my idea, right?"

"Yes, lieutenant colonel," the soldier hurried to reply.

"Fine," Nenashev concluded. "Go join the team."

The soldier saluted and went out.[4]

There have been quite a number of documentary films, about the Special Forces, in general, and the Vityaz detachment, in particular. In those films, SWAT soldiers easily perform even the most difficult Jackie Chan-style stunts, crushing bricks to dust, running multikilometre marches as if they were just leisurely walks, crossing water obstacles, crawling across swamps, shooting targets from any position and with any weapon, and so on. Naturally, having seen some fifteen minutes of such a film, where everything seems so easy, glamorous, and romantic, an ordinary man from the street would never think of how much effort it takes to achieve this. In fact, it requires a hellish routine, which brings mostly pain, sweat, and blood rather than pleasure. I doubt one can find any pleasure in running oneself to death, bathing in icy water, sleeping amidst the forest under the rain and puking with bile because of extreme physical exertion.

So why on earth would anyone want to have such a job?

There is something inside these soldiers, which they can't ignore and which makes them go for it. This something is what people would call "Special Forces spirit." And then there is also this feeling of contentment once you come to realize you've made it; you've overcome all your fears, laziness, weaknesses, rising to a whole new level to become the warrior of warriors, your power and your courage dazzling and inspiring.

During the hostage release mission at Sukhumi infirmary, one of the assault teams, comprising Vityaz and Alpha soldiers, was to enter the building. As they were sneaking toward the infirmary entrance, a guard dog, an Ovtcharka, suddenly appeared from around the corner. The soldiers froze up, as they expected the dog would attack them or, at least, start barking, giving the team away. But then a Vityaz soldier fell out, approaching the dog to establish eye contact. For some moments, the dog and the man were intently staring into each other's eyes, and then, suddenly, the dog wagged its tail. The soldier patted it on the back of the neck, and it just ran away, without barking a sound.[5]

And you would speak of some Crocodile Dundee.

---

1. *It was sort of an honour to be "pepped up" by the detachment's commander. For that, you needed to do something really outstanding.*

2. *Until 1998, each operational regiment had its own SWAT teams.*

3. *A friend of mine once took an APC to ride it with his team, and the division's deputy commander saw them riding back and forth about the training ground. So, he stopped the APC, trying to make the guys understand who was boss. And it happened that, just at that moment, the detachment's commander arrived at the training ground. On seeing the situation, he*

approached them. The big boss, of course, started complaining about the bad officer, but the detachment's commander responded at once: "Comrade colonel, this officer was fulfilling my order to improve their driver's skills. In fact, it's one of my best officers." After this speech, the division's deputy commander had no other option but to wind up the discussion and, murmuring something to himself, retired from the ground. Of course, my friend has also had his punishment, not that he felt offended in any way.

4. *Of course, the commander had no intention of sending the letter. This was just a tactical trick, and quite an efficient one, as you might see; enough to make the soldier think better of his actions.*

5. *An Alpha veteran told about this adventure at some TV show.*

Chapter 7

In the gym, seated on a bench, Yegor and Nenashev were testing another Vityaz contender. Oyama, a contract soldier, was sparring with the contender and assisting them with the test. A hygiene instructor was also there.

From time to time, they could see the contender falling as Oyama attacked him. The contender's nose and lips were already bleeding, and severe bruises started to appear under his eyes.

Yegor, glancing at his stopwatch, announced, "Time!" and Oyama stopped his attack.

The contender's arms fell feebly to his sides and, out of breath, he jerked his head up. Yegor turned around to face the soldiers who were sitting beside him, ordering, "Help him."

The soldiers were up in no time, running toward the contender. They helped him take off the guards—the helmet, the gloves, and the vest, all covered in blood.

"You've got three minutes to wash and dress yourself!" Nenashev commanded, his voice sounding harsh but calm. "Countdown!"

Yegor restarted his stopwatch as the contender, limping, ran out of the gym.

"Well, what's your opinion?" Nenashev turned to ask Yegor.

"Not bad, I'd say," Yegor commented. "He's got the brains, and the guts, too."

Nenashev nodded in agreement.

"How many times has he tried?"

"It's his fifth or sixth time, as far as I remember," Yegor answered.

"Good," Nenashev nodded again.

Right then, the contender, still limping, ran into the gym, fastening his shoulder belt. He approached Nenashev and froze to a standstill, waiting for the commander to decide on his fate. One could see he was wearing a senior lieutenant's shoulder straps and, though he had washed off the blood, his face looked like he'd just been in a serious crash -- the nose and mouth swollen and deep bruises under his eyes.

"Well, brother, you look better this time, I say," Nenashev commented impassively on the test results. "So, see you some other time," and he looked up at the contender. "What's your name?"

"Senior Lieutenant Lazarenko."

"Okay, so, your name is?"

"Sergey."

Nenashev nodded.

"Well, how about seeing you in a week, Seryoga?"

"Aye!" the contender's voice sounded firm, though a bit tired.

"So, then, that's it for today!" and Nenashev let him go.

The senior lieutenant saluted and headed for the exit, while Nenashev and Yegor got up from the bench and followed him slowly.

"If he comes, take him," Nenashev announced his decision. "No more beating."

Vityaz accepted only the deepest-dyed fans, those who were really into this Special Forces stuff. This is why the testing was extremely hard, the selection criteria far beyond any reasonable limits.

At each call-up, Dzershinskogo Division accepted about five thousand people, the selection following pretty much the same procedure as for the assault forces. The selectees were not only physically and psychologically fit, but there were numerous sportsmen of various kinds among them — both belonging to certain categories and having certificates of mastery.

And it was out of these five thousand that Vityaz headhunters chose their soldiers, accepting everyone (of their own free will only) who really wanted to join the Special Forces.[1] So, those who were willing enough to be SWAT soldiers were subject to tests aimed to reveal whether they were suited for special missions. They looked for coordination, speed, and endurance. Usually there would be about a hundred who survived the tests.

All the freshers who were lucky enough to get accepted were first sent to the Training SWAT Team, where they had a half year of initial training. Once the initial training was over, the selectees were ordered to their combat units. Usually, in half a year, only 40 to 60 percent of freshers remained. The rest of them, going crazy with stress, were transferred to regular (infantry, artillery, and other) units, or reduced to the Hans, as SWAT soldiers used to call it. So, whether to join the Special Forces or not, it was rather a question of one's will, no strings attached. To get to serve there, one had to really go beyond one's limits.

Also, one could quit any time, without any difficulties. A soldier, whether a fresher or an old-timer, just needed to write an application. The next day he would be gone and serving his term in some other unit. However, they needed to bear in mind that, once they made their bed, they actually had to sleep in it. There was no way back.

Selection of officers was quite another matter. Before a Military Academy graduate got to join Vityaz, he had to serve at an infantry unit. It was only after he had served his term that he was granted the privilege of joining Vityaz.[2]

They also had to pass some tests, mostly to check their physical fitness. At that, physical fitness was understood to be integral to moral qualities and would be revealed through physical endurance. To pass, they had to comply with some physical fitness targets with an excellent grade, of course. The tests included a 100-metre race, a 3000-metre race, and a set of exercises.

Exercise 1

From the squat rest position, take the leaning support position and then go back to the initial one.

Exercise 2

To immediately follow exercise 1.

From the leaning support position, lie down on the belly and turn over, belly up, raising one's feet up without bending the knees to touch the floor ahead with the toes (touching the floor was obligatory) and then return the feet to the initial position.

Exercise 3

To immediately follow exercise 2.

Lying on the back, turn over, belly up, taking up the leaning support position, bend the elbows, touching the floor (or the ground) with one's chest, and straighten the arms.

Exercise 4

To immediately follow exercise 3.

Taking up the squat rest position, crouch, one knee down and hands up, the palms over the nape, then jump up, straightening the legs, and land on the other knee.

Each exercise was to be repeated ten times. The four exercises made a complete testing set. And the tested contender had to cope with seven of such sets.

After these merciless workouts, the contender's hands and feet grew heavy as lead, and it was time to test them in a hand-to-hand fight: full-contact sparring, six minutes in all, two minutes for each sparring partner. And the hand-to-hand fight test was of major importance, rather resembling ultimate fighting. The contenders were "worked over" to blood to see whether they were going to break down and give up or survive through it all, no matter what.

Ordinary soldiers had to test officers, and should the officer survive the testing, these same soldiers were to be his subordinates. Nonetheless, the soldiers never hesitated to recognize the officer's authority whenever, and if, he proved to deserve it.

The tests were mainly to see if the contender was determined and strong enough to make it till the end. Some gave up in the first round, while others were tested six to seven times, always worked over to blood. However, it was the only way to know for sure whether they were worth accepting, the tests revealing how far they could go in their commitment.

Vityaz has *always* been short of qualified personnel. Should a person fail the tests, he would never be accepted. Only the best of the best could deserve the honour!

This is another good reason why Vityaz has always been number one. Often, it happened so that one team included ten soldiers and one to two officers, but the twelve people could tear up *any* enemy.

However, it didn't mean that to be a good officer one had to know only how to fight and endure; not at all. An officer was, first of all, someone who could teach the contingent and manage it throughout the daily routine and battles. Thus, an officer also had to be a qualified professional.

Besides the physical targets, a contending officer had to pass some credits to confirm his knowledge of weapons, tactics, military topography, and the charter.

There's a saying often heard from Vityaz soldiers. Roughly translated, it goes like this: "To be a cool guy is not an occupation." (Of course, they would use some other word instead of *cool*.) The essence of it is that you can be a good guy, or rather, you must be a good guy, but it's not foremost, as *professionalism* overshadows it all.

A friend of mine from the school times, who also served in a SWAT detachment, was shocked at what I had to do to join Vityaz. He really got confused with the story. First of all, it was the testing itself (he was just admitted without any tests) that confused him, and then the fact that officers were tested by ordinary soldiers. "What the hell is going on with that Vityaz?" I remember him saying.

Once, we got a bunch of "fresh" lieutenants applying to join Vityaz. One of them came to Moscow with his family. So, one day, the whole family appears at the division's premises. The lieutenant leaves for the division's headquarters while his family stays to wait for him at the CP to later take a tour of the capital together. At the division's headquarters, the lieutenant mentions he wants to join Vityaz, so he is sent at once to see Vityaz commanders, who tell him he needs to pass some tests and give him some time to get ready.

So, the lieutenant runs straight to the CP, asking for a pen and a copybook. "I need to pass some tests," he explains to his family. "I'll get the answers ready and we will be on our way."

Two hours later, he is back, limping, his lips and nose bleeding and his eyes turning into dark shadows. I doubt he was able to do any sightseeing that day.

Got the answers ready, I say.

In 1985, when S. Lysuik was appointed the detachment's commander, one more selection round was introduced. All the freshers, once they were accepted, were to spend three days in the "villie." During the three days, they had to live in tents, practising intensively. At night, of course, they had to go on guard. There were about thirty to thirty-five guard posts, three soldiers each. While the freshers were on guard, the soldiers from action units attacked them, all night long. So, for all the three days, the freshers hardly got more than four to six hours of sleep. The rest of their time was taken up by practise and guarding. Finally, in the end of the term, they were assigned some mission that was impossible to complete. For example, in winter, when it's twenty-five below zero outside, they were ordered to dig a trench full height to hide them. The soldiers tore their gloves to pieces. Skin was coming off their hands, and when shovels got damaged, they simply had to grab the ground with their hands.

The commander understood perfectly that the mission was impossible. However, it was not the trenches he was after. He needed to test their spirit to see what the freshers were really worth.

And while the soldiers were digging the frozen ground, the instructing warrant officers were sitting right beside them, comfortable on their chairs, warming up with tea. Of course, they were offering the steaming potion to everyone, seducing them to give up on the stupid assignment.

Another ten people were eliminated, having failed the test.

However, after 1988, they had to omit the testing, as the USSR got involved in all these hot-spot conflicts. The detachment got to stay in Moscow for only three to four months a year.

---

1. *Vityaz has long enjoyed the right of first choice. Unfortunately, not anymore, so now they have to be content with whatever is left, relying only on special training.*

2. *By the mid nineties, the rules had become obsolete, as officers were selected right upon graduation. However, selection criteria remained just as tough and categorical as ever, so only the best got to join the Special Forces.*

CHAPTER 8

The 2nd SWAT team was lined up right in front of the orderly room. The door opened, letting Artur out. Having looked over the line, he asked Kisel, "So, Kot is nowhere to be seen, is he?"

"No, he isn't," the sergeant said sullenly.

Artur nodded. "Fine! So now, team, you are to find the soldier. And you," said Artur, pointing at Kisel and Lebed, "you take a chair each and follow me to the room. That's all; dismissed!"

And, turning around, Artur headed for the orderly room.

The orderly room of the 2nd SWAT team (just like any other orderly room within the building) had a Spartan spirit to it. Arranged in a T-form, there was a table for the commander and a table for the record clerk. Also, the room had a bed, a couple of chairs, cabinets, and a TV set. On one of the walls hung a national flag, while the opposite one had a poster on it, drawn by some soldier.

Reclining on a chair and sipping tea from an iron cup, Artur was watching TV, looking completely uninterested in what was going on. His APS was beside him on the table. His expression didn't change even when he heard someone knocking on the door. Then the door opened, and Lebed and Kisel, holding chairs in their hands, came in.

"May we come in?" Kisel asked.

It was only then that Artur turned his head leisurely to give them a cold look.

*TERRORIST REMEMBER! GO AGAINST SWAT — DIE LIKE A
MOTHERFUCKER!*

"Horse stance! Now!" Artur was in no mood for long talks.
"Arms outstretched, chairs up."

The sergeants took the horse stance (it's a karate head-on stance,
with legs bent in the knees and apart at a distance wider than shoulders), then picked up the chairs, stretching their arms out. This
stance gave a good load on the hips, the shoulders, and the back.

"Stand like this till they find that soldier." That was the near
perspective for both the sergeants.

Meantime, "that soldier," namely Kot, was having a good time
with a nurse from the medical battalion. He was lying comfortably

on the couch, while his tongue was "studying" her mouth and his hand searching under her blouse.

But then, out of the blue, there thundered Talanych's voice, and this was a total meltdown.

"Hey, Kot!"

Kot, feeling outraged with the invasion, took his tongue out unwillingly, peeling off his body from hers, and, tucking his trousers, went to open the door. By the time he opened the door, the nurse was all dressed, sitting at the table. She was a military woman, too, so she knew how to do things fast.

"Hey, Andrey, Artur is looking for you everywhere!" Talanych was panting and sweating, exhausted by the search raid as the division's premises allowed some space for action.

"Damn it!" Kot cursed, jumping over the threshold. His body already outside, he turned around to say, "Call you later, honey!"

And he sprinted off after Talanych.

Artur was still watching TV and the sergeants were still holding their chairs frozen in the horse stance, their faces red with tension and their hands shaking, about to fall feebly to the sides. They finally (and alas!) heard a knock and "that very soldier" appeared at the door.

"May I come in, comrade senior lieutenant?" Kot blurted out as he entered the office.

In no hurry, Artur turned his head to award him a meaningful look, a look that promised no easy way out.

"Hands down," Artur ordered, not bothering to look at the sergeants.

Sighing with relief, the sergeants put the chairs down, while Artur, back to the TV set, enquired, his tone icy cold, "And you, soldier; where have you been?"

Kot shivered a little at the ice in the commander's voice and answered, "Had to visit the nurse, comrade senior lieutenant," Kot began, feeling unsure. "My arm, you know; might have dislocated something."

Again, Artur turned his head around, "blessing" Kot with a cold gaze, which made him cringe. "You may go." Artur made a long pause, which seemed to go on for eternity, and added, "We need to make sure his arm is all right." And, as if having lost interest in the entire situation, he turned back to the screen.

Already out in the corridor, Kisel, passing by Kot, threw at him, his voice suspiciously calm and even, "You are so wrong, Andrey."

"Alex, I just …" Kot, his voice thick with guilt, tried to find a plausible excuse.

Kisel just ignored him, making his way to the bay. Lebed, though, had his own opinion of the "issue," which he was not going to keep to himself. So, he grabbed Kot by the hand, dragging him along toward the washing room.

"Well, Kot, let's have a little talk with you!" Lebed was almost hissing as he pulled Kot inside the washing room.

"Wait, Lyosha," Kot was still trying to justify himself.

However, Lebed gave him no opportunity for that and, taking a swift turn, just punched him on the jaw. Kot fell on the floor some metres away.

"You son of a bitch! How many times are you going to set us up like that?" Lebed said angrily between his teeth. "I'm asking you!"

Whimpering and holding his jaw, Kot sprawled on the floor. For some seconds, Lebed stood there, staring at him, his eyes blazing with angry fire, and then he turned around and left the room.

If the team's commander were ever to get to know about the showdown, Lebed would have to "go through the line," and then, completely disgraced, be transferred to another unit, reduced to a Hans, because fighting with fellows was a "Hans thing." Even if there were any internal disagreement among Vityaz soldiers, those were dealt with in the gym, in a fair fight, hands in gloves.

In fact, Vityaz was in many ways different from regular Hans units, or rather, Vityaz has never had much in common with regular troops.

Unlike Hans troops, where the power was in the hands of the older bullies, Vityaz forces were under sergeants' command, just as the charter had it.

As I was talking to one of the veterans, he told me that when he was admitted to Vityaz, he saw an army, which they showed on TV, where things were neat and clean and in order. And, most importantly, there was no bullying!

Even when a sergeant happened to be a year or so younger than an old-timer, the old-timer would work his brains out whenever he got an order from this tenderfoot sergeant, just like his younger fellows. Of course, occasionally there would emerge an old-timer who didn't quite like the state of things. Then the problem was dealt with using the boxing gloves at the gym. And as sergeants were chosen from among the best-trained soldiers, and best trained in every respect, the problem vanished in a blink of an eye. Vityaz sergeants enjoyed real power, their skills beyond any doubt. Officers never worried about leaving sergeants in charge when they went home. They knew things were going to be okay, if not great. And there has never been a problem.

It was taboo for Vityaz soldiers to have freshers make one's bed, catch up the undercollar, wash up, or do any other things, whatsoever.

Making freshers run for cigarettes or tea — those were the Hans things, which were absolutely out of question for a SWAT soldier. Those were punishable things, and sometimes these were not the commanders but fellow-soldiers who punished the defaulters.

Vityaz old-timers were really like mentors for their younger fellows.

The only thing a sergeant (mind you! never an old-timer) was allowed to do was to send a fresher to the kitchen to have some potato fried, but it had to be a portion big enough for everyone, freshers included. But such assignments were rather an exception than regular practise. Besides, the ever-hungry freshers really enjoyed this kind of assignment.

All the more, bullying freshers was the greatest taboo!

Of course, as you might have seen from the above, one couldn't do without some physical exercise for educational matters. It often happened that soldiers could be running and doing press-ups for two to three hours without interruption to redeem their sins. However, to wake freshers up in the night for some cheap humiliation tricks — those were the Hans things and to be avoided!

In 1998, a program on TV showed two old-timers waking up freshers at night to have some fun, scoffing at them. They made it look as if they were really cool SWAT guys, just back from the battlefield. Those were soldiers from the 4th SWAT team of the Independent Special Designation Division (ISDD). Several months later, the two "hardball dogs" were finally found (though the recording was made back in 1995). The ISDD held a court session, and those cool guys went to prison. And here's what the team's commander told me about them.

One of those guys, right after his first mission, stole some urine from a guy in the medical unit who had the yellow sickness. So, diagnosed as having the yellow sickness (jaundice, or whatever is the right medical term), he went back to Moscow, where doctors, of course, couldn't confirm the diagnosis.

The other one scratched his hand and got infected — a usual thing whenever someone isn't careful enough in the field. So, when his hand was swollen, he approached his commander, complaining, "My hand hurts." The doctor said he only needed to make a slight cut and clear the wound. However, the commander sent the wounded warrior right back to Moscow, commenting, "I don't need you here."

In Moscow, their health seemed to improve really fast, so when they recovered, they were sent to monitor the training process, as back then, there were not enough people to do that. And then came their lucky hour.

The team's commander got to know about their feats from the TV broadcast. One of those freshers was then already a contract soldier in the detachment, so the commander, naturally, had a heated discussion with him. "Were you out of your mind or what? How come you let those suckers treat you like that? Couldn't you just hit them back a couple of times so that their brain would work better?"

And the soldier answered, "Well, we were really new to all of that, and we thought they saw real stuff, smelled some blood. For us, they were like heroes, or something."

These were the Hans people the Special Forces would be ashamed to have. I believe prison is the only right place for them!

Castes like "spirits," "crows," "dippers," and "old-timers" were all lousy Hans stuff. Ceremonies where soldiers had to have their asses beaten with plates or were made to eat bread, sitting on a bed arch, his fellows hitting him with pillows — all of these was Hans stuff!

So, as Vityaz has never had anything of the kind, it was really an elite unit against such a lousy background!

These were the criminal-style douchy concepts that made the Hans who they were. These practises were the reason the Special Forces always looked down on these people.

In the Special Forces, they use the "Hans" word (or the "Hans stuff" expression) a lot. You might have developed your own idea of what it should mean. However, I'd like to give a more profound interpretation.

Raiders from the Assault Forces often say, "Those who've never parachuted, let them all be called Mabutees." Mabutees is the name the Assault Forces use to denote soldiers from all the infantry troops, except for the Special Forces, the frontier guards, and the marines.

So, for the SWAT of Internal Troops, the Hans would be about the same as the Mabutees for the Assault Forces.

But again, it would be too simple a definition, as the Hans are not those who serve in troops other than the Special Forces. Rather, they are the carriers of the Hans philosophy, the latter synonymous to the lack of the Special Forces spirit. And the Special Forces spirit means high professionalism, esprit, brotherhood of people sharing weapons, and strict discipline (self-discipline, first of all). It excludes and never tolerates any Hans traditions, whatsoever.

It is that spirit that the Hans lack.

The Hans can be found in those units where old-timers are totally out of control, where soldiers get drunk and get involved in other military offenses, where, instead of training, the soldiers are either preoccupied with fatigues or just doing nothing at all. The Hans never care to think of such things as commitment and morale. And this can apply to both soldiers and officers. Hans philosophy is all about the criminal stuff, like senior to junior subordination.

This shit is just what one expects to find in the infantry troops and the like (the Tank Corps, the artillery, etc.).

One can also draw a parallel with the theatre, where we talk about amateurship, which stands for lack of professionalism and originality.

In fact, the Hans word came into use back in the 1970s. At first, it was just a facetious name that grew to be a common noun, denoting all the negative aspects of the army.

Finally, it all comes to this: dozens of soldiers are killed during field marching because they are totally ignorant of the battlefield security rules and prefer to sleep (mostly drunk) rather than watch out for danger. Again, insurgents have no trouble with seizing military checkpoints and massacring soldiers while they are fast asleep or drunk. Sometimes, they don't bother to kill, as soldiers would, of their own free will, give up their weapons, surrendering. Another example of negligence is when a squadron of over a hundred people cannot maintain the school building they have occupied for more than twenty-four hours, even though the position has been properly fortified and prepared for defense. They just throw their weapons away, running in all directions.

By comparison, SWAT 8 of the Internal Troops' Special Forces of the Ministry of Internal Affairs, which is known as Rus Team, its contingent numbering about forty people, had maintained control over a huge clinical center in Grozniy for two days and nights, fighting against five thousand invaders. As a matter of fact, it has *never* been the case with the Internal Troops' Special Forces that they would surrender and leave their positions without a fight.

In fact, it all depends on commanders. Internal Troops' Tactical and Police Units often had their own nonorganic SWAT sections. Then, the commander in charge would be an officer who used to work with a regular unit; however, it would be an officer close in spirit to those one could find in the Special Forces. So, these non-organic sections used to become hardcore SWAT units.

Let's go back to the 1980s, when Vityaz (back then — the Train-ing Special Operations Battalion [TSOB]) was on a mission in Nagorniy Karabakh, involved in the Armenia–Azerbaijan conflict. One day, a military truck approached the TSOB soldiers, its step plate occupied by an officer in a crimson beret looking like a brave Hussar, the truck body in the same crimson colour.

"Hey, bro, come here," the battalion's commander called out to the officer. "Who are you guys?"

The guys turned out to be from a nonorganic SWAT section of the Internal Troops' Tactical Brigade. It was totally their initiative to put on the berets. As the crimson beret tests proper were intro-duced only in 1988, there were not so many people who knew about those.

"So, now, guys," the commander ordered, "you'd better take the berets off."

All the officers and soldiers took off the berets at once and with-out demur. The battalion's commander set a term for them to pre-pare for testing, and as the time came, they were all, Captain Larin included, tested. Their examiners were the world's most experienced

SWAT soldiers. Only one third of the section passed the tests, which is, actually, an excellent result, proving they were really well trained. The SWAT detachment's commander described them like that: "The guys were diehards. You should've seen the mess they caused."

Unfortunately, real SWAT teams have their own Hans, as well, and Vityaz is no exception in this respect. These Hans are usually outsiders (from the division's headquarters, mostly) who are absolute strangers to all the SWAT traditions. Of course, they try to break the special SWAT spirit and get the others to cave in to their own standards. However, such people have two options only: either they get used to the new rules and accept them as their own, or they are simply driven out of the team. Naturally, it all depends on whether the team's sprit is strong enough to fight the strangers' invasion.

So, now, based on the above, you can make your conclusions about the Hans people.

Naturally, the classification is rather obscure. There are such Hans units, only by name, where things are totally different. Such units have real officers, who, their spirit strong and their beliefs unwavering, deserve to become Special Forces soldiers.

In 1995, the 3rd team was assigned a tank, the tank's mission being to destroy the enemy's firepower and the buildings where insurgents maintained their positions. But it's no easy task for a tank in the city. It takes just one shot of a grenade launcher for a tank to catch fire. So, the SWAT team's assignment was to make sure the tank was safe, clearing the ground for its operation. The SWAT soldiers and the tankers were so good in teamwork that RPG[1] remained silent for as long as they worked together, and the tankers completed their mission successfully. As a matter of fact, the tankers and the SWAT soldiers shared one dugout and treated each other like brothers.

This was what could be called a true unity of forces, a unity based on recognizing each other as professionals.

As the operation was launched, the SWAT soldiers were the first to set off, their moves fast and perfectly coordinated. There was not a blade of grass or a crack they hadn't examined. Two soldiers covered the tank from the back. Once the sectors were under SWAT control, they communicated it to the tankers so that the tank could move confidently along the route, razing to the ground *everything* that could pose a threat to the engaged forces.

As the first working day was over, the tank commander commented to Yegor, evidently surprised at how the SWAT acted, "Yegor, I suppose it was a special show that you put on today?" (It was clear he had never seen such a cover team.)

Yegor was puzzled. "What do you mean, Lyokha? War is no time to show off."

Vityaz soldiers, in their turn, appreciated the way the tankers did their job professionally. Nothing was left where the tank passed, not a firing point, not even a shooter's shelter.

So when the operation was over, it was hard to say good-bye.

That's why it would be wrong to think that SWAT soldiers are arrogant, high-qualified shit-asses, caring nothing about the rest of the world. As they say, if you are not willing to become a Hans, just don't be one. Whether you are a cook or a driver, you just need to be a military professional, sticking to the military ethics and moral principles (being a professional is just part of it all). There's only one way to deserve SWAT grace: be a professional.

Here's another example of a non-SWAT professional, my father.

During his compulsory military service, he served as a sergeant in the Space Forces. So he and the rest of the sergeant contingent who were transferred to the unit from the training regiment eliminated all the bullying crap.

Once his compulsory service term was over, he was transferred to the Internal Troops with disposition in Pyatigorsk. He stayed with the Internal Troops for over thirty years. It was due to him that

I got to know about the Special Forces and the crimson berets. It was he whom I looked up to when searching for my way to become a good officer and a good SWAT soldier. My father served in an escort guard regiment, which was later reformed into Pyatigorsk Tactical Division Headquarters. He was not a SWAT soldier, but a communicator and a true military man! I'm calling him that not because he is my father, but because it is true to the last word. If it were flattery, I wouldn't even bother to mention it.

My father was a professional with the highest qualifications.

I remember visiting his regiment one day; there was a line break. And, just then, the signal officer in command for North-Caucasian Okrug happened to be there, and he, being a colonel, was very polite and respectful as he spoke to my father, a warrant officer. He always addressed him as Volodya, avoiding the official "comrade warrant officer." Having heard of my father's reputation, he finally ordered the regiment's commander to follow my father's advice. It did the signal officer justice that he actually listened to his subordinates. Evidently, he was a knowing specialist, so he never tried to pretend to be a big boss, rather focusing on a productive dialogue to resolve the problem at hand.

Besides, my father was a good shooter, always fit as a fiddle. He had a category in fighting, and had won some prizes at the division's championship.

As for my father's relations with his subordinates, he behaved much the same as they did in Vityaz. I remember him arranging big parties at home whenever someone left military service. And I know that some of his soldiers kept in touch with him even after their retirement.

When the so-called First Chechen War broke out, he had a lonely middle-aged mother to tend to, so he could have just refused to go, using his authority and the good commendations of the commanding officers. However, he did go there. And in the letter I received from him after his return (at that time I was in my second year at the military school), he asked me to never shy away from my assignments; he was perfectly aware of my determination to join the Special Forces and of the kind of assignments SWAT soldiers were given.

The regiment where my father served had a nonorganic SWAT section under the command of the warrant officer who, back in the seventies, was recognized as the *professional of professionals* by all Vityaz soldiers. The man still keeps in touch with the veterans. So, back to my father, my father and this warrant officer have been friends for as long as they have known each other.

My father is not an exception for our army. If you are like him, this means you are not a Hans.

There are stories of when soldiers and officers from regular infantry units got special prizes — crimson berets — from their SWAT fellows.

* * *

After the evening roll call, Artur summed up the results of the day. "Private Koshkin!"

"Here!" and Kot appeared to the call.

"Front and center!"

"Aye!" Kot did as ordered, turning around to face the team.

"Today, Private Koshkin," and Artur started reading the verdict, "is your lucky day. You've won the prize and the wheel of fortune, too, I believe. Meet you on Saturday, the HKD^2, at the vehicle pool." Artur glanced at Kot and continued. "So, your prize is an extended weekend doing the fatigues. Dima!" and Artur turned to Shevchenko. "You are to instruct him on the scope of work."

"Aye," Chef admitted impassively.

"And give him the Hans outfit," Artur pointed at Kot, turning back to him. "This outfit, you are to take off! No training! And, also, you are not allowed in the gym. So, Saturday is the awards ceremony. Don't forget! Any questions?"

"No." Kot was sullen but calm.

"Fall in."

"Aye!" and Kot joined the line.

Vityaz had its own system of punishments and encouragements, unrecorded in the charter.

For SWAT soldiers, their uniform and the crimson beret were their pride. So, should a SWAT soldier do something wrong, they were made to take off the uniform and the beret (depending on the gravity of their misdeeds, of course). Instead, they were given regular soldier's uniforms, a pair of tarpaulin boots, and a cap — all Hans style.

Special workouts were also a privilege, notwithstanding the fact that loads at such workouts went up as high as 200 percent. Anyway, it was a severe punishment for a soldier to be banned from such workouts to do the fatigue duties, such as washing, painting, digging, cleaning, etc.

Defaulters were banned from the gym, too. Special Forces soldiers were supposed to be constantly improving their physical abilities. So, whenever they had a free minute, they spent it in the gym, pumping their muscles up or practising punches and kicks. Keep in mind their special workouts gave them more than enough physical strain.

Given this, to be banned from the gym was a serious sanction for a SWAT soldier. On the contrary, whenever someone deserved an encouragement, they were given extra time at the gym.

The charter prescribed addressing a soldier as "soldier" or "Private Petrov;" however, SWAT soldiers used this kind of address only for defaulters. It was a punishment in itself to be addressed in this way, as officers, as a rule, just called their soldiers by their name or nickname, or in rare cases, by the surname. Most frequently, soldiers addressed each other as "bro" or "brother," which emphasized the brotherly relations among all the SWAT soldiers. Of course, senior commanders were rather unhappy with this state of things, as they had none of the Special Forces spirit in their heart: "What are you, living in a monastery or something? Brethren? You must be kidding!"

"For a Russian officer, a soldier's life must be more important than his own; he is the little brother, the legendary knight, the hero." (Russian Officer's Code of Honour).

Sometimes, it happened so that a soldier could be both punished and awarded for the same action, like in the example with the CP attack.

Also, a SWAT soldier could be awarded with a set of army photos. As the Special Forces have been special regime units for quite a long time, on most occasions, photos were forbidden. However, a SWAT soldier could get a prize, presented with a set of photos (sometimes five, sometimes ten or fifteen) from their special workouts.

---

1. RPG: light antitank weapon

2. HKD: the housekeeping day, which meant overall cleaning. It was usually scheduled for Saturdays.

Chapter 9

Having sorted things out in the city, Yegor headed for the detachment's premises. Going through an arch, he glanced inside the yard, his body automatically coming to a halt.

"Damn it!" Yegor cursed to himself.

He saw two shaven-headed guys pushing a girl into their car. The girl was trying to escape; however, her chances were close to zero. Besides, there were two more guys inside the car, a driver and a passenger. Yegor came closer, hoping for a peaceful agreement.

"Hey, guys!" Yegor called out to them. "She seems to be unwilling to join you."

Everyone, surprised at the sudden interference, turned to see who was speaking. One of the two guys made a step toward Yegor, leaving the girl alone. The girl was staring at Yegor, hope vivid in her eyes.

"Look, you, hero!" The man's manner was impudent. "Just leave it! We know what she's up to." He gave Yegor a level look.

"Okay, guys, I'm on my way." The officer seemed to agree to the arguments. "No problem. You let the girl go, and I'm outta here in no time."

The rascal, obviously running out of patience, was now approaching Yegor. "Hey, you, the Red Riding Hero!" He was bluntly aggressive, his tone scornful. "You'd better go home, and that's my last warning! You grandma must be worr—"

These were the last words he managed to say, as he was stopped short by Yegor's hand crashing into his throat (Yegor used the "fork" — the palm section between the thumb and the index finger). The shaven-headed guy, his instincts driving his hand to reach out for his throat, moved somewhat back to "shoot his major weapon." Yegor, giving him no opportunity to recover, threw a right kick in the head so the rascal sank down to his knees. Yegor used the pause to take off his beret, carefully rolling it up and putting it in between the buttons on his chest. By this time, the driver was out of the car and approaching Yegor. His attack started with a head-on right kick in the belly, which was followed by a left-side kick in the head and a straight right-hand punch in the head. Yegor blocked the kicks and the punch easily, and, diving under the hand, used an uppercut in the liver, then, losing no time, took a turn to throw a left-hand hook in the head. Finally, the driver's attack was smashed with a right-hand elbow punch in the bridge. The driver flew off, hitting the car. The third one, leaving the girl, attacked from the right. Yegor threw a right kick, knocking the guy down.

The passenger jumped out of the car with a club in his hands. He decided to cut off the distance, sliding over the car hood. Yegor, reacting to his move, made a step with his left leg toward the car and then took a 360-degree turn. His right leg, drawing an arc in the air, went up to chop the baseball fan down at his knees. A moment later the man was flying, his feet high up in the air, landing with his back on the hood.

One of the scums, already up on his feet and taking out a knife, approached Yegor from the back. The girl cried out, warning Yegor, "From the back!"

Yegor turned around, jerking back. The man almost got him, the blade making a cut on the palm. The assailant did some feints and attacked from above. Yegor, coming closer, caught him and threw him over his back, the man's body smacking against the asphalt. To calm him down, Yegor punched him in the chin and then saw the baseball fan approaching. So, throwing a kick backward, Yegor smashed his heel into the man's solar plexus, the man's body doubling. Turning around, Yegor took a step closer and jumped, throwing his knee forward to hit the man on the chin, and then it was over.

Having checked the gangsters, who were now enjoying their rest on the ground, Yegor turned to the girl. "Are you all right?" The question automatically sprang up in his mind.

"Yes, thank you!" the girl responded quietly, and pointing at his body, added, "You're bleeding."

And it was only then that Yegor noticed the cut on his hand. Naturally, focused on the fight, he felt no pain. Taking a handkerchief out of his pocket, he gave himself first aid.

"I live not far from here. So let me take care of the wound," the girl offered.

Giving it a thought, Yegor nodded, accepting the offer, and they headed for the girl's house.

"You know them?" Yegor asked, just to keep up the conversation.

"No, of course not!" the girl responded as though frightened at the thought of such an acquaintance. "I was just passing by, and they offered to give me a ride. I refused." For a moment she was silent, the unpleasant scene rewinding in her mind.

"Actually, I never use the road." Finally, the girl was back to reality. "It was just an unfortunate accident. My car is in repair, so I had to use the public transport." She glanced at Yegor, adding, "Thank God you happened to be there."

* * *

Vityaz soldiers had a special attitude to hand-to-hand fights.

The Vityaz emblem (which is almost the same as that of the Special Forces) has a fist with a machine gun on it, its prototype being the emblem of the Cuban Special Forces of their national Ministry of Internal Affairs. Their emblem features a Kalashnikov machine gun and a fist above it against the background of a parachute, and there's also the signature, *Tropas Especiales*. It was this image that prompted a Vityaz commander with the idea for an original emblem for his detachment. The commander just added an NFFSD (noise- and flame-free shooting device, commonly known as the "silencer") to the machine gun, making the fist a little bigger and bringing it somewhat forward.

The NFFSD weapons pertain to the special weapons category and, as such, are usually used by the Special Forces soldiers. The fist is the symbol of respect for hand-to-hand fights.

And all of the above together emphasizes the *special* status of SWAT teams — their special weapons, tactics, and their special attitude to hand-to-hand fighting.

The special attitude could be actually called a cult, as hand-to-hand fights are practised daily, for several hours on end. The first workout is usually at six o'clock in the morning, right after the wakeup, and lasts for one hour and ten minutes — sort of morning routine, where kicks, punches, and blocks are practised. The workout is a must for everyone — even the day-shift orderlies. Even if a SWAT soldier has his leg or arm broken, he has to attend the workouts. With a leg broken, he could just practise punches and blocks, sitting on a bench, and with an arm broken, the kicks. It is due to these regular morning exercises that SWAT soldiers' technical skills at fighting are excellent, up to the highest standards. The formal hand-to-hand workout is held after the work formation. However, besides daily formal workouts that go on for hours, soldiers hone their fighting skills in their free hours.

Also, Vityaz has its own, unique test. Based on the test, the best fighters are awarded the A-Level Hand-to-Hand Fighter badge.

A contender is given some time to prepare. And as the appointment is due, the gym doors are closed from inside, a boxing ring is put up, and the test proper starts. It is a twenty-four-minute, continuous, full-contact fight, with only minimal restrictions!

Eight opponents change every three minutes; the only protection

device is a helmet!

Over the entire history of Vityaz existence, only seventeen people have been awarded this badge, and those were the greatest masters of hand-to-hand fighting. And should they happen to be involved in ultimate fighting, they would, undoubtedly, be among the winners.

Here are some examples, proving SWAT soldiers really respected martial arts.

After the obligatory service term was over, a number of Vityaz soldiers became martial arts instructors in other Special Forces detachments.

After retirement, a number of Vityaz soldiers became champions, either national or international, in various martial arts — karate, boxing, kickboxing — even though most of them started practising martial arts only when they joined Vityaz.

One soldier, while on his day off in the city, "calmed down" some criminals — and it took him only three minutes, while his only injury was a torn great-coat collar.

And then let's take, for instance, in the mid eighties, the Armenia-Azerbaijan conflict.

Enemy forces — a crowd of over a thousand people willing to tear everyone to pieces — blocked a refugee escort. The Internal Troops' soldiers, accompanying the escort, could hardly manage this crowd of wild animals, hungry for blood.

So they asked for help via radio, and soon two MI-8 helicopters were landing beside the escort with twenty-five soldiers, wearing cammies, sneakers, and crimson berets, rushing to help, their wrists in boxing wraps. A moment later, they were arranged in a line, facing the wild pack. The officer in command, a whistle in one of his hands, was quietly strolling behind their backs. And then he blew the whistle. The line came on the run, hands and legs crashing the pack at a whirlwind speed. A minute later, there sounded another two whistles, and the SWAT soldiers stopped at once and made a step backward, waiting patiently for the next command. Their wrist wraps were all wet with blood, while, on the ground, one could see at least several dozen extremists, knocked down and broken.

After a minute's rest, the commander blew the whistle again, and the fight started over. Then another two whistles, and the fight stopped.

They had quite a number of rounds like that, each time the crowd getting scarcer. Some were lying on the ground, injured, while, for most of the crowd, the show had been an awakening; they remembered their basic instincts of running.

In some twenty minutes, the crowd was gone, and the escort proceeded along the route, while the SWAT soldiers, all alive and intact, went back to their helicopters and flew away.

In the late 1980s, Vityaz was on a mission at a USSR hot spot. To keep their identity secret, Vityaz soldiers dressed like policemen. At that time, they were allocated at the premises of an Assault Forces regiment. The regiment's raiders, those stout fellows, looked down on the self-invited guests (who were cops, by the way) and never missed an opportunity to show them who was the boss, always ready with an excuse to demonstrate their power. And though, for the SWAT soldiers, it was strictly forbidden to react to provocations, there was no way to avoid the contact.

In the end, some Vityaz soldier, having run out of patience, started a fight with the raiders. Fortunately, the commander happened to be passing by, so he ordered, "Break! Take your corners," and invited the generous hosts to the gym.

In the gym, the commander lined up all the Vityaz soldiers by height, and ordered the last ten soldiers in the line to fall out. These were the smallest ones.

"That's our team," he explained to the opponents. "Now you can choose your dozen."

The opponents were happy, of course, and, grinning, chose their ten athletes. And the martial arts contest began.

There were three rounds only, each of them lasting for less than a minute and ending with a knockdown. After the third knockdown, the hosts announced, "That's it, guys. We got it — you are not cops. Sorry! How can we join your unit?"

* * *

"What's your name?" they were already in the elevator when the girl asked.

"Yegor," Yegor responded, looking calmly at the girl.

"And my name is Kira," she introduced herself.

"Pleased to meet you," Yegor added, just to be polite.

"Me, too," Kira smiled at him. "Thank you, Yegor."

"You're welcome." Yegor shrugged his shoulders as though making it clear that he just did what he was supposed to do.

Kira had a large, luxuriously furnished apartment. While Yegor was taking off his boots, Kira dropped in at the bathroom. Yegor could hear water running. As he got out of the boots, he also went to the bathroom to wash the wound. The wound was not deep (only a skin cut), but it needed to be taken care of.

He dried his hands with a towel and headed for the kitchen, where Kira was already waiting for him with iodine, cotton wool, and bandages.

"Give me your hand, will you?" Kira asked him, sitting down at the table.

Yegor obeyed, and Kira, taking his hand in hers, examined the wound. Yegor was watching Kira with interest.

"You can't imagine, Yegor, how frightened I was," the girl shared her impressions while tending to the wound.

"Me, too," Yegor said after a pause.

"Really!" Kira looked up, surprised. "I can't believe you were. You didn't seem scared as you came to my rescue."

She took some cotton wool, wetting it with iodine.

"Well, you know," Yegor began quietly, "only fools are afraid of nothing. Fear is a normal reaction. It helps to survive. It's just some people can overcome it, and that's what I'd call courage, to enter a building on fire to save a child, or to risk one's life under bullets to help your injured friend."

Kira applied iodine to the wound, and Yegor winced involuntarily. Kira blew on the wound lightly, as if she felt something. Yegor was silent for a moment, his look changing as he watched Kira do it.

Looking up, the girl met Yegor's stare. "Or else, to save a stranger from four creeps," Kira said, staring into his eyes, her voice almost turning into a whisper.

Yegor shrugged a little. "Well, dunno."

Kira looked aside and, taking the bandage, started dressing. "Honestly, I was afraid you wouldn't make it," she confessed. "You just look so …"

She struggled for the right word, and Yegor prompted, "Flimsy."

Kira smiled guiltily. "Well, not flimsy, but, you know, not big. Something like that. Besides, there were four of them. But you coped with them all right." She shook her head with obvious admiration. "I guess, Yegor, you are from the Assault Forces?"

Yegor couldn't help smiling.

"Or maybe not," she corrected herself. "As far as I remember, the Assault Forces have blue berets, and the one you're wearing is red."

"It's crimson," Yegor qualified the colour.

Kira looked at Yegor, obviously at a loss.

"Crimson? Never thought it makes any difference."

Yegor, having examined the bandage, grinned again. He'd heard it so many times. This time, he felt he had to explain it all over. "Actually, it does. It's the blood colour."

"Blood?" Kira looked puzzled. "Whose blood?"

"Well, if you speak about my beret, then it's my blood," Yegor explained, though Kira was evidently not sure how to understand it.

"How do you mean?"

"Well, it's something like this," and Yegor paused, choosing his words carefully. "To get this beret, one needs to spill some blood, to make it the right crimson shade. So, that's why blood. Understand?" and, smiling, added, "This kind of beret is the Internal Troops' Special Forces privilege."

Kira, her eyes on Yegor, was processing what she's just heard. "Internal Troops' Special Forces, you say?" Kira repeated thoughtfully. "Never heard about any of that."

Yegor answered in the tone of a lecturer. "Serious guys prefer to remain in the shadows." And then he smiled at her playfully, winking.

Kira smiled in response and reached out to take the beret. "May I?"

However, Yegor turned her hand off, trying to be as soft and gentle as he could. "Sorry."

"I'll just have a look," Kira was honestly surprised at such behaviour.

Yegor shook his head, causing even a bigger surprise. So he had to proceed with the explanations. "Only those people who have a crimson beret of their *own* can touch it."

Kira got up to put a kettle on the stove. "It means they're not given to everyone."

"Yes, you are right," Yegor confirmed her guess.

"So, what do you need to do to get it?"

"Are you really interested?" Yegor enquired, grinning.

"Well, you know, Yegor, after you almost broke my hand when I attempted just to touch it."

Appreciating her sense of humour, Yegor excused his being defensive about the headgear. "Sorry, again, Kira, but you can't, really."

"That's what I'm talking about," Kira agreed. "It's the first time ever when I came across a headgear which is, well, I don't know …" Kira struggled for the right word, "like an icon or something."

On hearing Kira's words, Yegor's face turned serious, as she had hit the score. "You are absolutely right, Kira. It is an icon for the Special Forces."

Kira thought she had made up a good joke, but Yegor's answer knocked her down again. Yegor, watching her expression change, had to add, "The beret is the essence of everything which is important for a man or a soldier — honour, courage, and brotherhood." Yegor stopped, struggling for words. "Words can't explain it. It's all in here," and he put his arm on his chest.

For a moment, the silence seemed dead, as Yegor and Kira were staring into each other's eyes.

"We have a special exam." Yegor was the first to break the silence. "If you are really interested, you can see it with your own eyes. It's gonna be in a couple of days — on the third of October."

"Where should I come?" Kira asked.

"Do you have anything to write on?" Yegor responded.

Kira got up and took a pen and a pad from the dresser, handing them over to Yegor.

"If you make up your mind to come," explained Yegor while writing, "here is the phone of the detachment's duty attendant. Ask for Lieutenant Menshikov. That's me. They will call me, and I'll tell you the details then."

"Okay," responded Kira, looking at the phone number.

She put the pad aside and filled the cups with tea, still turning over Yegor's explanations in her head.

CHAPTER 10

Finally came housekeeping day. Jobs were distributed, and all took their proper places. Once Kot was over with his scope of work, Artur accompanied him to the detachment's vehicle pool.

"Here's your wheel of fortune." Artur pointed at the APC tire as they entered the pool. "So, while I'm checking the machines, I want to hear you work it. Go!"

Artur turned around and headed for the workshop while Kot, his face wearing a sour expression, approached the tire lying near the workshop, did some rounds about it, and finally attempted to lift it. Having struggled some to lift it, he set the tire on edge and pushed it in the opposite direction. The wheel, giving a *puuuum* sound, fell to the ground. Then Kot approached the tire again to pick it up. Some seconds later, Artur heard another *puuuum*. In twenty more seconds, yet another, and so on.

The "wheel of fortune" was Artur's original invention. In the late nineties, they started to broadcast the *Strongest Man Ever* show. Artur used to complain jokingly that the TV producers had stolen the idea from him.

Besides the wheel, other "wonder devices" of encouragement have been used, for example, a "happiness tree" — a log near the detachment's headquarters. The tree was designated to train teamwork. A group of soldiers, picking the log up, had to do a variety of exercises: squats, running, handling the log from shoulder to shoulder, holding it in a static position, etc.

Artur entered the workshop approaching one of the APCs assigned to his team. The power section hatches were up, and a driver was stirring in the engine.

"Kochetok!" he called out to the driver.

The driver immediately straightened his back, and on seeing the commander, responded, "Here, comrade senior lieutenant!"

"What's up with the spares, Sanya?" Artur enquired.

"No spares yet, comrade senior lieutenant," the driver answered, shrugging his shoulders with obvious discontent. "I ask the technical deputy every day, but …"

Artur sighed and nodded. "Got you."

"I found a tube at the dump." Kochetok added some "sugar coat." "Installed it; seems to be all right."

Artur nodded again and complimented the driver, "Good job, Sanya."

Then, opening the personnel compartment, Artur climbed inside while Kochetok went back to the engine.

For a long time, the commanders hadn't considered the Internal Troops, its Special Forces included, to be the army. The Internal Troops were perceived as the police, the National Guard, the escort guard units; in fact, anything but the army, which meant they knew not how to wage war. Hence the attitude, different in all respects: the logistics (uniform and meals), ammunition, machines, engineering support, etc. Unlike the units under Defense Ministry supervision, where the personnel got whatever they wanted, drivers from our units had to work magic to repair their vehicles promptly with whatever they could find, say, at dumps.

Once, in 1989, the detachment's commander visited the Defense Ministry's Engineering Department to make a request for radio circuits to blow hollow charges and plastic explosives. He was invited to a huge cabinet, where he saw some engineering department officers, who, having heard his request, only sneered. "Charges, you say?" the department's head began. "Hey! You are escort guards! All you need is a reel of barbed wire and some tractors!"

"Fine," thought the detachment's commander. Pretending he hadn't heard the offensive comment, he told the big boss, "Comrade general, tomorrow we are having demonstration training. I'd like you to come and see it."

Of course they planned nothing of the kind. The detachment's commander just wanted the smarties to come and see it for themselves. His guys were always ready for demonstrations, as delegations never stopped coming!

The department's head accepted the invitation. The next day, a group of Engineering Department officers arrived at the training area in Novaya village.

As for Vityaz demonstration trainings, they deserve a special mention.

For Vityaz, these demonstrations were an art in itself, an art that could be compared, perhaps, to Cirque du Soleil. You know, there are a great many circuses, but Cirque du Soleil always stands apart, giving a show that makes people all over the world catch their breath in admiration.

The same applies to Vityaz demonstrations — there are army demonstrations, there are Special Forces demonstrations, and there are Vityaz demonstrations. I think Jackie Chan's stunt crew might be jealous of the things Vityaz soldiers pulled at their shows. And it is, indeed, how things are.

In 1990, the wife of Austria's chancellor paid a visit to Russia's Minister of the Interior, as the chancellor himself was not able to come. So, Vityaz was ordered to prepare a showcase. Later, Austria's first lady, giving an interview, remarked, "From all the things I've seen in Russia, I liked most the Bolshoi Theatre and the Special Forces show." You can imagine what kind of a show it must have been for the refined European lady to be that impressed to rank the demonstration as equal to the Bolshoi Theatre performance. Actually, it was then when friendly relations between Russia's Vityaz and Austria's Cobra started to develop.

When, early in the 2000s, I started working with film companies as a stunt director, I involved Vityaz soldiers. It caused quite a number of mishaps like that.

I showed a director what hand-to-hand combat would look like, and the director, having distributed assignments, cried out, "Action!" And we began — the soldiers got immediately involved in the action (their ability to involve themselves in the action could be envied by many professional actors). One could hear furious yells and the harsh sounds of clashing bodies. So, as the last punch was thrown and the stunt (my soldier) was on the ground, we expected the "Cut!" command. However, the film set was in dead silence. One of the soldiers fell to the ground, the other stood over his body, his teeth bared, looking like an animal on a hunt. Still no reaction! Only the same dead silence!

So, I turned around and saw the entire film crew frozen! We were at a loss, not knowing what to do next. Finally, after a very long pause, when the soldiers started looking about, their faces wearing interrogative expressions, everyone recovered and there came the "Cut!" command. Panic-stricken assistants rushed to the damaged soldier, while he just got up from the floor, healthy and intact.

"How are you? What happened?" I heard their excited voices.

"Well, I'm fine," the soldier replied impassively, shrugging his shoulders, perplexed, and shaking it off. For him, it was no big deal! They always worked like that at their training sessions.

As a rule, my soldiers needed just one shot to get a stunt done properly. So, when either directors or cameramen emphasized it was one take only, I used to say, "It's not like we ever have more."

And here's another example. I was invited to join a project as a stunt director for hand-to-hand combat, or the punching, as they say, while the rest of the stunts were supposed to be directed by a professional stunt director with a stunt crew of his own. So, as the filming was almost over and on the day when the last fighting scene was shot, the producer decided to leave us out to save some money (though our rates were much lower than those of the professional stunts), and just asked the professional stunt crew to deal with the fighting scene. Later, I got to hear the following story. As soon as they started filming, the faces of the entire shooting crew grew sour, and the director shouted at the producer: "Who are these creeps? Where are my Special Forces guys?" In the end, the scene was rejected and cut out.

When Vityaz soldiers were done with their routine, the detachment's commander lined them up in front of all the colonels and the generals from the Engineering Department, who were still trying to recover from the shocking show they'd witnessed.

"Those with a medal and an order," the commander cried out. "Fall out!" Two soldiers took two steps forward.

"Those who have two medals." Another command sounded. "Fall out!" Some more soldiers stepped forward.

"Those who have a medal or an order, fall out!" Only two soldiers stayed where they were, while all the rest of the line was now two steps forward.

And those were the peaceful times!

Getting up, the department's head approached the soldiers and paced along the line, staring into the faces of the heroes. Then he made a brisk turn and ordered, "From now on, you are to give them whatever they want!"

However, not only army officials are so prejudiced against the Internal Troops but also ordinary Russian citizens. Most think that the Internal Troops are not military at all, rather the police or escort guards — nothing serious, really. And, at war, those are mostly used for retreat blocking (back then NKVD Troops [People's Commissariat for Internal Affairs]).

However, the Special Forces are far from being the only Internal Troops' achievement. It was during the Great Patriotic War where the Internal Troops earned their deathless fame. Long before the feat of Alexander Matrosov, who covered up with his body a permanent fire position firing port, a similar feat was accomplished by a soldier from the NKVD troops. A detached battalion from the NKVD troops was fighting for Brest Fortress, and it was a soldier from this very battalion who wrote the famous words: "Farewell to you, dear Motherland. I'll die, but never surrender."

Should one go deeper, then the first Russian soldier slain in the first battle of the 1812 Patriotic War was Nikolay Ivanovich Ivshin, a warrant officer from Grodno Demi-Battalion of the Russian Empire's Internal Guard. It was the unit that had to meet Napoleon's attack first.

Besides, the Internal Troops' Central Sports Club gave us a great many famous sportsmen — Europe's, the world's, and Olympic champions and repeated European and world-record holders. Of course, listing them all here is impossible, so I'll just mention some of them:

Lev Yashin, Anatoliy Byshovets, Oleg Blokhin (football); Alexander Tikhonov, Sergey Chepikov (biathlon); Yulia Chepalova, Vasiliy Rochev, Evgeniy Redkin (skiing); Alexander Karelin (Greco-Roman wrestling); Alexander Popov (swimming); Alexander Maltsev (hockey); Shamil Tarpistchev, Marat Safin, Nikolay Davydenko (tennis), to name a few.

In 2012, at the London Olympics, members of the Internal Troops' Central Sports Club won eight gold medals.

* * *

Kot, his face tense and sweaty, was having a difficult time trying to pick up the APC tire and turn it over.

Having checked the machinery, Artur left the workshop and came up to Kot, watching him leisurely. He saw Kot struggling to lift the wheel. He did lift it, about half a metre above the ground, his mouth distorted with tension; however, that was about it — he was exhausted. Of course, he didn't stop trying, panting and puffing, but all his attempts were in vain.

"Come on, Kot, go for it!" Artur encouraged him good-naturedly.

Kot snarled like an angry animal, but his fingers failed him — and the wheel fell to the ground. Panting, Kot crouched, leaning on the hips.

"So, how are you doing, Kot?" Artur asked him, his voice quiet and level.

Kot raised his right hand, thumb up.

"Good for you!" Artur grinned. "Take the broom and sweep the workshops and then put the wheel back."

Kot straightened up and, sighing, headed for the workshops.

CHAPTER 11

Nenashev was practising with his unloaded gun when Yegor knocked on his door.

"May I come in, comrade lieutenant colonel?"

Nenashev put the gun down and turned around to face Yegor. "So, Yegor," he began, "get your team ready. You are to be at the theatre in an hour," and then he gave Yegor a meaningful look.

"Got you," Yegor replied after a short pause. "May I leave?"

"Yes, go."

Yegor went out of the cabinet, while Nenashev went back to the exercise.

Three minutes later, Yegor was standing in front of his team, announcing solemnly the commander's order. "Attention, team! For your excellent results in battle and special training, the detachment's commander decided to award you! In fifty minutes, we're off, leaving for the theatre! So, you are to be in full dress, clean and shaved. Line up in forty-five minutes! Any questions?"

The team was silently looking at Yegor, so he finished the speech. "Dismissed!"

The soldiers scattered, and Kirei, embracing Phil happily, said, "Cool, isn't it?"

"Not sure about that, Sanya." Phil's enthusiasm left him unaffected. "I'm not a big theatre fan, you know. I'd rather practise punches and kicks than sit my ass off there."

"Come on, Diman," Kirei tried to explain his point. "We can

catch up some really nice chicks there!"

"You think so?" Phil gave Kirei a distrustful look.

"Believe me!" Kirei assured him. "Girls like going to theatres."

"Well, if you think so!" On second thought, Phil agreed and they entered the bay.

There were few people who felt the same as Phil, because, notwithstanding all of their Special Forces commitment, most missed the city lights and were willing to show themselves and see stuff. So, the soldiers cleaned up and shaved thoroughly and brushed up their full-dress uniform.

Half an hour later, Kirei, already dressed up, was standing at the orderly post.

"Seryoga!" he called out to Mironov, who was passing by with a towel around his hips. "Lend me your cologne."

"Check the bedside table," Mironov replied, entering the washing room.

"Sieda!" Kirei called out to the soldier who happened to be running by. "Bring me Miron's cologne from the bay. It's on his bedside table."

Sieda ran on, while Kirei dropped in at the utility room to have another look in the mirror. Sieda was back in thirty seconds.

"Well?" Kirei asked him as he saw no cologne in his hands.

"It's under his beret!"

"Okay," replied Kirei calmly and headed for the bay.

Coming up to the bedside table where Miron's crimson beret was lying, Kirei lifted the beret and took the cologne flask. Having sprinkled some on his body, he put it back under the beret.

Only those who wore crimson berets themselves could touch the others' berets. An ordinary soldier would never touch the beret, even when he knew there was no one around and the door was closed — this is how strong the respect was of the Special Forces relic and its traditions. However, things could go too far sometimes.

It happened sometimes that a crimson beret soldier would put his headgear on a bedside table or a bed and leave. Later, either unwilling or short of time to come back in before the formation, he would ask the orderly to bring him the beret. The orderly, seeing no crimson beret soldiers around and realizing he has to fulfil the order anyway, would bring out the bedside table, the table, or the bed with the crimson beret on it.

Of course, I believe that's a twist! And the Special Forces should get rid of stuff like that.

In cases like that, the detachment's commander imposed strict sanctions, starting from a month's ban of wearing the beret. First, it was a punishment for leaving the beret unattended on some bedside table, instead of wearing it close to the heart. Second, giving someone an order to bring the beret might be considered a Hans thing, almost bullying.

However, even these negative aspects illustrate well the special attitude soldiers had to the crimson beret.

Sometime later, Yegor and his team got on the bus, all dressed up in new camouflage outfits. Some soldiers had their awards on. Yegor was the last to get on the bus.

"Comrade lieutenant!" Kirei addressed him. "What's the performance?"

Yegor, taking a quick count, glanced at the sergeant. "*Dead Souls*, by Gogol," he replied, turning to the driver. "Go!"

The driver started the bus, and it slowly left the detachment's premises.

* * *

As agreed, Lazarenko came back in a week, and Nenashev accepted him at once, just as promised. Some days later, he was appointed the commander of a platoon from the 2nd SWAT team.

Lazarenko went out of the orderly room and looked around. "Kiselev!" he called out to Kisel, who was standing at the bay entrance.

Kisel approached the officer.

"Sanya, find some fast runner!" Lazarenko commanded. "Tell him to go buy some cakes at the snack room."

"Aye!" Kisel heard the order out impassively.

"Here's the money." Lazarenko handed him the money. "But tell him to speed up. I'm in a hurry, okay?"

Kisel took the money and, in the same impassive manner, said, "Yes, got you."

Lazarenko nodded and went back inside the orderly room, while Kisel headed for the bay. Just at that moment, the bay door opened, and he saw Talanych running out.

"Talanych!"

The soldier froze in front of the sergeant.

"Here, comrade sergeant!"

"So, Andrey," Kisel began instructing, "now you go to the snack bar. No need to hurry, take your time. Sit there as long as you can, perhaps, until it's closed. And buy anything you want — a cake, some lemonade. Just enjoy your meal, okay?"

Talanych was shocked. He, being a fresher, didn't hope to visit the snack bar (soldiers' café) for a year, at least. And now his commander was sending him there, telling him to have a cup of tea with a cake. Talanych couldn't believe his ears.

"And right before it closes," Kisel continued, "buy some more cakes and bring them here; no need to hurry, as well. Understand?"

"Yes, comrade sergeant!" Talanych was completely at a loss.

"Here's the money," and Kisel handed him the money Lazarenko gave him. "Go!"

Talanych took the money and darted off.

"Stop!" Kisel cried out.

Talanych turned on his heels and went back to where he was.

"I said no need to hurry!" Kisel emphasized. "Now go!"

Talanych, still incredulous about the whole situation, turned around and, at an easy pace (whereas usually everything was done running), headed for the snack bar to fulfil the most fabulous order he'd ever been given his entire military career.

* * *

The bus of the 3rd SWAT team drove into a hospital's yard and stopped at the entrance. Yegor jumped out of the bus, and, running up the stairs, disappeared inside the building.

"What is it? A hospital?" Phil voiced his question, addressing it to no one in particular. "Why are we here?"

"Maybe Yegor has some business to deal with here," Kirei suggested.

Yegor was back in some minutes. "Out!" he commanded, standing on the step plate.

The soldiers, having no idea why they were there, began getting out of the bus, lining up.

"From the right, one by one, forward, march toward the building," Yegor commanded calmly, and soon the team was inside the hospital building.

Catching up with the team, Yegor took his place at the head of the line to show the direction. When they were down in the basement, Yegor stopped at one of the doors. Having examined the line to make sure everyone was present, he opened the door.

"Come in," he ordered with decision, and the soldiers, still at a loss, entered the room.

When they were all inside, the soldiers' expressions changed — the room was full of corpses.

"Come up here, to this table!" Yegor encouraged them loudly, giving them no time to recover their senses. However, the soldiers' brains worked well enough for them to understand that the theatre performance was off.

The soldiers approached the table to see a corpse of a young girl lying on it. Phil turned to Kirei and whispered to him, "Hey, Sanya, those are your chicks."

"Don't be shy. Come closer, please," invited the doctor who was standing right beside the table.

The soldiers, moving hesitantly, surrounded the table while the doctor began his speech.

"This is a woman's corpse. Thirty-two years old. Our provisional diagnosis is that she died of acute cardiovascular failure," and, glancing at the soldiers, the doctor shared another suggestion. "I think it was an aortic aneurism rupture, or, as common people say, a heart break. We need an autopsy to confirm our suggestions." The doctor looked at the woman's corpse, some thought obvious on his face. "Pay attention, please, colleagues!" He finally returned to his colleagues, pointing at what caught his eye. "Her chest is damaged, because her ribs have been broken. Also, we can see an abdominal distension, which is due to some air present in her stomach." He looked at his colleagues again, explaining. "It's all because our people know nothing about emergency care –artificial respiration and closed-chest cardiac massage," the doctor said, back in his musings again. "Well," he sighed, "here we go."

Taking a lancet, he started making a cut, and the soldiers all went dumb.

Yegor, having already been through it, was watching his guys intently. "Watch the doctor carefully!" The soldiers soon heard his loud voice.

Such visits were designed to strengthen the soldiers' psyches, as Vityaz commanders were extremely serious about ensuring a comprehensive training. Since battle missions usually meant immense psychological strain, such psychological tricks were of no less importance than physical training. In addition, there was a firing-assault course (FAC) where soldiers were tested with deafening explosions and flames. In both the FAC and the building assault practise, they used only real explosives — trotyl and plastid. Such tests also included shooting with service tracer bullets over crawling soldiers and setting soldiers on fire, which they had to extinguish all on their own, and trial runs with dogs, and so on.

Back at Novosibirsk Higher Military Command School of the RF MVD Interior Troops, I read an article about the Special Forces (I'd read about everything I could find on this topic). The article said that one of the big bosses, having a tour of the premises of the Independent Special Designation Division, saw SWAT soldiers practising. The article mentioned nothing about what kind of practise it was, but I suppose it was a forced march (or a regular cross-country). While practising, the SWAT soldiers were crying out a camp chant, something of the kind: "We are the SWATs! We are the best!"

The big boss was naturally indignant. "What's wrong with them?" he boiled over. "Are they trying to put themselves before all the rest? Where does this arrogance come from?" Something like that.

In fact, the chanting (or slogan shouting) is no more than a mere tune-up. In this way, SWAT meant to bring up their soldiers to think like winners. This is the very thought (I'm the best, consequently, "Who else but me?") that makes SWAT soldiers rise to the occasion and conquer new heights. This is the very thought that gives them courage to enter a basement full of terrorists.

Occasionally, SWAT soldiers visited Sklifosovskogo Institute for Emergency Medicine to watch an autopsy.

Moreover, these visits were always unexpected for soldiers (to make the psychological training more efficient, of course). Soldiers were usually told they were going out — to the theatre, cinema, circus, museum, etc. Naturally, this surprise effect was of major importance because, being at war, one can never know when to expect such horrors.

* * *

Nenashev was sitting at the table, cleaning his gun, when he heard a knock on the door and saw Yegor at the threshold.

"May I come in, comrade lieutenant colonel?"

"Sure, Yegor," the commander invited him in. "So, how did it go?"

"Well, two had to go out for some fresh air; the rest were all right."

"Fine," Nenashev concluded. "Tomorrow, Team Four is going to a circus show. Get those two to join them."

"Got you," Yegor replied. "May I go?"

"Go!" Nenashev nodded and Yegor left the room.

In the morning, Kisel knocked on the door of the orderly room.

"May I come in, comrade senior lieutenant?" he asked Lazarenko. "You asked me to buy some cakes yesterday, right?" and, coming up to the table, he put a package with cakes on it. "May I go?" the sergeant asked, looking calmly at the officer.

"Seems like I did something wrong," Lazarenko replied with a question. "Am I right?"

Kisel looked at him for some seconds, thinking over the answer. "Well, yes, I could say." He decided to make the young officer clear on this.

Lazarenko gave him an enquiring look, waiting for a more precise explanation.

"I mean," Kisel began, "to give assignments like this, moreover, using this kind of tone, you have to be something more than just an officer. You have to be a hardcore SWAT officer. Such assignments are a privilege of those SWAT officers who've seen real stuff, whose authority is without question." Kisel looked up at Lazarenko once again. "You are all right, of course, if you made it into the detachment. However, it's not enough. For one, anyone of our team is now a better SWAT soldier than you are, let alone the old-timers and the sergeants. So, to earn their respect you have to prove you are harder than they."

Lazarenko listened to Kisel attentively.

"In our detachment, respect is not about your rank. Rather, it's about your deeds and professional attitude," Kisel concluded.

Lazarenko was evidently processing what he has just heard from the sergeant. For him, everything was so different from his former regiment, but, in fact, he realized he liked it better. "Got you," he nodded. "Thank you." He reached out to shake the sergeant's hand. "May I use your help then, if I need?"

"As a matter of fact, you can ask anyone," Kisel replied, shaking his hand. "Don't be shy to learn from soldiers. There's nothing shameful about learning. It's shameful to know nothing and leave things as they are."

"Sure," Lazarenko agreed. "Thank you once again."

"May I go?" Kisel asked, saluting.

"Yes." The officer gave his permission and Kisel went out.

Indeed, to be an officer was hardly enough to earn a soldier's respect. One had to be a true professional and a real man.

So, once an officer proved to have all the qualities needed, his authority became indisputable. Later, Lazarenko proved himself to be a true Vityaz officer, his name forever recorded in its history.

* * *

We've had no special training at the military school. I had no idea of vehicle and building assault tactics as well as that of altitude and special missions. So, when I joined Vityaz, whenever I had some free time, I asked a soldier to help me with those. I learnt from my soldiers, actually. I remember myself dangling like a worm from a rope and saw my soldiers giggling. Many officers have no nerve to cast themselves in such a light before their subordinates; therefore, they prefer to leave it as it is, catching only the "tops" without understanding the essence. I had no fear like that, so, in just a couple of months, I was way ahead of all the gigglers, becoming their teacher. And they always followed my orders. However, even later, whenever I saw someone doing something better than me, I was not ashamed to ask them to teach me.

Thus, learning isn't shameful. It's shameful to know nothing and leave things as they are.

The Hans would, of course, be outraged at this state of things, but what else could one expect from those people? It's because of this attitude that officers in Hans units are called jackals, whereas the Special Forces have never had a thing like that. In fact, Vityaz officers and soldiers felt more connected with each other, their relations far beyond what's prescribed by the charter, rarely to be seen in the rest of the army.

* * *

October 3, 1993

It was the putsch date. Vityaz soldiers were among the few units who remained loyal.

It's due to Vityaz soldiers that the putsch gangsters failed in their attempts to seize Ostankino TV center. On that day, they saved a lot of lives.

As commanders got the information about tanks moving toward Ostankino TV center, they decided to leave all the senior and warrant officers and contracted soldiers, while private soldiers were to be transported to the permanent location point.

The order was announced to all the soldiers. However, those refused to obey, explaining they would stand by their officers till the end!

In the morning, when things were back in their proper places, a lot of journalists arrived at the center. They saw a soldier sitting on the steps, opening a can with his bayonet knife. They all rushed to him, poking their microphones in his face.

"Are you for Yeltsin or for Khazbulatov?" they shouted, vying with each other.

The SWAT soldier looked up at them impassively and answered in the same impassive manner, "I'm for my platoon's commander."

Or the 1980s, Nagorniy Karabakh. The Armenia–Azerbaijan conflict. The SWAT platoon of the Internal Troops' Tactical Brigade, which was located in the conflict area, held the opposing insurgents tight under their control (I've already mentioned the platoon before). They either arrested or eliminated dozens of insurgents, confiscating their weapons. As long as the platoon was there, the insurgents couldn't come close to the civilians.

Once, on a day off, Captain Larin, the SWAT platoon's commander, heard his doorbell ring. He went to open the door and, as he was turning the key, a gun fired, the blast going through his chest. The heavily injured officer sank to the floor. The bullet entered right under the heart.

His platoon's soldiers, his deputy sergeant Tikhonov in charge, brought him to hospital. In the hospital, the personnel laid him down on a stretcher and took him to the surgery. As the surgeon came into the room, he recognized the injured SWAT officer immediately. The surgeon was from an extremist paramilitary group, and, some months before, Larin and his guys gave them some trouble. So, he thought it was the right moment for revenge.

"I'm not going to do the surgery," the surgeon announced.

"What do you mean?" The sergeant was shocked.

"I am definitely not," the surgeon insisted. "I'm not a heart specialist. Take him to some other hospital."

He was perfectly aware that the officer's time was running out and he wouldn't make it to some other hospital. Sergeant Tikhonov realized it, too. So, after exchanging a long look with the doctor, he made his decision. He took a grenade and pulled out its safety pin, crying out loud, "I'm not putting it back until you to do the surgery," and, coming up to the door, he added, "and I'm not letting anyone out!"

At first, the surgeon tried to pretend like he didn't care. However, on seeing the sergeant's determination, he finally started the surgery. And the sergeant kept standing by him, the grenade in his hands, for as long as the surgery lasted.

So, Larin was saved.

Both of these stories illustrate the unrivalled courage of SWAT soldiers and the way they were all for their commanders.

CHAPTER 12

The detachment's commander's car stopped at the shooting range. Nenashev got out of it, accompanied by another inspector from the central administration.

Nenashev and the inspector entered the shooting range, where soldiers were practising shooting in threesomes comprising a machine gunner and two rifle shooters. The soldiers were moving by short bounds, covering each other. As soon as a threesome reached the destination, they threw themselves down.

"Retreat!" one of the rifle shooters shouted.

The second shooter fired a smoke agent, throwing it forward, and the threesome set out to retreat. The retreat was also by short bounds, the soldiers covering each other.

Vityaz was the first to realize that to retreat backward, occasionally shooting at the enemy, is neither convenient nor reasonable. First, it's almost impossible to hit a target from such a position. Second, the retreating speed is too slow, so one is going to be too easy a target for the enemy. Third, one can trip over something, hence, the fourth argument against such retreat tactics: one can accidentally take down one's fellows.

That's why Vityaz opted for another retreat tactic, making it an asset for the rest of the army as well. Some soldiers have to give cover, providing for precise fire, while the rest retreat by bounds. Once the first group is at its due position, it orders the second group to move, covering its retreat. Vityaz even had a special pistol technique for the action.

Artur was at the limit of opening fire, watching his guys moving. Another threesome was standing beside him, at the initial limit.

The inspector was horrified at the mess he saw.

"Lieutenant colonel, it's unacceptable! You are breaking all the safety rules! Are you nuts here?" He gave Nenashev a reproachful look, proceeding with the safety instructions. "All the shooting soldiers must be at the same limit! When it's shooting in motion, then it should be one by one. And, while moving, the weapons must be set at safe. And what's going on here?"

Nenashev heard him out and offered his explanation, his voice calm and even, "Comrade colonel, their safety locks must be in their heads because, in a battle, there will be no safety locks, no limits of opening fire. They will have to shoot over the heads of their fellows."

"However, it's no war now!"

"It's gonna be too late then!" Nenashev objected coldly. "Too late to teach them anything then, while, now, they can experience how it's gonna be in a real battle under an officer's supervision, the situation entirely controllable."

It was evident the explanation left the colonel unaffected, but as he couldn't find any arguments to defend his point, he just preferred to keep silent.

One of the threesomes finished the routine and Artur commanded, "Stand up! Middle close march!"

The soldiers got up, holding their weapons barrels up, and did as ordered, their actions swift and precise.

"Inspection arms!" there sounded another command.

Meantime, Nenashev and the inspector entered the neighbouring shooting range.

There, the 3rd SWAT team was shooting, their exercise being the rapid fire. The targets were fifty to one hundred metres apart, and the inspector made a sour expression again.

"What is this? Where did you get the exercise from?"

"It's our original development," Nenashev explained impassively, "for rapid fire."

"You are always doing it your own way, lieutenant colonel! You have a course in marksmanship, and those people who developed it were no fools. So why do you need to invent anything else?"

"The course in marksmanship has only long-distance shooting exercises."

"That's right! You should teach your soldiers shooting from three to four hundred-metre distances!"

Nenashev listened to the inspector's reproaches calmly, finally shaking his head. "Comrade colonel." He once more referred to the inspector's logic thinking. "Can you tell from a three hundred metre distance whether it's your enemy or your fellow?"

The inspector was at a loss.

"To identify a target, one needs to be as close as one hundred metres," the detachment's commander continued. "This is first. And second, judging by Vietnam War experience, up to seventy percent of targets are missed in close-up action. Close-up actions are always rapid fire. Soldiers have no time for target identification. Most are not trained enough to cope with that, so we thought the exercise might be useful for the purpose."

As the inspector had nothing to object to, he just moved on.

At the shooting range exit, he saw three targets, the distance to them some ten metres. "Well, and here, what do you have here?"

At that moment, two explosions sounded near the targets, making the inspector duck down, hunching. The next instance, he heard the iron doors of the shooting range clattering open and saw two soldiers running in. They had black masks on, special NFFSD weapons in their hands. They fired a couple double shots and froze in front of the targets, holding their barrels up.

"Clear!" the first soldier cried out.

"Clear!" the other one confirmed.

"Stop!" Yegor shouted.

And the soldiers took the attention position, holding their weapons barrels up.

"Arms inspection!" Yegor commanded, approaching them.

"Shooting range, retreat!" Once the arms were inspected, he voiced another command. "Double time, march toward the targets for inspection!"

The soldiers ran up to their target, Yegor following them to check the hits.

"Situational shooting," Nenashev proceeded with explanations. "Releasing hostages in a building."

"And what are these targets?" The inspector made another bureaucratic-style enquiry.

"These are situational targets[1]," Nenashev replied patiently. "The terrorist–hostage one. Why?"

"Well, the targets are no good," the inspector said, demonstrating his expertise.

"So, what are good targets then?" Nenashev asked, a reasonable question.

"Those that are green and rectangular," the colonel clarified knowingly.

Nenashev made a careful enquiry, just to make things clear.

"Comrade colonel, have you seen green and rectangular people?"

The inspector realized he was making a fool of himself. "Still, targets must comply with control samples!" He made one last attempt to maintain his authority and headed for the exit.

Done with another exercise, Yegor commanded to retreat, and the soldiers rushed toward their targets.

As all the soldiers were positioned at their targets, Yegor started checking the hits. When it was Lis's turn, Yegor examined the target carefully and turned around to face the shooter. All the hits were at the center mark.

"Hey, Yura!" Yegor lifted his hands in surprise. "Why do you always hit the score at training, and whenever we have a test, your bullets go sideways? What's up with you, man?"

Lis only shrugged his shoulders. "I wish I knew, comrade lieutenant."

"Fine," Yegor decided to leave Lis alone. "Double march, to the starting position!"

And the soldiers ran back routinely to the starting position.

Some minutes later, the entire group was lying at the limit of opening fire, ready to proceed with the second part of the exercise. Yegor, having surveyed the group, gave an order to open fire, "Shooting range, fire!"

Soldiers unlocked the safety locks, and the sounds of shooting filled the range. Lis, lying beside Yegor, was confidently processing the shot through the optics, while Yegor was watching him thoughtfully. Suddenly, as if some important idea struck him, he shook up, speaking up, "Lisitsyn, up!"

Lis, putting his SWD down, hurried to get up and froze in front of Yegor, who, metal in his voice, all of a sudden was yelling at him. "What's wrong with your uniform, soldier? From the rear!"

And Lis plummeted forward.

"As you were!"

And Lis jumped back up at once.

"Your belt is loose!" Grabbing by the belt, Yegor pulled at it, using all his strength. "Take care of your outfit, soldier!"

Hastily, Lis undid his belt. As Yegor saw Lis losing control, he piped another command, "Action! Faster!"

Lis, his uniform unbelted, plummeted to the ground, taking the shooting position, while Yegor was already shouting another order, "Fire!"

Lis, having fired three quick shots, reported, "Comrade lieutenant, Private Lisitsyn is done with the shooting."

A minute later, as Yegor was checking Lis's target, he found only two hits out of three. Moreover, both were within the "milk" area, at the target's edges.

"Well, well, well!" Yegor was looking at the suddenly sullen Lis, his voice sounding content. And the contentedness in Yegor's voice was because he now knew why the shooter missed his targets.

"Those emotions of yours, Lis. You can't control them! I think we need some emergency therapy."

And Yegor got down to the therapy, which included the following treatments:

- Lis would start with doing press-ups, and then Yegor would command, "Action!" and Lis would have to fire his shots.
- While Lis would be lying at the limit, taking sight, Yegor would be gunning, the bullets whistling right above Lis's head. Then Yegor would command, "Fire!" and Lis would have to shoot under Yegor's dense fire.
- Yegor and Lis would start with a sparring. Yegor would throw a body punch, Lis's body doubling, and then would at once command, "Action!" So, Lis, his hand on the plexus, would run toward his SWD, strip for action quickly, and fire a shot.
- Lis would be taking sight to shoot, while Yegor would be pouring water onto his head.
- Lis would be taking sight while Yegor would be tearing a package with flour over his head.
- And then Lis would be shooting over and over again!

The purpose of it all was quite simple — to teach the shooter how to ignore all the external irritants.

It took some time till Lis returned the target with all hits at the center mark.

"Finally!" Yegor was content with the result. "Good job! If you go on like this, the 'five' is yours."

For Vityaz shooters, it was the highest level of mastery to hit a five-kopecks coin at one shot from a hundred metres. After this, they drilled the coin to make a hole in it, and threading a string through the hole, wore it around their necks.

Someone might say, "Big deal! A kilometre — that's a wow!"

However, Vityaz shooters have never had to hit targets at a longer distance.

Of course, I've heard there was a Vympel shooter (a graduate of the Internal Troops' School, by the way) who sent a bullet right into a gangster's forehead from a half kilometre distance when the gangster showed his head a little through a brick-size firing port, and the other one got a "bullet pill" for his ass, which he dared to exhibit to our soldiers.

This sure is the highest level of mastery!

Nevertheless, a Vityaz shooter (or from any other antiterrorist unit) must be able to easily hit a terrorist in the eye from some one or two hundred metres without hurting the hostage.

So, shooters were usually chosen from among phlegmatics, as those had to be able to lie still for hours on end, unresponsive to any irritants, watching the terrorist through the optics, ready to smoothly press the trigger upon order to shoot the bastard's head off.

Yegor turned around, facing the group, "Group, line up!"

"Comrade lieutenant, may I try the SWD, just once?" Phil approached Yegor.

"Next time."

"Comrade lieutenant, please," the soldier's eyes pleaded. "I just have to."

"Why?" The soldier had got Yegor interested.

The soldier wavered for a moment, but then showed a photo of a girl. Yegor smiled at him, shaking his head. "Lis," he called out to the shooter, "give this Othello a rifle. Sanya, you give him three bullets."

"Aye!" Kirei, who was responsible for the ammunition, responded.

"You've got three minutes," Yegor looked up at Phil.

"Aye!" Phil replied and went to hang the photo.

Done with shooting out the photo, Phil removed it and joined the line, satisfied.

"Feel better, huh?" Yegor grinned at him.

"Yes!" Indeed, the soldier sounded relieved.

"Thank god," the officer added, still grinning. "Arms inspection!"

Soldiers took their weapons in their hands and, pointing the barrels at the targets, pulled back the bolt carrier assemblies. Looking from behind the soldiers' backs, Yegor checked breech pieces.

"Inspection over!" he gave an overall order.

As the soldiers were done with control pull-off, they set their weapons at safe and slung those over their shoulders.

"To the right!" Yegor gave another order, and the group turned toward the exit. "Forward, march to the exit!"

---

1. *Back then, soldiers made these situational targets with their own hands since they were not available ready-made.*

CHAPTER 13

It was a beautiful autumn morning, sunny and dry. The weather was just right for the day, as this day was about the most important for SWAT soldiers. Some guys had spent years to prepare for that day — the day of the crimson beret qualification exam, or as SWAT soldiers say, "The Exam."[1]

For every SWAT soldier, the exam is an Olympics of its own, a crimson beret being just as precious an award as the Olympic gold for sportsmen. And it's no exaggeration.

A car parked beside the detachment's premises, and Kira and Yegor got out of it.

"Kira, you'd better wait here," Yegor said. "I'll sort things out and we'll be on our way then."

"All right," Kira nodded, replying.

Yegor hurried to the ground where the preparations for the exam were in full swing.

Contenders wanting to get a crimson beret were lined up, each wearing an armour vest and a helmet. They were holding their weapons in prebattle positions — barrels up in their right hands. Artur was facing the contenders' line, checking if everyone was present.

"Kiselev?"

"Here," Kisel replied.

"Philatov?" Artur proceeded to the next name.

"Here," Phil hurried to confirm his presence.

Yegor, in his turn, was giving each contender a blank bullet, pacing along the line. The bullet was for checking the weapons after the march. The contenders put the bullet into the magazines and attached the magazines to their machine guns.

Standing at the entrance to the detachment's premises, Nenashev was supervising the last preparations, his eyes intent on the soldiers. Suddenly, a soldier, the one on the very fringe of the line, caught his eye. He had his finger on the trigger, which was a violation of rule two: "Hold your finger on the trigger guard."

"Soldier!" Nenashev pointed at him.

"Yes?" the soldier responded, as he understood Nenashev was talking to him.

"Finger!" Nenashev commented briefly, and the soldier got what he meant at once.

The soldier shifted his finger quickly onto the trigger guard. However, Artur had already noticed him. "Your name?"

"Antipov," the soldier replied, his voice wobbling a bit.

"Dismissed," Artur announced the sentence unemotionally, without even looking at the soldier anymore and crossed his name off the list.

"Well, brother," Nenashev made a helpless gesture. "If they say dead, then she's certainly dead."

A soldier in a crimson beret rushed toward Antipov. He detached the magazine from Antipov's machine gun, took out the bullet, and gave the magazine back to Antipov. Taking it, the soldier headed for the barracks, his head drooping. That was it for his exam — the price he had to pay for the mistake.

There's an army instruction booklet detailing weapon handling rules. The rules are numerous, but one can mention the three basics: "Don't breech," (breeching when needed only), "Don't point," (never point weapons at people, even if the weapons are not loaded), "Don't leave," (never leave weapons unattended).

However, Vityaz has one more important rule (and from Vityaz, the rule was inherited by the rest of SWAT detachments), which I think should also be included in the said instruction (at least, in 2012, it was not there): "Hold your finger on the trigger guard," (shifting it onto the trigger only immediately before shooting). There are a number of world-famous films where a character would either trip over something (or just shudder) and shoot himself in some body part (sometimes, even in the head, like in *Pulp Fiction* or *Out of Sight*). And the army is abundant with such illustrations — one stumbles over, shudders, catches one's outfit on something and shoots his fellow soldier in the leg, hand, or head. So, to justify the unprofessional behaviour, people then have to invent exclusive stories of heroism for the parents of the deceased.

This is what the rule is for. It's the rule each soldier gets to know at his first acquaintance with arms. This is the small thing that distinguishes a true professional, because in a battle, when the arms are loaded and off safe, the only safety device is your head, which is to make sure the finger is on the trigger guard. So, if a soldier's finger is off the trigger guard, it means he can't control the situation and must not be allowed to take part in special missions.

Once, on a detached service, we learned there was a group of gangsters hiding in an abandoned cultural center. We were at the destination in no time and, having surrounded the house, began the "cleaning" procedure, trying to be as fast as possible. As this was a major mission, we had to approach the house simultaneously from several sides. I and one more officer were approaching from the right, exterior side, taking up the first floor and the side exits. As we were checking an exit, I swung my body forward, sticking the barrel out into the passage, and saw a man holding his machine gun at the trail. It was at evening, dusk, so I could see only his silhouette. While I was shifting my finger onto the trigger to shoot (it was a moment only!) I managed to recognize him and he managed to cry out, "Friends!" I put my finger back to where it'd been and went on with checking the surroundings. However, if I were holding my finger on the trigger, the old good friend of mine could have been long dead. So, "Glory to the special forces! Glory to professionals!"

* * *

Yegor approached his soldiers, five at this exam. Taken that his group included twelve soldiers, and three of them already had crimson berets, it was an achievement in itself.[2]

"So, guys," he started his speech. "Don't expect the march to be easy. It's gonna be way harder than you can imagine. At some moment, you might think, 'That's it! I can't stand it!' and then you will want to quit the race. However, don't forget that 'can't' is always about collapsing and coming around smelling ammoniac. That's what I understand as 'can't,' whereas, if you can still see, hear, think, and move — that's about 'I don't want!' only. So, just clench your teeth and deal with it! And remember; you've all had enough training. You are all equally capable to do this, both physically and professionally. The crimson beret exam is, first of all, a test to see if your *spirit* is strong enough. Those who are strong in spirit and determined to win will definitely succeed! Keep it in mind!"

He paused and, emphasizing each word, added, "Do or die! I might die, but I'll make it!"[3]

Yegor looked over his subordinates, who were listening to him attentively. His tone became more relaxed, almost light-hearted, and he concluded, "If you need the WC, then use your pants. Don't worry about it much — later, we'll throw your rags away anyway."

Some minutes later, as the preparations were over, the entire detachment lined up, waiting for the readiness report the detachment's commander was to hear out. The detachment's Deputy Commander for Special Training, Major Putilin, looked over the line and ordered, "Dress! Ready, front! Dress middle!" and then, saluting, he reported to Nenashev. "Comrade lieutenant colonel!" he began. "Vityaz, the 6th SWAT Detachment, is lined up ready for the crimson beret qualification exam! Detachment's Deputy

Commander for Special Training Major Putilin, reporting!"

"My greeting, soldiers!" Nenashev greeted the line.

"Greeting, comrade lieutenant colonel!" thundered the voices of the soldiers.

"Stand easy!" Nenashev commanded, lowering his hand.

"Stand easy!" repeated Putilin.

"Soldiers!" the detachment's commander started his speech. "My fellows! Today, you are taking the qualification exam, but there's another reason to remember this day. It's been a year since we've lost Nikolay Sitnikov, a soldier from our detachment, who was fatally wounded in a mission. Let's honour his memory with a minute of silence."

Nenashev, taking off the beret, put it down onto the right arm, and bending his right knee, dropped his head, the soldiers acting the same way. A minute later, everyone was up, putting on their headgear.

"That's it," Nenashev concluded. "Go ahead!"

"Contenders!" Putilin commanded. "Form a column, officers ahead!"

The contenders were soon done with the task and lined up in front of Putilin. The line was surrounded by soldiers in crimson berets, Chef, Kot, Kirei, and Lebed among them. Those were the instructors who were to accompany the contenders, evaluating their actions. Artur gave them his last directions.

"And remember!" he said harshly, "let them show what they're worth! No mercy! The berets are for the best only!"

The instructor on the front edge of the line, who was to be in charge of the march, cried out, "Double, march!"

And the contenders, surrounded by instructors, marched off toward their dreams, while the rest of the "spectators" got into vehicles — some on the bus, and some on the Ural. The bus would be waiting at the finish line, while the Ural would be picking up those who would fall out of the race. Of course, not everyone would make it to the end.

Yegor, having sorted things out, came up to Kira. "We can go now."

"Shall we follow them?" Kira beckoned toward the marching group.

"No," Yegor shook his head. "We'll inspect the control points only."

The exam begins with a twelve-kilometre march. It was not just running, but "smooth" running, as close as possible to a warfare situation. The route went across a forest, some hills, and a number of water obstacles. From time to time, it was interrupted by different tasks, such as carrying a casualty, destroying an ambush, and passing a contaminated area.

Contenders had to pass the dirtiest road sections crawling on their stomachs, without missing the smallest puddle.

It was not only physical strain that instructors used to "kill" contenders, but also psychological pressure, making them break down and give up.

A group, for example, was doing press-ups on their fists, waiting for the rest to cross the river. "Guys!" Kirei called out to the contenders. "What the hell do you need this for? Get inside the bus, have some tea, take a rest! I'm sure you can do it some other time."

 Because of the ragged running, which is constantly interrupted by various events and the cold water, soldiers go completely out of breath; their legs grow heavy and cramped. With all of this, plus the instructors getting on their nerves, some of the soldiers prefer to quit the race.

However, most contenders, clenching their teeth and pummeling their cramped legs, growling and grating their teeth, move on.

Some don't give up but can't handle the strain and pass out, the accompanying instructors and the medical men attending to them.

Artur, Yegor, and Kira were waiting together for the group to arrive at a control point.

There are a number of control points along the entire distance. The points are where instructors order soldiers to put their weapons up in pre-battle positions (hold their weapons in their right hands, barrels up) and speed up.

Not far from where the officers and a girl were standing, a group of foreigners, some wearing military uniforms, were also waiting for the soldiers to arrive.

"Are these the foreign guests we expected?" Yegor asked Artur.

"Yep. The ones wearing uniforms are Austrians, Cobra guys, and the ones with caps and sunglasses are Americans, the Marines."

"And the camera guy?" and Yegor beckoned toward one of the guests.

"That's a French journalist."

In some minutes, they could see the contenders approaching, wet and dirty. Some even had their uniforms torn. It was obvious they were dead tired. As the group was crossing the control point, the guests started cheering them on. Two soldiers were some fifteen metres behind the rest of the group.

As soon as Artur saw the last contender from the basic group running past him, he gave an order to the two instructors standing beside him. "That's it!" he said to the ones who were falling behind.

The instructors at once blocked the road in front of the two soldiers, and they came to a halt, looking miserable.

"And why have you stopped them?" Kira turned around to Yegor.

"The ones who fall behind the basic group at a control point are eliminated," Yegor explained.

The instructors took the blank bullets out of the eliminated soldiers' magazines, while Artur crossed them off the list. Their heads dropped in despair as they got in the Ural vehicle.

"Let's move on," Yegor invited Kira to join another adventure.

"And how long do they have to run?" Kira asked as they approached the car.

"Twelve kilometres in total. They're in the middle now — at the sixth kilometre mark," Yegor made simple calculations.

The marching was immediately followed by the FAC test. So, while the marching test was in progress, the field engineers were getting the FAC ready to meet the contenders, setting up charges and running wires. A UAZ arrived at the site. Nenashev got out of it and came up to the senior field engineer. "So, brother, are you ready?"

"We need five minutes more, comrade lieutenant colonel."

"Have you checked it yourself? Everything is fine?"

"Yes," the field engineer was positive.

Nenashev nodded and stepped aside. He decided to check it himself, just in case, to make sure everything was all right. Strolling along the FAC, Nenashev examined the charges, and one of them made him stop. A trinitrotoluene block was not on the stick as it was supposed to be (it was supposed to be hanging down from a stick, exploding in the air); instead, it was tied to the fittings sticking out from the ground. Nenashev turned on his heels and called out to the field engineer, "Sanya, come up here! Quick!"

Leaving what he was doing, the field engineer rushed to the commander.

"You say you've checked everything?" Nenashev gave him a menacing look. "What is this, then?" and he pointed at the charge.

The engineer had nothing to say, realizing his fault.

"Well, then, I'll tell you — it's a fragmentation mine!" He suddenly caught hold of the field engineer and threw two traditional stomach kicks. "Fifty press-ups!" he added, letting the man go.

The field engineer, taking the leaning rest position, started doing the press-ups.

"Are you out of your mind? You want this iron piece to smash someone's head off, do you?" Nenashev hovered over the engineer menacingly.

Vityaz was very strict about safety matters, as they were all "written with blood." If a soldier would breech when he was not supposed to, his gun would go off — and there you go! A corpse! Again, a reminder one should keep in mind, the "don't breech" rule! If one would point at someone and push the trigger by accident, the gun would go off, killing someone. Hence, the "Don't point at people!" rule, and so on. This is, of course, an exaggeration, but still, one needs to be careful.

Vityaz commanders could forgive lots of things (if not forgive, then, at least, close their eyes to these things, play things cool, or use some minor penalty), except for safety violations.

This is why Vityaz has never had non-battle casualties or severe injuries. Unlike other troops, which were given munitions only when in the action area, Vityaz soldiers loaded their guns right on the training ground, before getting on the bus to the airport, and gave back the munitions on the same ground upon return.

Someone might say it's a violation, a violation of the kind you've mentioned before. Of course, a young, inexperienced soldier might do something wrong, contradicting safety rules. However, officers and sergeants were always at hand to correct the mistakes of freshers, and the defaulter himself would be "awarded" with such a punishment that he would never ever dare to do a thing like that again.

Also, let's not forget the "don't leave unattended" rule. When on a detached service, soldiers always had their weapons with them, behind their backs, even during their meals, in the WC, and at workouts. Whenever there happened to be such a "lucky" soldier who would leave his machine gun (even guarded), he would have to dig a standing trench.

Done with the press-ups, the field engineer got up to his feet and reported, "Comrade lieutenant colonel! Warrant Officer Fomin has completed a set of fifty press-ups and realized his fault!"

"Hang it onto the stick as it is supposed to be," Nenashev commanded harshly. "And to improve your memory, dig the fittings out and carry it with you for three months." Then, giving the field engineer a level look, Nenashev added, "Everywhere you go! Be ready to show them upon order! And beware; if you don't have those on you, a three-kilometre race. Got my idea?"

"Sure, I do," the field engineer replied somberly.

Nenashev moved on along the FAC while the field engineer got down to fixing the charge.

Two and a half hours after the start, once this hell of a march was over, the contenders' group was finally at the training center, all dirt and mud from head to toe. Some could barely move their feet. They had about three hundred metres left to the finish, but those were the hardest three hundred metres! The soldiers were straining their will to the ultimate.

To encourage them, one of the instructors took off his beret and almost poked it into a contender's face. "Go!"

The contender understood the instructor wanted him to last

some more.

As soon as the soldier saw the crimson beret, he felt as though something clicked inside him. His teeth bared, he made an animal sound, and using whatever was left of his powers, sped up.

The FAC test started right after the marching was over.

The guests could hear simulation charges exploding around them. The noise was so unbearable the foreigners had to put their hands over their ears. The only one who seemed to have lost nothing of his enthusiasm was the French photographer. Kira, following Yegor, was also wincing, covering her ears with her hands.

In the beginning of the FAC, soldiers had to crawl under barbed wire. It was at this control point where Artur eliminated one more contender. The soldier struggled to his knees, while the instructor

took the bullet out of his magazine, throwing it carelessly down to his feet. The instructor held no interest in the soldier anymore.

"Single rank!" Artur, who was in charge of the testing, commanded.

The contenders rushed to do as ordered, their ranks not as numerous as before.

Yegor, walking along, was punching each soldier lightly in the armour vest. Throwing another punch, he stopped to add one more

and heard a sound that was not of a metal plate at all. Yegor looked up at the soldier. The soldier looked down. His gaze growing stern, Yegor detached the magazine and, maintaining eye contact, extracted the bullet and hit the soldier with the magazine, almost slamming it into his chest.

"Plywood is no good against a bullet!" he snapped. "It seems you've just been killed. Dismissed!"

The soldier put down his machine gun, turned around, and staggered toward his group.

Facing the line, Artur started naming contenders, calling them out for arms inspection. After the marching, arms should be in good condition and ready for shooting.

"Kiselev!"

Kisel fell out of the line and, breeching, pushed the trigger. The machine went off, and Kisel, throwing his fist up, roared joyfully.

"Philatov!"

Phil fell out, and his machine gun went off shooting, too.

"Kononov!" Artur proceeded to another name.

Another contender fell out of the line. He set his machine gun off safe, pulled back the carrier bolt assembly, and released it. The bolt carrier assembly, being under the spring action, is supposed to return at once, sending the bullet into the chamber. However, the contender's machine gun was so dirty that the assembly couldn't return. The soldier pressed the trigger, but no shot followed. He tried to push back the assembly; however, it stuck.

"Good-bye!" Artur commented unemotionally, crossing the soldier's name off the list.

The march was nothing like a sports race, where all one needs to do is run. The qualification exam is, actually, a warfare simulation. A unit is supposed to march up to the action area and complete its mission, eliminating its enemies. Marching, the unit also has to deal with quite a number of obstacles while keeping its arms safe. Otherwise, its enemy elimination mission would be questionable.

So, when a soldier's arms were not ready for action, it meant the soldier failed the test.

The same procedure was used for the rest of the soldiers, too. Artur would call a soldier's name, the soldier would fall out of the line and check his arms. Some had to push their bolt carrier assemblies back with their hands. Some succeeded, and then a shot would sound, while others failed, as they had not been careful enough about their weapons during the march. You can image what the result could be if those careless soldiers were engaged in an action right after the march. Anyway, Artur didn't bother about those failures anymore.

"Dismissed." Artur's sentence sounded as he crossed the soldier's name off the list.

Fortunately, most of the contenders handled their weapons with care. Their next assignment was to eliminate the enemy, so they rushed to the shooting range and lined up to carry out the mission.

No one had any trouble with that, since SWAT soldiers were real masters of shooting.

Back from the shooting range, the soldiers froze up in front of Artur.

"Ten minutes to prepare for altitude training!" Artur announced, starting the stopwatch.

The soldiers scattered, hurrying to take off what they had on and change into another uniform. They finally got to drink some water and wash away all the dirt and mud from their faces. Some were quick enough to strip their machine guns and were now cleaning them. Those who were done with everything were helping their fellows.

Artur looked at the stopwatch and stopped it.

"I'm counting to ten now for you to line up! One!"

The contenders hurried to put on their armour vests and helmets. Then they stripped their guns, put on their boots, and rushed to the line-up position.

"Ten!" Artur cried out.

As "Ten!" sounded, one of the soldiers was one step away from the line, however, not in the line yet! Artur, pointing at him, announced the sentence, "Dismissed! Your surname?"

Yes, Vityaz tests had very strict criteria, as everything was supposed to be as close to a real battle as possible. Soldiers must always be alert, no matter what, ready to accomplish their mission within minimum time!

Then there was the next stage — altitude training and eliminating terrorists in a building.

Kisel and Phil were standing at window openings, their armour vests, helmets, AK, and suspensions on. The suspensions were connected to a rope. Lebed was working with Kisel, while Kirei was with Phil, monitoring their entrance though the windows.

"Ready?" Artur enquired.

Kisel and Phil raised their right hands, fists up, confirming they were ready.

"TA!" Artur commanded.

Kisel and Phil put their feet quickly onto the windowsill and, turning around, pushed themselves off it to go through the window, pulling their machine guns from behind the back to shift into their right hands. On the fourth-floor windowsill, they gave a squirt, pointing their machine guns at the silhouettes of the terrorists. Then they pushed themselves off the windowsill once more to go down to the third floor, snatched simulation grenades off their chests and jumped down to the second floor. Smashing a window simulation with their legs, they threw the grenades into the room and pushed themselves off the sill. As they reached the ground, they disconnected the rope and put their hands up to show the mission was accomplished.

At the edge of the training ground, right in front of the building, there was a table where Artur and Chef were sitting. Two stopwatches in their hands, they were recording the contenders' timing.

"Kiselev — twenty-nine. Philatov — thirty."

Chef signed off the results. Kisel and Phil ran up to the table.

"Get ready for the next assignment," he cheered the soldiers up.

At this stage, it was rare that anyone had any trouble. The soldiers were all moving precisely, coming through the fifth-floor windows and going down to the ground, simultaneously clearing the floors, shooting, and blowing up the terrorists. They all managed to comply with time targets.

There was only one Artur paid special attention to. Landing on the fourth-floor windowsill, the soldier started pulling the machine gun from behind his back.

"Dismissed!" Artur called out to him.

Why dismissed? Well, it's as simple as that. First, we should remember that the exam is actually a warfare simulation; in this case, eliminating terrorists in a building. Naturally, it means there's an armed terrorist hiding out on the fourth floor. So, if a soldier starts looking for his machine gun when he is already on the windowsill, the terrorist won't wait a second to kill him. That's why, going through the fifth-floor window, the soldier must have his weapons in the battle position to be able to start shooting once at the fourth-floor level.

Next were the acrobatics. And, despite everyone being exhausted, they successfully coped with all the three elements: the up-kicking movement (when one was jumping up to one's feet, swaying one's legs abruptly), the "silhouette" (kicking a human silhouette on the wall with two legs and rolling over), and a somersault forward. Those were the basic elements each soldier had to master.

The acrobatics was followed by four hand-to-hand sets (the fourth one with arms).

The hand-to-hand sets, comprising all the necessary attack and protection techniques, were originally developed by Vityaz. The sets were obligatory to know. For Vityaz, as I have already emphasized, usability was foremost. The techniques for hand-to-hand fights were based on several martial arts. The attack elements were taken from boxing, while the leg movements and the protection elements from karate. Some of judo techniques were used, too. Actually, SWAT has eliminated all the excessive elements, leaving only the essential and efficient ones, combining those in the said four sets. We talked about the efficiency of such a system when discussing the special attitude SWAT soldiers had toward hand-to-hand fights.

And, finally, the concluding stage started!

The final test challenge was a twelve-minute full-contact hand-to-hand fight with three changing opponents, one of them being an instructor. The contenders were lined up, facing Artur, their safety vests, plastic helmets, and boxing gloves on. They were enthusiastically kneading their noses, rubbing their brows and cheekbones. Artur made a quick round of the line, breaking it down into threesomes. Finally, all the threesomes were on the test ground, with an instructor assigned to each. The instructor had only boxing gloves on. The threesomes were then broken down into pairs, one of the pairs comprising two contenders, the other one a contender and an instructor. A crimson beret soldier was then appointed for each of the pairs as an umpire. The detachment's commander looked over the pairs once again and gave his order to begin, "Time!"

And the sparring started.

The fight was always full-contact, with almost no restrictions. The soldiers were putting out, trying to make each punch and kick efficient and precise. They totally forgot it was their fellow who they were fighting against. They used all they could — the hands, the legs, the elbows, the kicks, the punches, and the throws. So, blood was usually soon to appear. And the instructors were especially tough. Sometimes it seemed like they were fighting an enemy they were willing to kill. So the contenders fell down a lot, the umpires giving them a helping hand.

One of the pairs was fighting half-heartedly. The umpire, naturally, didn't like it, so he raised his hand, pointing it out to Nenashev, "The guys are like frozen!"

Nenashev called for reserve instructors at once, "Two!"

And two instructors joined the frozen pair to heat up the fight. A minute later, when the instructors were torn off the contenders, the contenders' faces were all covered in blood. They went on fighting with each other, delicacy aside.

The foreigners were actually horrified at the things they saw.

"If they are like this to each other, then what's gonna happen with their enemies?" one of the marines commented.

Despite the way it might look to the outsiders, no one was going for a kill here. The major aim of it all was to let the soldiers feel the value of a crimson beret so that they would cherish it as the biggest treasure they ever had. Another aim was to show a contender what to strive for. However, once, an instructor was deprived of his beret for being too violent.

Crimson beret soldiers, in their turn, got an opportunity to prove their right to wear the beret. It was a way for them to show they have kept themselves perfectly fit, because there have always been people who would think they needed no training once they passed the test. So, sometimes, soldiers were deprived of their berets if they failed to demonstrate they were fit enough.

Kira, standing by Yegor's side, was speechless.

"Oh, my God! Now I can see why it's crimson!" She turned around to face Yegor. "But why do the tests have to be so tough?"

"You know …" Yegor struggled for a better explanation, "as a rule, SWAT teams get those missions which are next to impossible, when all the other variants proved to be no good. However, we are expected to be able to make those missions possible, so we have to stretch ourselves to the limit, sometimes even beyond." He glanced at Kira and added, "And, through these tests, soldiers learn to use their abilities to the maximum and above it."

"So, it's like a must for everyone to pass the test?" the girl asked.

"As a matter of fact, no. It's always of one's own free will," Yegor answered, but hurried to add, "However, those who are willing never dwindle in numbers. Besides, to be accepted for a test one has to earn this right."

Nevertheless, however well Yegor explained things, it was beyond Kira's understanding. "But why? Why has one to go through it all?"

Yegor shrugged his shoulder and, on giving it a thought, replied, "Some say it's a test which proves men to be men." Looking up at

Kira, he added, "And I do agree with them."

A SWAT soldier, indeed, has to earn the right to take the crimson beret exam: his SWAT service must be at least six months long, he must be exceptionally good at battle and special training, and his discipline must be impeccable. It's only when a soldier complies with all those criteria that he is allowed to take control tests. If he succeeds in these tests and the doctor finds no problems with his health, the soldier can be recognized as an eligible contender.

The willing ones were, indeed, numerous. And everyone had to go through the same procedures — heads of procurement services and Special Department officers alike!

I had been dreaming of having a crimson beret of my own since I was a schoolboy. However, when I joined the detachment ...

You must remember A. S. Pushkin's lines: "All breathes of Russ, the Russ of Old ..." I can say the same about Vityaz. The "breath of Russ" was almost tangible; one could almost cut it with a knife. This breath was omnipresent, penetrating into every cell of your body, transforming you from the inside. And this desire to get a crimson beret was so wild it could be compared to the agonies of a drug addict. Even though my test was scheduled two months after I joined the detachment (the Board did me a favour, giving me permission to take the test as an exception) I couldn't wait for the day!

All the more, those crimson berets were constantly before your eyes. It was such an unbearable torture when you could see the thing but you couldn't touch it!

Naturally, all those who wore crimson berets were idols for me, if not gods! Who needs Thor, Zeus, or Mars? Who are they against the crimson beret soldiers? I remember meeting my friend and my first tutor when I just joined the detachment. He graduated only a year before me (and I knew that) and he was only a senior lieutenant (while I was a lieutenant). However, I addressed him by the rank only, paying all the respect I could. It's because he was a Vityaz officer wearing a crimson beret! Indeed, my respect for these soldiers was immense!

Every four minutes, foursomes (three contenders plus an instructor) would change. Occasionally, a reserve instructor would have to intervene, heating up the fight.

One of the instructors, holding a contender by the neck, threw some knee kicks into his upper body, then pushed him away, adding some kicks in the head. The contender fell down, unable to withstand the severe attack.

Now, all the contenders' faces were covered with blood. From time to time, a doctor would appear on the ground to wipe off the blood from under their noses, to give them a sniff of salmiac, or to rub their temples. To somehow solve the bleeding problem, the soldiers had to insert cotton plugs into noses, which helped little, as, just a few seconds later, those plugs would be sent flying out of their noses, and bleeding started anew.

Kisel had Kot as his last opponent. Kot, grabbing Kisel by the neck, threw two kicks into Kisel's hip. After the second kick, Kisel's leg failed him, and he fell down to the ground, crying with pain. Artur helped Kisel up, Kisel's pain coming through all the blood stains on his face.

"Giving up?" he said, looking into Kisel's eyes.

"No!" Kisel was determined to win, notwithstanding the pain.

"Hands up! Go!"

And the fight continued. The soldiers, watching Kisel's fight, were doing their best to cheer him on.

"It's the twelfth minute now!" Nenashev announced.

"Hold on, Kisel!" Kot whispered to Kisel, kicking him in the upper body and then punching him in the head.

Soon, Kisel was back on the ground, exhausted. Again, Artur came to his rescue.

Meantime, Yegor, being an umpire, was watching the pair where Phil was fighting against an instructor. Phil was about to drop down, his hands failing him. He missed a tough kick in the head, the instructor's leg hitting Phil right in his mashed up face, the blood splashing to the sides. Kira closed her eyes tightly and turned away.

Yegor helped Phil up and looked into his eyes to see if it was a knockdown. He raised his hand, holding it right in front of Phil's face, and showed him two fingers.

"How many fingers?"

"Two," Phil struggled some, but finally answered.

"Giving up?"

"No," Phil replied, his voice showing no sign of hesitation.

"Hands up! Hands up!" and once Phil managed to move his hands high enough to cover his head, Yegor pushed him toward the instructor. "Go!"

One of the Americans shook his head, horrified at the show, while the French journalist, overexcited, hurried to take a picture of it. Indeed, this was a show he'd never seen before.

"Time's up!" finally sounded, the command everyone was waiting for.

That was it! The twelve minutes of hellish torture was over, and the exam was over, too!

Then everyone was applauding. Kot gave Kisel a joyful hug, happy for his victory. The instructors were helping contenders up to give them a brotherly hug and congratulate them on their success.

Phil, his face smashed and red with blood, threw his hands up, shouting with joy.

One of the soldiers who passed the crimson beret test was kneeling, his hands limp, and his face up, eyes on the sky. Happy tears were streaming down his dirty cheeks.

Fellow soldiers hurried to the successful contenders to give them a hug and congratulate them.

Yegor approached Kira. "Russian style, huh? First we use our fists to beat the hell out of people, and then, just as wholeheartedly, we congratulate them and celebrate together."

The crowd was rocking the crimson beret freshers, cheering up those who failed.

* * *

As preparations for the awards ceremony were still in progress, Yegor had some time to talk to the foreigners. The Austrian guys were the first to ask their questions, and the interpreter addressed the question to Yegor: "They thought it was too cruel. What is this all for?"

"To bring them up to the SWAT standards," Yegor replied calmly. "Besides, the exam is meant to be as close to an actual warfare situation as possible."

The interpreters translated Yegor's words, and the foreigners started nodding, realizing his point.

Then the American marine enquired, "And what's your pay, if you don't mind telling us?" The interpreter rendered the question into Russian.

Yegor kept silent for a couple of seconds, calculating. "Well, if in dollars, that would be about one hundred twenty."

The interpreters translated the answer, and the Americans, having discussed it among themselves, asked the interpreter to tell Yegor their conclusion.

"Given the intensive workouts you have, they think one hundred twenty a day is not enough."

Having heard the translator out, Yegor looked at his foreign colleagues and, sighing, addressed the interpreters. "Tell them I can't but agree. However, what I've told you was our monthly pay."

On hearing what the interpreter had to say, the visitors looked up at Yegor immediately, their faces saying, "What? You must be kidding us!"

And Yegor added, "And this is the money an officer is paid. Soldiers' pay is hardly more than one and a half dollars per month."

The foreigners were incredulous.

"Yegor!" Artur called out to him.

Yegor turned around, nodded, and was turned back to his colleagues. "Let's go; the award ceremony is starting."

Yegor left, while the visitors, barely conscious after what they'd heard from the translator, followed him to the ceremony ground, discussing the things they'd seen and heard.

"Indeed, only psychos can wage a war on these people," an Austrian said, expressing his opinion to his friend.

The second Austrian, deep in thought, kept silent — the words might well have missed his ears.

"Well," a marine speculated. "I haven't seen bears walking in the streets here, but still, I think the Russians are crazy."

"They are." His friend was of the same opinion.

Of course, our way of thinking might seem strange to most people. An acquaintance of mine who studied at the Military Medical Academy once saw a video of our exam and asked me to let him take the tape to show it to his psychiatric department so that they could use it for their graduation papers. Naturally, it was only a joke, but …

* * *

The entire detachment was lined up under the Vityaz banner waving in the breeze. In front of the line were the soldiers who had passed the exam, some twenty in all, which was about one third of the initial quantity. The detachment's commander was facing the line. A crimson beret soldier stood behind him holding a pile of crimson berets. Artur, a list of that day's heroes in his hands, was right beside him.

"So!" Nenashev began his speech. "We've been through another SWAT exam where you were given a chance to earn the SWAT symbol of honour and valour." He looked over the line of soldiers and continued. "Based on the exam results, twenty-seven SWAT soldiers have proved they are worthy to wear crimson berets!"

The exam is usually held two times a year, in May and September. Also, Vityaz has the "three attempts" rule: when a Vityaz soldier fails his third qualification attempt, he is transferred from the detachment as insufficiently qualified.

Initially, about 80 percent of contenders passed the exam successfully. However, in the second half of the nineties, the call-up selections grew worse and worse, so the percentage of successful contenders at this exam was down to 30 to 40 percent.

Nenashev turned to face Artur and motioned him to step out. Standing beside Nenashev, Artur started reading the names of those who had passed the exam and were now to receive crimson berets.

"Senior Lieutenant Ushakov!"

An officer stepped out of the line and came up to Nenashev, who, taking a crimson beret from the soldier behind him, shook the soldier's hand, gave him a hug, and handed over the crimson beret. The officer turned around to face the line, and kneeling on his right leg, kissed the SWAT relic and put it on. Then he stood up and, saluting, cried out loud, "Honour to the motherland and the SWAT!"

Accompanied by vigorous applause, the detachment's officer took his place beside Nenashev.

"Sergeant Kiselev!" Artur proceeded to another name.

Another round of applause, and Kisel stepped out of the line. Limping badly, he came up to the detachment's commander. Nenashev hugged him and patted him on the back. Kisel took the beret and, overcoming the pain, kneeled and pressed his face against the dream he was now holding in his hands. A moment later, he looked up. One could see tears running over his mashed up face. Then he put on the beret and, struggled up to his feet, saluted. He couldn't speak, feeling a lump in his throat. So he inhaled and exhaled once to stifle tears and, finally, managed to speak up, his voice shaky and hoarse, "Honour to the motherland and the SWAT!"

One more round of applause accompanied him to where he was

supposed to be standing beside Nenashev.

The same procedure was repeated for every soldier. Soldiers would fall out of the line and approach Nenashev, who would give them a brotherly hug and hand over the beret. Then soldiers would kneel on their right leg and kiss the relic, put the beret on, and, back up on their feet, cry out loud, "Honour to the motherland and the SWAT!" Soldiers' faces were all mashed up. Some had cotton plugs sticking out of their nostrils, and almost everyone had difficulty walking. However, all of them looked perfectly happy. As the award ceremony was over, the entire detachment lined up as a single column and made a congratulation round of the new crimson berets.

It might be a tough challenge to pass the exam, but it got soldiers to know that crimson berets never give up, which was confirmed by later events.

On my first leave after graduation, I came to visit the academy, my schoolmates, and former teachers. In the evening, we gathered round the table in the office of the battalion's commander and I shared some stories about Vityaz, its traditions, and the crimson berets.

One of the officers told us the following story. During the First Chechen War, when the army was short of officers and new ones were requested from military schools, he was sent on a three-month detached service to one of the Internal Troops' motorized rifle units. The battalion he joined was then maintaining a high ground. So, one day, the ground was attacked by a gang of insurgents, the gang being quite numerous. Their fire was so dense that the entire battalion had to hide out in trenches, afraid to stick out even an inch of their body. The insurgents, no fire in their direction, were quietly approaching the location. They were actually only some metres away from the trenches. The battalion had a machine gunner, transferred from a SWAT team. So, when the insurgents were close to the location, he took his helmet off his head and fished out his crimson beret out of his bosom, then put it on and, standing up to full height, started shooting with his machine gun. The battalion, inspired, followed his example, and the attack was defeated. I have no idea why he was transferred and why he still had his crimson beret on him in this case. However, I believe his deed was reason enough to consider his possible return to the crimson berets. Undoubtedly, it's a good illustration to what I'd call the SWAT spirit.

Now you might understand why SWAT soldiers are so reverent about their crimson berets and why it is considered the symbol of SWAT honour and valour. It's a true relic, invaluable treasure — to own it, one will have to give up a lot. For each Internal Troops' soldier, getting a crimson beret of their own is a major goal.

I know some examples when soldiers were offered a choice — either a state award ("For Valour" medal or the Order of Courage) or a crimson beret, and the soldiers chose the second variant since, for the Internal Troops' Special Forces, those are of equal importance.

However, there seems to be a contagious virus spreading in the Special Forces, a virus originating from movies like *Soldier Jane*; the Soldier Jane syndrome, as S. Lisyuk calls it. If you've seen the movie, you must remember sergeants humiliating soldiers — yelling, kicking, hitting them on the head, calling them unpleasant names, such as "piece of shit," "assholes," "morons," etc.

"Remember you're all pieces of shit! Who are you, now?"

"Shit, sir. I'm a piece of shit!"

"Come again!"

"Shit, sir. I'm a piece of shit!"

"Can't hear ya, soldier!" a sergeant would yell a fresher in the face, spluttering.

"Shit, sir! I'm a piece of shit!"

"You're the most miserable creature I've ever seen! Twenty press-ups!"

"Yes, sir!" the soldier would cry out, taking the lean support position.

"And what are you doing, you stupid-headed assholes?" the sergeant would bellow. "Twenty press-ups, everyone! I'm gonna teach ya all, pieces of shit, real soldier stuff!"

Such dialogue is close to the scenes in such movies. By the way, you come across this kind of behaviour in *The 9th Company* film, too, with freshers humiliated in various ways, their dignity coming off in pieces. Whoever saw the *Soldier Jane* movie surely remembers how the freshers were made to eat waste.

In fact, it has nothing to do with real crimson SWATs; it's rather Hans stuff.

In Internal Troops' Special Forces, soldiers treat each other as brothers. That's why, at exams, one could hear soldiers cheering on their fellows: "Come on, brother! Hold on!"

This is the true crimson SWAT spirit!

From its first days, Vityaz soldiers, unlike those from other units, have worn their berets on the left. And it's not because they want to stand out, but rather because it is practical. Commanded to rest, a soldier starts from the headgear. Naturally, as his right hand holds a machine gun, the soldier has only his left hand free. Hence, for convenience, the easiest variant would be to wear the beret on the left side. And there's nothing unusual about it. However, all the Internal Troops' Special Detachments formed thereafter wore their berets on the left side, it becoming a distinctive SWAT feature.

By the way, Vityaz soldiers wear crimson berets only — nothing green, olive, black, etc. It's either a crimson beret or a cap.

In 1999, Vityaz formed an officer's team comprising seventeen graduates of Ryazan Air Assault Forces Military Academy. Just at the time they arrived, I happened to be on duty and was to meet them. They came, of course, wearing blue berets. I stopped them, at the entrance, explaining that, in Vityaz it's either a crimson beret or a cap. The day hardly finished as they were all wearing caps.

A friend of mine, Bajo, from that lieutenant team, always told us this story as his first impression of Vityaz and me, in particular, when toasting to Vityaz whenever our detachment met at a festive table. And after the toast, he would add, "When, after the graduation, we were told we would not be serving in the Assault Forces, but would be sent to the Internal Troops' Special Forces, we were all disappointed, of course. But now we can only thank our lucky gods we had a chance to serve in Vityaz."

Since 1997, Vityaz crimson berets have been issued Crimson Beret Certificates. Before, it was only a special note in the service record book or an officer's ID that proved the right to wear the crimson beret. But somehow it has grown into total crimson identification, with Hans soldiers simply buying SWAT outfits and crimson berets and changing into them upon retirement. Of course, if those happened to walk into real SWATs, their punishment would be severe. So, the certificates were meant to prove a person really had the right to wear a crimson beret.[4]

In military outfit shops, one can buy a crimson beret only if one has the certificate.

Crimson beret is the exclusive privilege of the Internal Troops' Special Forces. And Vityaz's Crimson Beret Brotherhood (comprising Vityaz veterans) has patented (acquired copyright for) everything concerning the crimson beret. Nevertheless, Special Forces of other troops can arrange (and do arrange) crimson beret exams. Such exams cannot be held unless allowed by Vityaz Crimson Beret Brotherhood and attended by Vityaz supervisors.

Most think that to earn the right to wear a crimson beret one has to be, first and foremost, physically fit. I've come across such statements on the Internet: "Basically, you have to cope with the running and the fighting." Well, first of all, to cope with the fighting is not simply to survive through the fight, but to be active all the time. Second, if you know nothing about the fighting techniques, you'll be disqualified. The techniques are practised in special hand-to-hand sets developed by Vityaz, for which one will also have to pass a test before one's actually eligible for the sparring. Naturally, if one fails in the tests, one is disqualified, too. I saw this happen once during my exam. There was an officer with a certificate of mastery in officers' quadrathlon. Those are really tough guys who can do all right at multiathlon, even at the Olympics. Of course, he coped with the running. However, he failed in the hand-to-hand sets.

A crimson beret is something that proves a soldier has achieved the highest level of professionalism and his spirit is strong enough to handle SWAT missions. Besides, a SWAT soldier must be excellent at all the subjects studied by the Special Forces (both in theory and practise) and, naturally, he must be exceptionally well disciplined. Also, a SWAT soldier must live up to certain standards, moral principles, if you will. The principles are detailed in the Crimson Beret Code of Honour, which I have provided at the end of the book.

A crimson beret soldier cannot afford most things others would take the liberty to do. Their worst punishment for misbehaviour is having their crimson beret taken away.

So, whenever I hear someone boast, "I'd have passed the exam! I was perfectly fit. It's just that I pressed those freshers a bit and got transferred. The rest was fine. I was sure ready to make it!"

I tell them, "No, you weren't ready for anything if you insulted those who are younger and weaker. You don't deserve to wear a crimson beret with principles like that!"

Since 2011, Vityaz Training Center has been holding special veteran crimson beret exams for everyone who failed to get their crimson beret during their regular service.

In addition to the crimson beret qualification exam, Vityaz holds the special uniform test and Vityaz ID tag test.

So, the general idea is that one has to earn honours. In this way, everything a soldier gets will be of special value to him. Besides, the uniform and the ID tag tests are like preliminary stages of the Major Exam.

The special uniform is special camouflage clothes. All units wear ordinary all-arms camouflage clothes in green colours. Besides, the engineering support has particular types of uniforms — summer, winter, and demi-season camouflage outfits, boots, and sweaters.

Nowadays, of course, there's a variety of workshops where they sew various uniforms, and the range of products in military shops is, perhaps, wider than ever. However, back in the nineties, the camouflage was in short supply and choice rather limited.

The special uniform was only given to the Special Forces, the Intelligence, and the Engineer General Service units. So, to wear the Vityaz special uniform, one had to pass a test.

Vityaz ID tag is, in fact, a regular metal ID tag, with the "Special Forces Detachment" inscription engraved at the top, and VITYAZ at the bottom, with the middle section taken up by the Special Forces emblem — a fist with a machine gun.

Unlike the exam, the tests were arranged by commanders of separate teams for soldiers of their teams only.

The uniform test is always the first one.

The test has no general criteria; rather, the criteria are defined by teams' commanders. The test can include physical targets only, such as a hundred-metre race, or a 3000-metre race, pull-ups and a set of muscle strengthening exercises. However, a concluding hand-to-hand fight of one or two full-contact rounds is a must.

A team's commander might, on his own initiative, introduce certain exam elements, such as a short-distance march (three kilometres), with interruptions for various tasks. Also, these can include shooting, some elements of altitude training, acrobatics, and sparring.

The ID tag test, on the other hand, has strictly predefined criteria.

It's a miniature exam, if you will, giving an opportunity to make sure soldiers are ready for the Major Exam. Teams have to cover the same distance as at the exam march. Furthermore, the FAC test is also obligatory, just like the acrobatics, the altitude training, and the sparring tests (in short, all exam elements). The sparring, however, is only six minutes long — three plus three, instead of twelve.

So, one might wonder how the ID tag test and the Major Exam differ. Well, first, the ID tag test is not as tough as the Major Exam: where a soldier would get a minus or eliminated at the Major Exam, at the ID tag test he would get a warning only. Second, teams' commanders are entitled to introduce into the test some additional elements they would like to work on, such as map orienteering and compass bearing motion. Or else, commanders might choose to train the trench digging target for shooting in the rest position and introduce into the altitude test (temporarily) some extra elements beyond the exam scope. Options are numerous.

I'd like to emphasize it one more time that those are actually preliminary exam stages, sort of intermediate tests. It's like this: a soldier joins Vityaz, learns something, refines his skills, and then takes the intermediate test to get the uniform, then learns some more, growing still stronger and achieving a higher professional level — and takes the ID tag test.

Thus, you can see the tests are arranged in increasing order — first the uniform, then the ID tag, and finally the beret exam.

Consequently, the one who passes the ID tag test gets the uniform, too, while the one who passes the Beret Exam takes it all.

Anyway, SWAT soldiers are always dead serious about whatever tests they take.

Once, at an ID tag test, I remember a soldier crossing a water obstacle and losing a boot (it got stuck in the mud). So, he ran for some kilometres cross-country, stones everywhere, with only one boot on. He cried and shouted with pain, but ran on and finished. And he went through it all for just a small piece of metal! So, perhaps, you can imagine how such a soldier would fight when his fellows are in danger or his detachment or, all the more, his motherland is at stake.

As a matter of fact, such examples of extraordinary will and determination can be found in various sports, football being, unfortunately, an exception. Though it was not like that before. In 1960, when the USSR national team won the European Championship, one of our players broke his collarbone but didn't leave the field, willing to win! I might be mistaken, but I think it was Viktor Ponedelnik. Such people have the true warrior spirit, in my opinion. Especially taken that, back then, sportsmen were playing not for millions of Euros, but for some Lenin Diploma, which was only a sheet of paper. So, what made them fight and endure?

It's that victory was a matter of pride for them.

Once, a Vityaz officer happened to be at a club party. Given alcohol and the relaxed atmosphere, people naturally want to show off some. So they start searching the club for adventures. This time, a company of drunkards came across a Vityaz officer. The police came right on time to take them away after the "antiagression therapy" the officer had just then finished. Of course, he might well have calmed them down forever, but he was a good guy and his brain worked all right. Naturally, the policemen arrested him, as well, taking him with the rest of the crowd to the police station. The officer realized they would report to his division what happened that night and his detachment would also be mentioned. It's not like such things were unusual for our country, and it's not like that could cause some catastrophe; however, the officer was so concerned about the pride of his detachment he ate his ID on the way to the police station!

I'm sure when our football players come to understand what pride is and what it means to defend the honour of their country, they will be the best not only in Europe, but in the entire world.

Other Internal Troops' Special Forces detachments have tests of their own — chevron or green or olive beret tests.

1. *As for me, I waited for this day for seven years, starting from the day when my father brought home a newspaper article about the crimson berets.*

2. *I know that, once, a Vityaz officer caught two Hans soldiers on a train, who, besides the crimson berets, had certificates. The culprits then confessed they had bought the certificates from some division's staff officer. However, it turned out impossible to find out who exactly it was.*

3. *Crimson beret soldiers are those who have the right to wear a crimson beret.*

4. *Some days before the exam, I saw a "SWAT assertions" print-out hanging on a wall. There were a lot of good statements; however, only one of them imprinted in my mind immediately, and I still remember it clearly: "DO OR DIE!" I've repeated it to myself hundreds of times during the exam.*

CHAPTER 14

After the exam, Vityaz soldiers, as the tradition was, gathered at the gym to congratulate the newly selected crimson berets, have a drink on this occasion, and remember Nikolay Sitnikov, who died a year ago. They took away the carpet, a group of tables taking its place. The tables were taken up by officers and contracted soldiers, sitting side by side with successful contenders. Of course, the drinks were mostly lemonade. There were also some simple snacks on the tables and a couple of vodka bottles — just for commemoration, so to say.

Right before the graduation, I was really worried about the alcohol issue, as my senior schoolmates seemed to be rather pessimistic about it. Back then, I barely had a taste of alcohol; I thought it could be a big problem for me. However, in Vityaz, I saw quite the opposite to what I'd been told. It was a month after I passed the ID tag test that I dared to approach the old-timers, asking, "Well, how about setting the table?" You know, it seemed like I had to.

They answered, "Don't worry about the drinks! Just bring something to eat. And no vodka! If you want alcohol, then wine would be the best." So, we, a crowd of seven grown-up men, just shared a bottle of dry wine. You can't believe how relieved I was! Of course, it would be wrong to insist we never drank alcohol — we were still human, even though we were SWAT soldiers. It's only we were all into sports and had our own, specific life attitudes, including to alcohol. Drinking was rare, and I don't remember anyone getting too drunk. Also, there were some people who didn't drink at all, such as Yegor, for instance.

Vityaz never had the caste separation so obvious in other units, when colonels would drink and talk only with colonels, and lieutenants only with lieutenants. Rather, people were celebrating within the close circle of their own companies. For festivities (and non-festive events), the entire detachment gathered at one table, commanders and contracted privates sharing the same food and drinks, while, on a detached service, it was usual for officers and soldiers to celebrate their birthdays together, sharing one table, like a big family (the detachment's headquarters couldn't house all Vityaz soldiers at one time).

I was surprised at this, but the surprise was a pleasant one. I immediately felt like I was among my brothers and we were one big and united family. It was the very attitude I had been looking for in the army. We, being newly admitted lieutenants, had to introduce ourselves to the detachment a month or so after our admission. We set the table at the conference hall and gathered there after the formation. I remember some woman secretary saying, "And what if some inspection arrives?"

The detachment's commander answered, "So what? That's how we usually have dinners."

However, it would be wrong to think relations among Vityaz soldiers were more like backslapping. We always understood the difference between a genuine brotherhood and backslapping.

The French journalist, accompanied by his interpreter, joined the SWAT soldiers at the table. The detachment's commander was at the head of the table, just as he was supposed to be. He was the one to open the event. Raising his plastic glass up, he said, "To Kolya Sitnikov and the rest of our brothers."

Everyone, following the commander's example, stood up. There was a silent pause, which lasted for some seconds, and then they just had their drinks, without clinking glasses.

* * *

Back to October 3, 1993, the putsch attempt. As I've mentioned, Vityaz was one of the few detachments who remained loyal till the end.

It was thanks to Vityaz that the terrorists failed to seize Ostankino TV center. On that day, Vityaz soldiers saved the lives of thousands who were inside the building.

For many years, Vityaz has had to deal with accusations of shooting a crowd of peaceful citizens. However, looking at the photos from those times, it's unlikely you'll be able to see anyone peaceful.

Vityaz soldiers were actually shooting at armed people. And they opened fire only after the RPG-7 shot that killed Nikolay Sitnikov, a Vityaz soldier, their actions in strict compliance with the law!

Federal Law No. 3534-1, dated September 24, 1992, On the Internal Troops of the Ministry of Internal Affairs of the Russian Federation:

Article 27. Usage of Weapons

The Internal Troops' soldiers shall be entitled to use their weapons in cases as follows:

 a) to protect civilians from attacks posing a threat either to their health or their lives;

 b) to hold off attacks aimed at the soldiers and employees of the Internal Affairs agencies and posing a threat either to their health or their lives as well as to stop attempts to seize their weapons and military equipment;

 c) to hold off assaults in concert or armed assaults (including with use of vehicles) on military communities, military trains (transportation vehicles), transport columns, guarded objects, special cargoes, communication structures, civilian accommodations, and the premises of governmental authorities, enterprises, institutions and agencies of whatever form of ownership, and public organizations;

d) to eliminate the opposition of armed people refusing to obey the Internal Troops' soldiers requesting them to stop their wrongful acts and hand over the weapons, ammunition, explosives, special and military equipment at their disposal;

e) to stop persons from attempting to enter, by any illegitimate means, guarded premises, pickets and other military service sites or leave those, whenever it is deemed impossible to stop the attempts by any other methods whatsoever.

It is allowed to use weapons without warning to hold off an armed attack, involving special and military equipment, vehicles, airborne devices …

Everyone was denying that an RPG-7 actually fired a shot at the TV center. Some proposed their own versions, saying that Vityaz had a variety of explosives acquired during its trips to hot spots, so they might well have blown some up. But that's insane!

The TV show *Marianna Maximova Weekly*, dedicated to the fifteenth anniversary of the events, invited Alexander Barkashov, one of the assaulters, for an interview. And the interviewee told them: "Sanya Petrov[1] was then passing by me, an RPG seven on his shoulder. … And he fired the RPG, by accident, scaring Vityaz soldiers to shooting!"

Well, first of all, "scaring Vityaz soldiers to shooting" was next to impossible, if not insane!

Second, those who had to deal with RPG-7 know for sure that firing it by accident is hardly possible! Its firing mechanism is much stiffer than that of small arms.

Still, even leaving the silly guesses aside, the interview proved there was actually a shot![2] So, Vityaz did nothing wrong or illegal.

At that, Vityaz acted basically unaware of what was going on, because if the putsch were a success, then on the following day, in the Bolsheviks' tradition, the detachment's officers would all be shot dead, and this is the best case. In the worst-case scenario, all the SWAT soldiers would be sentenced to death, too.

So, if the Petrograd of 1917 had at least one such unit as Vityaz (which would remain loyal to its oath), then there would have been no seventy years of Red Terror in the history of Russia. However, all the combat units were at the front then, Petrograd disposing only of training regiments, which actually started the revolution.

To sum up the topic, Nikolay Sitnikov was awarded the title of the Hero of Russia (postmortem). The date of October 3, 1993 has some universal significance, obviously. On the very day when Vityaz fought against terrorists in Moscow on October 3, 1993, American special forces showed examples of courage and a military fraternity in Magadishu. The movie "Black Hawk Down" was filmed about these events.

* * *

Then there was talking and laughing, eating and drinking. The French journalist listened to it all, his eyes vivid with interest. Sometime later, already pretty drunk, his sympathy to crazy Russians growing every minute, the journalist decided to spit it out.

"In western countries," he started with deliberation, "they all think Russia's an easy target and they can have it with just bare hands. They think Russia has actually lost its army." The interpreter was rendering the Frenchman's monologue, while others kept silent, listening. "However, today I saw for the first time that there is a force that can oppose NATO."

The journalist stopped speaking, giving a glance around the table. "Be sure I'll tell them about it," he stated.

Everyone was interested in what the French comrade had to say, and once the heart-breaking monologue was over, Nenashev stood up, saying, "So, 'No *pasaran*!' as they say," Nenashev suddenly switched to French. "To SWAT!"

Everyone, the Frenchman included, stood up shouting out loud in unison: "To SWAT!"

"TA!" replied a choir of voices.

"To SWAT!" Nenashev repeated.

"TA!" the soldiers echoed back.

"TA!" This time they had to change replies.

"To SWAT!" and the table drowned in loud shouts.

"Glory to the SWAT! Death to the terrorists!" Nenashev added, and everyone took their drinks.

The story with the French journalist actually happened in 1999. It was a journalist from one of the leading magazines. I don't remember which one exactly. At that time, NATO forces were bombing Kosovo and he dared to publish an anti-NATO article, so his management exiled him to Russia. I wrote here, almost word-for-word, what he said after he had seen the exam. When he came back to France, he showed his management the photos he made at the exam. The managers were shocked! Sometime later, on another visit to Russia, the journalist brought us a copy of his magazine. The photos they chose for their article were the least shocking. However, even with that, the article drew a response no one expected.

When the gym part was over, Vityaz soldiers continued their celebrations in store- and waiting rooms. In the storeroom of the 3rd SWAT team, one could see a table with lemonade and a variety of sweet treats on it, and Chef, Kot, Kirei, Phil, and Kisel seated around it. Phil and Kisel still had their berets on. Their noses were swollen, lips smashed, and they had deep bruises under their eyes. Nevertheless, there was no suffering in their faces — pure delight only. Kot filled the cups with lemonade.

"So, guys, to you!" Kirei toasted. "Good job!"

Clinking the cups, they drank them up, and once the cups were back on the table, Kisel, at last, took the beret off, putting it down onto his knee.

"Sanya, brother," Kirei called out to him, "if you take the beret off, you should keep it right here," and he showed Kisel his own beret, which he hid against his chest, between the buttons. "I know some idiots who carry it under the shoulder strap or, even better, in the pocket of their pants." He shrugged his shoulders and shook his head to show how he was confused by such people. "You just can't do that. You know, it's like a sacred relic. So, if you take it off, you'd better keep it at your heart. That's the only right place for it." And he once again showed Kisel where he kept his beret.

"Sorry, guys," Kisel apologized, rolling the beret up with care and putting it between the buttons on his chest.

It was already getting dark when Yegor and Kira left the gym, walking leisurely along the alley.

"You know what," Kira said musingly. "On the day after I met you, I told a friend of mine about you. Her response was, 'Are you crazy? Those SWAT guys are all nuts. He'll twist your neck; you wouldn't even notice'!"

Yegor gave a mirthless smile, shaking his head.

"Honestly, I really got frightened." The girl looked up at Yegor. "It took me a long time to pluck up the courage to come here."

Yegor looked back at Kira, sighing. "People think that a SWAT soldier is some crazy monkey, crashing and destroying whatever comes in his way," he paused, as though trying to remember something. "In fact, however, a SWAT soldier must know how to use his brain," he continued, "think fast and be creative. It's something which we need to win over our enemies." He glanced at the girl, grinning, and to calm her down, said, "So, you don't need to worry. We are mostly adequate."

"Well, I actually understood you were not going to twist my neck." She smiled back at Yegor, "Well, of course, unless I touch your beret."

Yegor laughed and responded to her joke, also jokingly. Raising his finger up meaningfully, he confirmed what Kira said with studied gravity, "Certainly, you must remember it."

So, laughing, they finally reached Kira's car.

"Look, I can give you a ride if you don't mind," she offered.

"Well, I actually live here, at the detachment's premises."

Kira fell silent, thinking over Yegor's answer. "You mean in the barrack, right?"

Kira was looking around the bay where Yegor lived, studying its Spartan-style appearance, bare walls, a self-made wardrobe at the door, and next to it an old electric stove lying on the floor. The bay had two beds, chairs standing beside them. Above one of the beds, she could see a crimson beret hanging on a nail. Some packs of Chinese instant noodles, basic products on the officer's menu, were lying on the windowsill.

"And you live here, seriously?" Kira looked at Yegor.

"Well," Yegor shrugged his shoulders. "As a matter of fact, yes."

Kira gave him an astonished look. "Just tell me if I am wrong somewhere," she said. "You are all, indeed, living for your work." Her intonations were far from being interrogative; rather she was stating facts as they were. "Today I've seen and heard it that your courage and professionalism are admired all over the world." She bent in another finger. "And you say this is how you live?"

Yegor had nothing to do but sigh and shrug his shoulders, realizing the truth in her words.

"I'd say," Kira shook her head, "you are, no doubt, out of your mind."

Indeed, SWAT soldiers had to put up with where and how they lived and how much pay they got, but they were all ready to sacrifice anything for what they got from SWAT service — a genuine brotherhood and understanding that their special mission was essential to their motherland. However pathetic it might seem, they really thought this way.

Officers' families lived in barracks together with regular soldiers. Their pay was miserable; however, notwithstanding all of that, they were willing to serve their country!

It's because Vityaz soldiers, just like those in the Tsar Russia, believed in the idea.

As the second Chechen campaign was launched, the army paid the so-called battle money, about 1000 USD monthly. And that was great news, of course, taken that monthly pay was as small as 80 dollars. However, we agreed to the detached service trips not because of the money, but because of who we were. For us, the money was just a pleasant bonus, our main encouragement being the slogan "Who else but us?" In the mid-2000s, the battle payments were cancelled. And it always offended me to hear some officers say, as they refused detached service trips, "Why should we go there? It's not like we are getting any profit from it." I believe those are really come-and-go people, absolutely unworthy of being called officers, let alone serving in Vityaz.

Artur told me that during the First Chechen War one of the officers withdrew from a detached service trip, pretending he had some "business to deal with in Moscow." The officer was at once deprived of his beret and transferred to some other unit.

The Russian Officer's Code of Honour says: "It's both challenging and noble to be an Officer, but it's an occupation essential and useful both for Russia, as a country, and its people. The career can neither make one rich nor does it present breath-catching opportunities for promotion. The pride of an Officer is in their dreams and aspiration to become a true military leader, to distinguish oneself with their deeds and service for the benefit of their motherland. Those who think otherwise should better go 'sell suspenders or beetroot marmalade.' It would be beneath an Officer's dignity to grow into a careerist, even a smart and knowing one, and to emphasize their careers over the interests of Russia!"

When, in 1991, the Soviet Union disintegrated, people saw the communist idols for what they really were, their former ideals crushed. Everything was in a hell of a mess, the army and the military service, too. Soldiers from other republics never came back once they had gone on leave, and the leave was their legal right no one could ignore. So they just had to let soldiers go, perfectly aware they were never coming back.

However, Vityaz has always had its own principles, the SWAT principles, which had nothing to do with the communist bullshit. So, every single soldier, after going on a leave, came back to finish his service in Vityaz, though, as they confessed, they were more than once asked to stay.

* * *

It was dark when Yegor and Kira finally approached her car. Kira took a calling card out of her purse and handed it to Yegor. "Here's my phone number. Call me, will you?"

"Sure," Yegor answered and the girl gave him a playful smile.

"Well, then ..." She faltered, lost for words, and Yegor came to her rescue:

"See you!"

Kira agreed, smiling, "Yes, see you." She reached out to open the door of the car.

"Do you remember the way back?" Yegor decided to ask, just in case.

Kira nodded, got into the car, and drove away. Yegor raised his hand to wave her good-bye and headed back for the detachment's premises.

Some minutes after he entered his bay, he heard a knock on the door.

"May I come in, comrade lieutenant?" asked Phil, emerging at the door opening.

"Sure," Yegor replied matter-of-factly. "Is there something you want to tell me, Vitya?"

"Comrade lieutenant," the newly admitted crimson beret began, his voice a bit wavering, "I wanted to ask you something." Phil faltered, casting his eyes down, and asked in a low voice, "Can you give me your old beret, please?" He looked up at Yegor and then added, looking down, "You are the person I respect most."

There was a dead silence for a moment, Yegor staring at his subordinate, studying him intently. Then he made a step toward the wall, took his old beret, and handed it over to Phil, saying, "Here you are!"

"Thank you so much, comrade lieutenant!" Phil's voice sounded suspiciously hoarse. "And thank you so much for what you told us before the start in the morning. It was of great help to us — me and the rest. We could have given up but for your words."

Yegor smiled and reached out to give Phil a hearty handshake. "May I go?"

"Sure," Yegor replied, and Phil left the bay.

---

1. *I don't remember the exact name.*

2. *Working on this chapter, I looked through numerous photos to select the ones you can see here. I came across the grenadier photo (at the top) at a website and its heading read: "The grenadier had long been setting his weapon, aiming at the SWAT soldiers defending the building from inside. It was evident those could see him, but, surprisingly, they produced no shots. Once the grenadier fired his first shot, the SWATs responded with massed intense fire." No doubt, whoever took the photo was a witness to the past events, his "surprise" at SWAT soldiers waiting for the shot proving that Vityaz acted in strict accordance with the law. By the way, on the Internet, one can find a bunch of video records featuring Barkashov's gang. He, himself, says the gang numbered around one thousand people, all well armed and determined to overthrow the government.*

CHAPTER 15

On the following day, the detachment arranged demonstration training for their foreign visitors. SWAT soldiers were to show how they release hostages from buildings or vehicles, pass the FAC in pairs and threesomes, and how they shoot and fight in hand-to-hand combats.

After the FAC, all the SWAT soldiers lined up in front of the visitors. An Austrian guy, having looked over the line, said something to his interpreter.

"Excuse me," the interpreter called out to Yegor. "But these are the same soldiers who were taking the exam yesterday, right?"

"Yes," Yegor answered calmly, not quite understanding what the man was getting at.

After the interpreter was done with the translation and the Austrian guy processed the information, he asked another question, and the interpreter, having heard him out, nodded and rendered his question into Russian. "Isn't it too much of a strain to be training this hard after yesterday's challenge?"

"Well, yesterday we had formal training. Besides, they had some time to rest in the afternoon. So," Yegor shrugged his shoulders, "I can see nothing wrong about today."

The interpreter translated Yegor's explanation and the Austrian guys, exchanging glances, said something else in their language.

"We are paid thirty times more than you," the translation followed, "but we hardly ever train as much as you do. In fact, if we trained this much, our country would go bankrupt paying for our treatment."

Yegor looked up at the Austrians, sighed, and shrugged his shoulders. "I hope there'll come a day when our country would care about us, too."

As the interpreter translated Yegor's words, the Austrians looked at Yegor and nodded, the curious one obviously intending to continue the conversation:

"As I understand it, you are a counterterrorism, that is to say, a police unit," the interpreter proceeded with translation. "However, some of the situational tasks you use in your training are beyond the scope of your police functions. What do you need that for?"

"Judging by our experience, at times we have to deal with this kind of situation, too."

As the Austrian guy was listening to the interpreter, his brows went up and another question followed.

The interpreter turned to Yegor and asked, "So, besides the police functions, you have to act as military special forces, too?"

"As a matter of fact, yes," Yegor answered after a short pause.

The Austrian guys had a discussion on what they heard from the interpreter, and then the curious one, making a helpless gesture with his hands, announced the results of the discussion, making the interpreter smile.

"They say you're supersoldiers."

Yegor thought a little and said, "Well, we are!" He grinned and, once the foreigners heard the translation, they smiled, too.

Indeed, Vityaz training included elements that were beyond what was needed for counterterrorism operations. Vityaz soldiers knew how to act in any situation and how to complete any mission, whatsoever. This is what was unique about Vityaz. It was simply unimaginable that Austrian COBRA or the American SWAT would assault settlements and high grounds, eliminate armed gangs in the mountains or woods. However, Vityaz was ready for it all! Maybe that's why the imminent tragedy has not become a total catastrophe for Vityaz.

In Russia, there's also this problem with the use of Special Forces — any Special Forces, I mean. Russian generals think too primitively. They are the Special Forces. They are well trained, and they would cope with tanks all right. But they forget somehow about the special anti-tank forces. Well, no doubt, SWAT guys are better trained than most of the other army, but they are the Special Forces, anyway. So, why would assaulting a settlement be a special mission? Regular motorized rifle units should be able to manage the task all right. The Battle Charter of the Land Forces also has it like that: "A special case fight is a fight within a settlement, in the mountains, in the woods, or in the Far North areas." Still, it is the Special Forces who would be sent to assault, as the efficiency of the motorized rifle units leaves much to be desired.

The same primitive logic makes our generals conclude: "You are, guys, bad warriors — no losses at all! Just look at that regiment, a hundred killed each month; those are the warriors!"

Unfortunately, the perverted logic is most common among our generals.

* * *

As soon as the visitors left for the training ground, Artur approached Yegor.

"So, how are they?"

"Shocked!" Yegor looked up at his friend. "How can we train after what we had yesterday?"

Artur smiled, nodding.

"When we visited them," he began telling Yegor about his Austrian experience, "we arranged some trainings. Once, in a hand-to-hand fight, some of us got an Austrian guy in the nose. Just a light punch — there were some drops of blood at one nostril, I believe. Not like it was a real bleeding or something. And you know — he was on a sick leave for three days. See what I mean?"

"Oh, right then," Yegor grinned.

"There was also another one," Artur continued, "who broke his finger at an altitude training, through his own fault. Pretty serious, huh? And I thought," Artur paused, calculating, "well, it's gonna be a month — maximum! But the guy was curing his finger for half a year. How do you like that?"

They exchanged glances, and Yegor shook his head, laughing, "That's a wow!"

Vityaz training is always on the edge of human limits (maximum warfare approximation) and is always full contact, live-or-die style. Naturally, we do care for safety, but bruises, smashed (sometimes broken) noses, some slight injuries, sprains, and blood coming out on the fists and feet — that's pretty normal for the Special Forces. Unlike our foreign colleagues, Vityaz has never paid much attention to such insignificant, in our opinion, things as pain, blood, exhaustion, injuries. It's against the Special Forces informal code to complain about those things. Our soldiers believe if one can move, then one is in good health and ready for action.

Neither did Vityaz soldiers care about a pilot flying higher or faster than the standards prescribed at airlift delivery. They just jumped down without giving it a second thought! Perhaps if those were people who had had less training, then the jumping could have ended up with lethal or severe injuries, but Vityaz soldiers rarely had anything more serious than a sprain or a bruise after such landings.

As a matter of fact, the training process can be thought of as a sort of mental conditioning since it is in the course of training that the SWAT spirit, the spirit of a true warrior, is moulded.

Chapter 16

In the afternoon, soldiers had some time to themselves, so they usually headed for shops and cafés to buy some treats. Kalinin was passing by the soldier's café when he saw one of the soldiers leaving through the door, a package in his hands.

"Stop!" Kalinin ordered.

The soldier stopped, turning around to the SWAT soldier.

"What's in there?" Kalinin asked, in an offhanded manner.

The soldier opened up the package for Kalinin to see. Having satisfied his curiosity, Kalinin reached out and pulled at the package. However, the soldier, even though scared, was not going to let go of the package so easily. Looking up, surprised at the resistance, Kalinin gave the daredevil a quick glance, and then, abruptly, threw a kick in his head. The soldier fell down, while Kalinin, the package in his hands, walked on leisurely toward the detachment's premises.

Unfortunately, Vityaz has had a number of cases like this, but those were rather exceptions than general practise, unlike in other units. Besides, Vityaz has developed its own efficient measures to fight this kind of behaviour.

On the following morning, Yegor, who took over as the detachment's on-duty officer on the previous evening, was waiting at the entrance for the detachment's commander to arrive. Kirei, Yegor's duty assistant, and Phil, who took over as the headquarters' courier, were standing at the duty room. They heard the door open and saw Nenashev coming in.

"Ready, front!" Yegor cried out the command.

Both the officers saluted to Nenashev, and Yegor reported, "Comrade lieutenant colonel, I've had no accidents reported while on duty, except for …" he paused, not sure how to tell the commander about what happened at the café, so they just stared at each other for some moments. "We have a problem, Alexander Ivanovich," Yegor finally said.

"Stand easy!" Nenashev commanded and reached out to shake Yegor's hand. "Hello, Yegor!"

"Stand easy!" Yegor repeated the command, shaking his commander's hand. "Good morning, comrade lieutenant colonel!"

And then they gave each other the traditional brotherly hug.

"Come on," Nenashev invited him.

And they headed for Nenashev's office. Passing by Kirei, Nenashev greeted him, too.

"Hello, brother!" he said and gave him a hug.

"Good morning, comrade lieutenant colonel!" the soldier replied formally.

The detachment's commander never thought it to be something extraordinary when he shook hands with his soldiers or gave them brotherly hugs. It's just that a soldier had to earn such an honour.

They entered the office and Nenashev, sitting down at his table, gave Yegor a level look. "Now, tell me what's happened," he said, apprehensive.

"Yesterday, at the café, soldier Kalinin from the second team stopped a soldier from the fifth regiment, kicked him in the head, and took away his package of bakery."

The commander's face lost its colour, and he sighed heavily. It took him some minutes to recover after Yegor's story. All this time he was staring somberly into space, silent. Dropping another sigh, he finally voiced his decision — evident and inevitable in such a situation. "Call the Crimson Beret Board after the formation."

The Crimson Beret Board is a public body comprising only those soldiers who have the right to wear crimson berets. At the Board, any crimson beret soldier can voice his opinion, irrespective of his rank. Naturally, major issues on the Board's agenda include arranging and holding the Crimson Beret Exam as well as awarding someone with a crimson beret or depriving someone of it. It's the Board's exclusive power to take such decisions. The decisions are usually taken by open voting.

The Board, however, has some other functions in addition to those. For instance, it discusses issues concerning the Special Forces traditions, and it's also a powerful disciplinary authority. Any soldier can be requested to appear before the Board. Such a visit is a sobering experience to defaulters, who usually start to think better of their behaviour and its consequences. The Board can be called not only to consider cases concerning Vityaz soldiers proper, but also those concerning crimson beret soldiers from other detachments.

So, as you can see, the Board is another efficient instrument providing for the unprecedented discipline the Special Forces are famous for.

CHAPTER 17

Artur was holding a hand-to-hand training, his soldiers practising fights blindfolded. Kalinin, his armour vest and helmet on, was frozen in the leaning rest position at the orderly post. He'd been in the position for quite a long time. His hands and legs were shaking with tension, his face red and wet. Beads of sweat were falling from his forehead onto the floor.

"Time's up!" Artur cried out, and the soldiers stopped the sparring. "Bandages off! Take a minute's rest!"

Taking off their bandages wrapped around their eyes, the soldiers tried to catch their breath.

"Now! The hammering!" he announced another exercise. "Ready! Go!"

And the soldiers started hammering each other in the hips, stomach, and chest to make them less pain sensitive.

Nenashev was also working out in the gym, practising kicks and punches on a punch bag.

Right then, a colonel approached the detachment's premises, holding a file in his hands. At the entrance, he stopped to read the poster above the porch: "Without action, SWAT get rusty like iron."

Sniffing disdainfully, he went up the stairs, bumping into Kirei at the door.

"Detachment's on-duty assistant, Sergeant Kireev! May I ask you about the purpose of your visit?"

160

"Colonel Soloviev! On an inspection from the Central Administration!"

He took one step forward, intending to make the sergeant move aside to let him in. However, the sergeant remained where he was, explaining politely, "Let me report your arrival, comrade colonel!"

The colonel, surprised at the impudence, froze in place, while Kirei turned around to Phil and cried out, "Phil! Will you tell the commander that Colonel Soloviev from the Central Administration has arrived to inspect us?"

And then he turned back to the inspector, who was still recovering from the shock.

"Sergeant!" the inspector pitched his voice higher. "Can't you see who you are talking to?" he said, emphasizing the who part. "Let me in!"

"I can see it perfectly, comrade colonel!" Kirei stayed calm and polite. "However, I can't let you in until I get the duty officer's permission."

"I'm telling you!" and the inspector's voice was now a tone higher, "Let me in!"

"Let the colonel in, Kireev!"

And Kirei at once moved aside as ordered.

"Will you come in, comrade colonel, please?"

The inspector, his feelings being a mixture of indignation and mild shock, headed for the detachment's premises, where Yegor was waiting for him.

"Comrade colonel, I'm detachment's duty officer, Lieutenant Menshikov!"

Yegor introduced himself.

"What's going on here, lieutenant?" the inspector complained. "Why should a Central Administration officer wait for your permission to enter?"

Yegor offered his explanation, staying perfectly calm, just like Kirei. "I'm sorry, comrade colonel, but that's the way things are here."

"But that's nonsense!" The colonel was boiling over. "Where's the detachment's commander?"

"He's in the gym, on the fourth floor."

"Call him, now!" the inspector grew impatient.

Yegor turned around to Phil, who took over in the duty room.

"Philatov, call the fourth floor. Tell them to report to the commander."

Nenashev was working the punch bag as he saw the team's duty attendant entering the gym.

"May I report to you, comrade lieutenant colonel?"

After throwing a hook, Nenashev turned around to the duty attendant.

"Comrade lieutenant colonel, we got a call from the first floor. Some colonel from the Central Administration is waiting for you down there."

Nenashev winced as though in pain.

"Okay, you may go, brother; thanks," Nenashev told the soldier and the soldier left immediately.

Nenashev took off his hand straps and, grabbing a towel, left the gym, heading for the washing room.

Yegor was standing at the duty room entrance, waiting for Nenashev to appear, while the inspector, with his hands behind his back, was pacing to and fro along the passage. Finally, the door opened, letting Nenashev in, dressed like a sportsmen — a T-shirt, camouflage pants, sneakers, and straps on his hands. His hair was still wet from the washing, so he was rubbing it with a towel. He approached the inspector and introduced himself. "Comrade colonel, I'm the commander of the 6th SWAT detachment Vityaz, Lieutenant Colonel Nenashev!"

The inspector, his hands still behind his back, first examined Nenashev's appearance, an annoyed expression appearing on his face, and then started a new round of complaints. "Will you please tell me, lieutenant colonel, why does a colonel from the Central

Administration have to wait at the entrance, arguing with some sergeant?"

Nenashev, giving the inspector a serene look, replied just as politely and calmly as Kirei and Yegor. "It's because the sergeant was executing my order not to let any strangers in without either my permission or that of the detachment's duty officer."

It looked like the inspector was going to make another comment, but, finally, he chose to not to pursue the subject.

"Get dressed, comrade lieutenant colonel!" he grumbled. "Let's see what else you have here."

He accented the word "else" on purpose, as though to show he was really going to reveal the truth.

In half an hour, Nenashev was standing at the entrance to one of the washing rooms, leisurely watching the inspector "trying to reveal the truth." At last, he managed to find something and, coming closer to the finding, pointed it out to Nenashev, announcing triumphantly, "You've got stubs lying all around here, under the radiators, comrade lieutenant colonel! Look here!"

Nenashev, who already understood what the inspection was going to be about, agreed impassively. "I believe you, comrade colonel. We'll do the cleaning."

Meanwhile, the inspector recorded the finding in his copybook.

As they came out of the washing room, he came up to the entrance door and, pointing at the orderly and the duty officer, enquired, "Why haven't the soldiers trimmed their uniforms?"

And, having made another note in his copybook, the inspector left the detachment's quarters. Nenashev chose to postpone his argument with the colonel till they were out. So, when they were on the stairs, he explained just as calmly and politely as before, "Comrade colonel, it's a special outfit. There's hardly an army in the world where soldiers would trim such outfits."

The inspector stopped abruptly.

"Comrade lieutenant colonel!" he obviously decided to take the lead in the argument. "Don't you think it's no use arguing with me? We're talking about the Russian army, where soldiers are supposed to trim their uniform!"

Then he just turned around and hurried down the stairs.

After the barracks, the inspector got down to the outside premises, looking for faults to find. He was almost sniffing the space around the entrance.

"You could have whitewashed the curbs better," he said, slowly eating away at Nenashev. "I'd advise you to follow the example of the 2nd Regiment." He was obviously enjoying the brainwashing. Adding another note into his copybook, he made one more acid comment. "The Special Forces, you say?"

On hearing the comment, Nenashev lost his temper, his face growing stern. Seeing no one around, he scored off the office rat. "You! Colonel! You have come here to look for stubs or what?"

A little further away, a group of soldiers was practising hand-to-hand sets and Nenashev beckoned toward them, saying, "I can call any one of them right now and order them to do a somersault. And you know what — they'll do it. Can you do it?" He leaned forward, making the inspector cringe unintentionally.

The voice and the cold gaze of Nenashev took the inspector down, and he fell silent, at a loss for what to say:

"No? Then just get out!" and Nenashev beckoned toward the CP, turning around to Yegor, who was standing at the entrance watching them.

"Yegor! Show the colonel out!"

Yegor was only too happy to execute the commander's order. For a few seconds, the inspector stared perplexedly at Nenashev, finally squeezing out, though without confidence, "I'm not leaving it this way!"

Then he turned on his heels and headed for the CP, while Nenashev, having glanced at his back, made his way toward the building.

As the inspector reached the group that was practising hand-to-hand sets, he tried to go right through them. However, two young soldiers suddenly appeared in his way. "Comrade colonel, can you please go the other way round?" they asked the inspector.

The inspector started to grow red. "You! Move aside! Quickly!" he yelled.

However, the soldiers didn't move a muscle, feeling the invisible support.

"You can't go through the line, comrade colonel!" The inspector heard Yegor saying. "And you should know it!"

The colonel turned around on his heels, meeting Yegor's hostile gaze. For a moment, they stared at each other, and then Yegor cried out curtly, "Grenade!"

Repeating the command, all the soldiers sprinted off every which way, throwing themselves down.

Commands such as Grenade, Rear, and Flash were practised not just for the fun of it. This practise was meant to develop a reflex when soldiers would execute the commands instantly, without even realizing their actions. So, whenever when executing a field command someone happened to see a discharge flash, the entire unit would fall down upon hearing the warning. Or else the first one to notice a flying grenade was to warn the others, and everyone was supposed to scatter around the area, pressing their bodies against the ground. (There's a real-life example hereinafter.)

All the commands — every single one — were to be repeated by everyone who heard them.

"You can go along now, comrade colonel," Yegor offered, his voice still calm and tone impassive.

The colonel moved along, pacing nervously and cursing. "You think it's funny? I'm gonna show you the fun!" he said.

"Fall in!" Yegor commanded, and the soldiers lined up, springing up to their feet.

Yegor turned around and headed for the detachment's headquarters.

* * *

Vityaz was basically a state within a state, with its own laws and traditions. Strangers were not allowed. And it was what made it so similar to the Kazaks, who, stewing in their own juices and following their own rules, formed an isolated society, almost an independent state. At first the government tried to fight this isolation, which caused Kazak rebellions and insurrections. However, in the nineteenth century, some wise emperor finally allowed the Kazaks certain freedom and autonomy. In return for the favour, the Kazaks became a secure foothold of the Russian Empire. It's due to the Kazaks' distinct traditions and rules that they were able to invoke a special esprit in their warriors, which made their enemies scatter in horror. The same story happened with Vityaz and, later, the entire Internal Troops' Special Forces. Due to their unique traditions, they have managed to become the cream of the cream, not only in terms of the Internal Troops, but the Russian Army on the whole. And, just like the Kazaks before, the Special Forces now awe gangsters and terrorists.

Actually, I've heard a lot of stories like this one. Say there's a motorized rifle unit, numbering several hundred people, located near some settlement. Besides the rifles, it disposes of an artillery arm and some dozens of combat equipment units. However, all the human and weapon power is wasted, the soldiers simply sitting out their time, because once two gangsters paid a visit to the unit's commander and made a statement: "If you dare to shoot, just once, we'll burn your camp down."

So, the well-equipped "heroes" chose to shut their mouths, letting the gangsters do whatever they wanted right in their own backyard. But the gangsters' rule lasted not long. Two Vityaz teams happened to drop in at the settlement. Over just twenty-four hours, the forty men, riding four APCs, turned the settlement upside down — some gangsters were killed, others scattered, horrified to death and trying to find a place to hide out. As a result, when Vityaz left, the settlement got a chance to enjoy peaceful life for some more months.

It's thanks to the special, non-charter rules and traditions that Vityaz, nowadays, is the most mission-capable and professional military unit in the entire Russian army.

From a book on acting techniques, I learnt that Stanslavskiy's followers were so different from the rest of acting companies that they were called the "sectaries."

I believe it's the most precise definition for Vityaz soldiers, too. Vityaz Detachment is like a sect, but in the better sense of the word, of course.

So, all the big bosses and all the army idols, who never had to ask twice for the doors to be opened, got used to the regiments' commanders appearing before them upon their first call. They all had to wait at Vityaz entrance for permission to come in.

Personally, I believe there's nothing unusual about it. It's only natural to restrict entry to military premises — the weapons, the ammunition, you know. To make it a revolving door would be unreasonable. No one feels indignant that it's impossible to get into a watchhouse unless allowed in by the captain of the guard. And if the captain happens to be patrolling the pickets at that moment, any inspector, whatever his rank, would have to wait for the captain to come back.

Naturally, the Hans were outraged at these non-charter rules since, unlike real officers, who even after their retirement remain both respected professionals and reputable individuals, they are no one and nothing without their shoulder straps and the charter. As a rule, such inspectors are only two spots. Both at school and at the military academy they used to be grey mice, always getting the most unpleasant assignments and always ready to be at your service, as they never had guts to say no to someone who seemed stronger. So, to pursue a military career was the only way they could gain influence and power. A high rank and impressive shoulder straps made them feel important.[1] They would never miss an opportunity to refer to the charter and to comment on how the Special Forces didn't care about the rules and the discipline and were crazy about their own traditions. But it was all a big lie! Vityaz, with all the specific traditions and non-charter rules, was even better disciplined than all those units that followed the charter. It's through these traditions and rules that Vityaz maintained order and discipline among its soldiers. Anyone who dared to go against the rules and traditions was to be exiled from the detachment immediately.

Some might think that Vityaz has no charter at all — they just live as they want, the laws and the rules for them being only a vox. But that was never the case! Vityaz is a military unit, not a gang, so they stick to the charter with even greater fervency than infantry units (remember the safety measures, the tests to check the knowledge of the charter, Vityaz sergeants). It's just that some rules and requirements seemed of less importance to them, which only improved their esprit, discipline, and professionalism. Some rules were simply absent from the charter, such as "Keep your finger on the trigger guard."

Three hours later, as Nenashev was reading an article in some military magazine in his office, he heard the phone ringing. He picked up the receiver without lifting his eyes from the article. "Nenashev speaking."

"Hello, Alexander Ivanovich!" Nenashev heard in the receiver, recognizing the voice at once.

"Greetings, comrade commander-in-chief!"

"What's up with you there, commander?" the commander-in-chief began calmly. "Why do I get complaints about you?"

"My bad, comrade commander-in-chief!" replied Nenashev. "However …" and Nenashev paused for a moment, thinking over his next phrase, "how can one evaluate professionalism by checking whether the curbs are white enough and the grass is mowed?"

The commander-in-chief sighed heavily, realizing what Nenashev was getting at.

"Okay, then," he concluded calmly. "I got you. Now, go back to work."

The commander-in-chief hung up and Nenashev, dropping a sigh, went back to reading the magazine.

The commander-in-chief, putting down the receiver, shifted his gaze to the inspector, who was now in his office. He stared at him for some moments, and then asked, still calm, "What else, you say? They don't want to trim the uniform?"

He turned his head to look through the window. It was silent for a few seconds, and then he spoke up thoughtfully, his eyes on the window. "Well, if it's more convenient to them," he broke the silence, "then let them leave it as it is." He turned around to look at the inspector, adding, "And, as a matter of fact," he paused to make the inspector understand he really meant what he was saying, "leave them alone. They know better what to do. Don't disturb them!"

Unlike with most other things, the Special Forces have always been fortunate in their commanders-in-chief. And that's a fact. I believe our luck in this respect was even greater than that of the Assault Forces. All the commanders-in-chief ever appointed for the Special Forces were knowing and wise leaders who did their best to make the state respect and appreciate the Special Forces. These wise generals have always understood the Special Forces — better than anyone else. The Special Forces, in their turn, showed them their respect and admiration, always ready and only too happy to obey their orders!

It's due to them that Vityaz actually appeared and lived on, doing their thing — training and improving their professionalism and fighting spirit.

Some of the commanders-in-chief, for their special merits in developing and improving the Special Forces, were honoured with the highest SWAT award — the crimson beret.

1. *Of course, not everyone is like this. There are really decent officers in the Central Administration, too. Once, on a detached service, we happened to work with a Central Administration officer. He was very respectful, treating us as his equals. Unlike most of his colleagues who earned their orders, hiding out in the headquarters tent, he always accompanied us during field trips, participated in our missions, and risked his life, coming under fire.*

CHAPTER 18

The detachment was lined up in two columns, facing each other. Kalinin, sulky and somber, was standing at the front edge of the line, wearing, instead of the camouflage outfit and the high quarter boots, a regular uniform and knee-high boots. His crimson beret was on him. Nenashev, facing the lined up soldiers, was pronouncing the fair and inevitable sentence: "For actions discrediting the honorable name of a Special Forces soldier, Private Kalinin shall be deprived of his right to wear the crimson beret and be transferred to a motorized rifle unit." He paused to give an order, "Team's commander, take off the beret!"

Artur came up to Kalinin and snatched off the beret, his movements harsh, even rude. Kalinin kept his head down, accepting his fate with humility. The drummer, standing beside Nenashev, stroked the beat, and Kalinin moved along through the line, looking like a criminal led to a scaffold. Everyone he approached turned their back on him. The line finished at the central alley where he could see his rucksack on the ground. Taking it up, Kalinin left the detachment for good, tears in his eyes. He didn't dare to look back.

Being a Vityaz soldier entails not only certain privileges, but also huge responsibilities — too hard to bear for some. Those who couldn't handle the responsibilities had to "go through the line" (were exiled), and those who once went through it were never to come back again. This was also a good warning for others. Vityaz, actually, borrowed the tradition from the American Green Berets, as it was completely in line with Vityaz general principles. In fact, Vityaz has never shunned such borrowings (even from their potential opponents) if those fit in with its own principles and could contribute to Vityaz growing still stronger. Often more than not, the borrowed elements were reprocessed — what Vityaz needed remained, sometimes growing into something really powerful, while the rest was thrown away. It didn't matter much what kind of things Vityaz had to borrow — whether the exile scheme or urban action tactics — as long as it made it stronger.

CHAPTER 19

"Team's orderly Private Guschin speaking!" the orderly for the fourth-floor picked up the phone. "Aye!" he cried out curtly and hung up. "Team One and Two, wake up! Assembly signal!"

"Team Three and Four, wake up! Assembly signal!" a few seconds later, the fifth-floor orderly resounded.

The floors at the detachment's headquarters came to life. Yegor jumped out of his bay, his armour and discharge vest on and a mask in his hands, and sprinted off toward the AS room. It took him almost no time to get his arms, and soon he was at the AS supervising his guys.

"Quick, quick, guys! Don't forget to take all you need!"

The soldiers grabbed their arms, magazines, and breathers and rushed to the training ground.

Teams' commanders, called by the courier, were gradually joining the detachment. All the officers put on their armour and discharge vests and masks, took their machine guns, and then rushed down to the duty officer's room to get their APS.

Then teams began lining up on the training ground, while the officers were checking presence and ammunition. Cases with ammunition had been brought down to the training ground from the AS room. APCs arrived in a couple of minutes, and the soldiers rushed to them.

When the entire detachment was seated on the armour, Nenashev joined them, too, his armour and discharge vest on, a machine gun over his shoulder and a mask in his hands.

"Commanders of the teams! Report on your contingent, ammunition, and weapons!"

All the teams' commanders hurried to the detachment's commander, jumping off the APCs. The formalities settled, everyone was back on the vehicles. Nenashev chose the APC of the first SWAT team, and as soon as he took his place, Vityaz column moved on along the central alley toward the division's headquarters.

When the APCs stopped at the division's headquarters, Nenashev jumped off the vehicle and, making long strides, rushed to the division's operational duty officer. He came back three minutes later and commanded, "Senior officers, come up here!"

The teams' commanders jumped off their APCs and hurried to Nenashev, who started giving them assignments. Nenashev's voice was quite loud, so the soldiers could also hear him.

"The on-duty unit is to go back to the detachment's premises! You are the reserve, so stay here and wait for further orders! Teams Two, Three, and Four, we're now marching to the special operations area, our route starting at the division's headquarters, then CP One and the twenty-third kilometre of Gorkovskoye highway. I'll specify your tasks once we arrive!" He looked over his soldiers once again, their eyes already blazing with thirst for action. "Take your places!"

Soon all the soldiers were back on the cold APC armour, looking forward to the battle. Nenashev changed the APC to join the 2nd SWAT team, looked over the column once more, and ordered the driver to move on. The first team turned right, heading for the detachment's premises, while the rest of the column took the left turn, toward CP One Northern Gates. The duty attendants were all warned by the time, so the traffic-control barriers were up and Vityaz column passed the CP right along, taking a turn to the right, toward the special operations area.

About thirty minutes later, the detachment stopped at the destination, near Gorkovskoye Highway.

"Detachment, line up at the vehicles!" Nenashev ordered.

The entire contingent jumped off the armoured vehicles and lined up quickly in front of Nenashev, breaking down by teams.

"Attention!" the detachment's commander announced. "Children of high-ranking officials have seized some hostages. Your task is to capture the terrorists and release the hostages. Considering that they are VIP kids, we need them alive!"

The commander looked up at his soldiers, who were listening to him attentively, adrenaline already rushing through their veins.

"According to the police, the criminals are cruising around Moscow suburbs now! The traffic police will block the roads, leaving them Gorkovskoye Highway as the only option. So Team Four — you're the first isolation ring! One platoon with an APC to move a hundred metres back! On command, you're to block the road with your APC so that neither a car nor a man could get inside the special operation area. Platoon Two, take the APC and move two hundred metres forward! You're to block the road once the car with the criminals passes us by! Don't allow civilians and their cars inside the area or the criminals outside it! That's it! So, now, go ahead!"

"Aye," replied the commander of the 4th SWAT team and, turning around, headed for his APCs.

"Teams Two and Three — you're the second isolation ring! Leave the APCs on either side of the road. Group Two, move fifty metres forward!" and the commander showed the direction. "Group Three, move fifty metres back!" and he specified their direction. "You're to block the road on command."

The APC of the 4th team passed by, heading for its destination.

"Teams Two and Three, provide a group of assaulters each!" Nenashev continued. "Team Three to assault from the driver's side, Team Two from the passenger's side. Remember, we need the criminals alive. So, only the officers have live rounds. Shooting is the last resort — and choose the legs or the arms! Assault teams, you have blank bullets only. Any questions?"

"No!" Yegor and Artur replied in unison.

"Then give your assignments to the contingent. Waiting for your reports in five minutes."

"Aye!" the officers cried out and, turning around, headed for their teams.

"Attention!" Nenashev announced via the radio handset. "Get APCs off the road and hide them in the forest."

Having joined their teams, Artur and Yegor briefed their soldiers on the task and assigned their duties. The 3rd SWAT team chose Phil, Kirei, and Miron as assaulters, while the 2nd SWAT team delegated Kisel, Lebed, and Kot.

Then, the APCs took their positions as ordered, while the soldiers located along the road, lying on the ground. The field engineers did a quick round along the road, putting up charges at the proposed seizure point to divert the criminals' attention.

As soon as the preparations were over, commanders reported their teams as ready, and the soldiers had to wait, the tension building up every minute. Sometime later, one of Nenashev's radio sets went alive.

"Got you!" he responded and, taking up another radio set, commanded, "Nine zero four, block the road!"

The APC of the 4th SWAT team, which had to move back, reacted at once, getting onto the road.

"Get ready! Everyone!" Nenashev gave his next order.

A few seconds later, they could see the headlights of the approaching car. There was almost no traffic on the roads at this time of the day.

As soon as the car with the criminals passed by the first control point, the APC of the 4th SWAT team blocked the road, while the soldiers, emerging from the forest, encircled the operation area.

The car kept moving and soon reached the engagement area, the tension reaching its highest point!

"APCs!" Nenashev commanded harshly via radio.

The APCs, leaving their hideouts, took off toward the road embankment, their front wheels first going high up in the air and then flopping heavily onto the asphalt — like submarines coming out of the water.

The driver hit the brakes and the car froze in place.

"Engineers!"

The charges put up on either side of the road exploded at once, both deafening and blinding.

"Assault!"

And the assaulters sprinted off toward the car.

As Miron and Kot reached the car, they started shooting with blank bullets to catch the car's passengers off balance.

Kisel ran up to the car, pointing his machine gun at the passenger, while Kirei hurtled to the driver's door and, without thinking twice, smashed the window with the stock of his gun. The window broke, and Kirei was now pointing his gun straight at the driver. "Don't move, you bastard!"

Phil and Lebed pulled the handles simultaneously, swinging the doors open. Phil grabbed the driver. Lebed reached out to catch the other criminal and realized it was Putilin.

"Comrade major!" was all he managed to say.

Next moment, the driver was out of the car, his body bumping into Phil's leg somewhere in the stomach area. The driver squealed and fell onto the asphalt, Phil pressing him against the road, face down.

"Stop!" Nenashev was shouting. "Stop!"

All the soldiers, engrossed in action, had to stop, perplexed at the order.

"Let him go, brother!" Nenashev told Phil.

Phil let go of the driver, who rose to his feet, not without difficulty.

"Back to your starting positions, everyone!" Nenashev ordered, and the soldiers, still wondering what was going on, moved back.

"Hey, guys!" the driver sounded off. "That was not the deal, man! What's going on here, anyway?"

"Okay, all right! Take it easy! We'll make things right!" Nenashev tried to calm the man down. "Officers, come up here!"

And the officers hurried to the detachment's commander. They had a short discussion, made their decision, and then collected some money.

The soldiers, already back at their starting positions, were also having a heated discussion about the embarrassing situation.

"Damn! Looks like we've mistaken the car!"

"Here you are," and Nenashev handed over the money to the driver. "It's for the smashed window and the emotional distress, so to say."

The driver took the money, trying to evaluate the amount by sight.

"Well, and …" Nenashev made a helpless gesture, "sorry for everything. Our guys are pretty quick, as you see."

"Indeed, they are." The compensation cheered up the driver a bit. "I was down on the ground before I realized what was going on."

"Well, then, bye." Nenashev reached out to shake the man's hand. "And thank you once again."

They shook hands, and then the driver got into his car and drove away.

"Retreat, everyone!" Nenashev commanded. "Back to your starting positions and line up!"

"Team Three, line up!"

"Team Two, line up!"

"Team Four, line up!"

Vityaz soldiers, barely making out anything, left their hideouts, lining up on the road in front of Nenashev. The APCs arrived, too, parking at the roadside with their noses home.

"Dress!" Nenashev finally gave his order.

The soldiers turned their heads to the right, composing themselves.

"Ready, front!" Nenashev said, saluting. "I'd like to thank the entire contingent who took part in the special tactical training! Stand easy!"

"What? It was a training?" The line came alive.

"Holy crap! And I thought, why on earth is Putilin here?" Kisel exclaimed.

"Now we're to march back to the permanent location point," Nenashev formulated the next assignment.

And this is how things were in reality.

The detachment's commander gathered his officers in advance, telling them the time and the idea of the training. None of the soldiers was supposed to know it was training. Also, they drew up plans as appropriate and then got the approval of the division's commander. To make the soldiers believe everything was for real, they even ordered some cases with the 2nd Regiment's administrative company. The cases looked exactly like those with ammunition that the detachment's duty attendant was responsible for. The cases were then painted and filled with bricks, and when the time came, were brought to the detachment's duty room.

All the officers went home and were sent for with couriers upon the assemble signal — as if it were a real alarm.

When the column stopped at the division's headquarters, the detachment's commander just walked in to greet the operational duty attendant and showed him the training plan approved by the division's commander. The duty attendant ordered the CP to let the detachment out at once.

As it was a regular training, the duty unit couldn't leave the premises. So, Team One, which took over that day, had to stay behind as the reserve.

Once they were at the destination, the detachment's commander fed the prepared legend to the soldiers.

To solve the blank bullet issue, the soldiers were told they had to detain some presumptuous VIP kids, naturally, alive.

Putilin left earlier than the others, on purpose, to find a crime car. When the column reached the destination, he got an order from the commander and stopped the first car he saw driving by, asking the driver to play along. Then, he told the commander the car make and its number.

This is why the special operation area was not blocked at once — not to hinder the regular traffic, and this is why the assault groups included no officers — to give the soldiers an opportunity to act on their own. And the soldiers proved to be real professionals.

The soldiers had no idea of what was going on; that's why they acted for real (as if it were a real battle mission). It took them a long time to believe the whole thing was only a training simulation.

The officers actually gave a wonderful performance, which is another example of the creativity and original thinking I've mentioned before. And such trainings were numerous.

CHAPTER 20

"You have been looking for me, commander?" Warrant Officer Naumov asked, entering the orderly room.

"Yep, Andrey," Yegor replied, picking up his work copybook from the table. "I'm gonna be out for a meeting. Take the team and practise the disarmament techniques — with knives and guns."

"Got you," Naum responded, heading for the exit. "Team Three, line up!" Yegor heard him shout almost at once.

And the floor came alive.

Vityaz warrant officers deserve a special mention, as those were usually the toughest SWAT soldiers.

It was usual for Vityaz to contract the most experienced and the best-trained regular service soldiers — that's how they became warrant officers. As these soldiers were usually good at special training, they were often employed as instructors. There were a number of warrant officers who later got an officer's rank, taking up the positions of special training deputies or teams' commanders. Yegor used to be a warrant officer, just like the legendary Detachment's Deputy Commander for Special Training — Major Putilin.

Meantime, teams' commanders were having a meeting at the office of the detachment's commander.

"Team One," Nenashev was distributing assignments. "Vanya, a bus will be waiting for you at the CP, Saturday, nine o'clock. Send one officer with the group to work at the plant. They promised us some paint for the gym.[1]

The commander of the 1st SWAT team nodded, making a note in his work copybook.

"Oleg," Nenashev called out to Rostigayev. "You and your team are joining the 8th Detachment tomorrow, for the altitude and the building assault training. The detachment has just been formed, so we are to help them with their special training."

Rostigayev nodded and made a record, too.

"Team Two, and what do you have for tomorrow?"

"Our team's taking over today," Lazarenko, who was substituting for Artur, replied. "Tomorrow we're shooting in the villie. And six three two is still out of order — no spares yet."

"I know, I do," Nenashev sighed. "I've been getting down on the division's commander's nerves for days now. So, just take the bus."

"Aye!"

"So," Nenashev concluded as he was done with the assignment, "take a sheet of paper and sign it with your name."

The officers tore out a sheet of paper each from their work copybooks and signed them, while Nenashev pulled out a table drawer, looking for something. They heard him shuffle things about the drawer, and, finally, Nenashev took out a part of a weapon, presenting it to the officers.

"So, write down what it is and then hand over the sheets of paper to me."

Lazarenko, who joined the detachment recently, had to take the part in his hands to have a better look at it, while the rest of the officers wrote down their answers without hesitation. Nenashev looked through the papers, putting one of them aside.

"Lazarenko!"

"Here."

"It's a KPWT extractor." Nenashev gave the young officer an expressive look. "Fifty press-ups, over there, in the corner."

Lazarenko got up and headed for the corner, then took the rest position, leaning on his fists, and started doing the press-ups.

"Things like that, brother, a SWAT officer should know by heart," the detachment's commander commented instructively.

It was commander's habit to hold tests like this, which made his officers always alert and encouraged them in their self-education — learning weapon make-up and parts, the tactics and other military disciplines. It was impossible to survive in a SWAT team without all this knowledge. In fact, Vityaz had created such an environment, the special SWAT spirit ingrained in it, that one couldn't but strive for more knowledge and professional growth.

Let's take me for example. When I graduated from the academy, I had just one "good" grade — the rest were excellent. However, my knowledge of certain things was rather superficial. It was only in Vityaz where I got to master those things fundamentally. Another example — a close friend of mine at the academy was a rather negligent student. He never cared much about studies — just did some sports occasionally and played the guitar. So, he used to say, "If only I were sent to some orderly room with a kettle and tea and a guitar. Believe me — that would be like my dream coming true."

But after graduation, he was sent to Rosich. A couple of months later, one of my former classmates told me, "You wouldn't recognize Volodya at all. He's training all the time and reading aids day in, day out, complaining he used to be such a fool at the academy!" In the end, he made an excellent SWAT soldier; he even graduated from Frunze Academy. This is how the special SWAT spirit changes a man.

"Comrade lieutenant colonel!" Lazarenko finally spoke up. "Senior Lieutenant Lazarenko is done with fifty press-ups as ordered! May I get up?"

"Go ahead," Nenashev replied and Lazarenko got up and returned to the table. "And the last thing," Nenashev addressed the officers, "you all watch TV, so you know the situation in the Caucasus. The Central Administration keeps silent, but I'm sure, soon ..."

And he fell silent, leaving the phrase unfinished. Everyone understood only too well what they had to expect soon. However, it was not because everyone understood what he was going to say that Nenashev didn't finish the phrase. It was as though he suddenly saw something, his eyes staring blankly into space. Maybe it was their future that he saw. It lasted for a short moment only, and then Nenashev recovered his senses and came back to reality. He glanced through the window and turned around to his officers, who caught the commander's mood at once.

"So, get ready."

In the silence, filled with apprehension, souls were brooding, thoughts a heavy weight on them. The sullen reverie was broken by the phone ringing. Nenashev picked up the receiver and said, "Lieutenant Colonel Nenashev speaking. Greeting, comrade colonel!"

Nenashev was listening to the voice from the receiver, his facing growing sour. He cursed wordlessly, with his lips only, and replied, his tone a little annoyed, "Yes, sure."

He threw the receiver down with anger and, taking a moment to recover, explained to the officers, "It was the division's logistics deputy. They need fifty people to dig a trench tomorrow."

He saw the officers were also unhappy with the news. And that was only understandable! The Special Forces should be doing what they were supposed to be doing — training, not housekeeping!

"Damn it!" Nenashev cursed. "And the commander-in-chief is on vacation."

The commander-in-chief was very specific about the purposes the Special Forces were to be used for.

Nenashev was staring silently through the window, speculating about something. As he made up his mind, he turned to the officers. "So, you know what? Tomorrow, I don't want to see anyone of you and your people here at the detachment's premises. Just get your travel rations and get your contingents going, say, to the villie, or the Mu-Mu,[2] or to the woods. Be back by suppertime, though. Got me?"

The officers replied to the pleasant announcement in a choir of voices, "Aye!"

"Any questions?"

"No!" the officers cried out in unison.

"Now I'm counting to three — and you should be all gone!" Nenashev commanded expressively and started the count. "One!"

The officers sprinted off to the door, overthrowing the chairs and jumping over the table. Reaching it simultaneously, they fouled, the door coming off under their weight. And Nenashev shouted after them, his anger rather studied, more fatherlike, "Damn you, guys! You've broken my door!"

The officers, roaring with laughter, fell out of the office and, springing up to their feet, hurried out. Nenashev followed them out to examine the damage.

"Hot damn!" he cursed good-naturedly and, turning around to the detachment's duty attendant, asked him, "Hey, brother, find someone to repair the door." Grinning and shaking his head, Nenashev returned to his office.

Back from the meeting, Yegor sent his copybook flying onto the table and set out in search of his guys. Passing by one of the bays, he heard someone playing the guitar. As he opened the door, he saw soldiers sitting around Lis, listening to him sing a song of his own making.

"Team, up! Ready, front!" Sieda, who was the first to notice Yegor, shouted out loud.

The soldiers sprang up to their feet, taking attention positions.

"Easy!" Yegor said and, coming up to Lis, reached out to shake his hand.

A bit embarrassed, Lis shifted the guitar into his left hand and shook hands with the commander. "Greetings!"

Yegor, still shaking his hand, looked into his eyes and said, a faint smile stirring his lips, "Give it to me, the guitar."

Lis was now completely at a loss. "Huh? Oh! Sure, sorry," he finally choked out, embarrassed, and handed the guitar to Yegor.

It all looked funny, of course, and the soldiers started giggling.

"You can finish the song later, Yura," promised Yegor, taking the guitar. "And I'll have to listen, too." He glanced at the soldier and gave his order, confidently and quietly. "Out to line up!"

The soldiers were now leaving the bay, a smile lingering on their lips. As they were passing by, Yegor made a quick look over the bay, checking its appearance. A framed photo on Phil's bedside table caught his eye. It was the photo Phil shot out with his SWD. The girl's face was undamaged by the shooting, yet the very fact that Phil kept the photo surprised Yegor.

"Oh, wow, Dima! And what is it doing here?" he asked, pointing at the photo.

Phil looked down, embarrassed. "Well, hmmm, comrade lieutenant," he muttered. "We're, you know, we've figured things out."

"Oh, okay!" Yegor smiled, giving his subordinate a sly look. "Now, move; join the line!"

Thirty seconds later, the entire team was lined up at the orderly post.

"Team, ready, front!" Naum commanded as he saw Yegor approaching.

"Easy! Is everyone here?"

"Yes, commander," Naum replied.

Yegor nodded.

"Follow me, everyone!" Opening the door, he headed for the stairs to the roof.

The team followed him up to the roof.

Kisel was walking out of the bay as he saw Talanych and Malysh collaring each other, apparently having a heated discussion.

"Hey, you!" he snapped at them.

As they heard Kisel calling to them, they let go of each other and turned around to the sergeant.

"Rear!" The sergeant offered them his usual treat and the soldiers threw themselves down to the floor. "Get up!" the sergeant shouted another command. "Run up here! Quick!"

And soon the soldiers froze in front of Kisel.

"Guys, I didn't get your point here. What was that all about, huh?" Kisel was reproaching his subordinates for their behaviour. "You could be sent on a detached service trip any day now, where you'll have to cover each other's backs. So why do you have to behave like that? Are you out of your mind?"

The soldiers were silent, casting alarmed glances at their sergeant.

"Let me be your peacemaker!" Kisel offered. "You! Now then, pick him up! And you, jump up here!" he commanded to Malysh.

Malysh nestled in Talanych's arms.

"Can you be a little more delicate? Imagine you're holding a girl," Kisel prompted. "Here you go! Now, you're to run around the floor, crying out loud, 'I love you!' You have to answer, of course, 'Love you, too!' So just run around like that to give your feelings a way out! And don't you dare to stop unless I order! Got it?"

"Aye!" the duellists replied.

"Now move!" Kisel gave his order, and the soldiers started their love marathon.

"I love you!" Talanych cried out his confession.

"Love you, too!" Malysh echoed back.

"I love you!" Talanych cried out again.

"Love you, too!" Malysh repeated.

In fact, gripe sessions like that one were quite rare for Vityaz soldiers, as they had neither time nor will for such stupid things after all the exhausting training and workouts. They could hardly make it to their beds! Besides, I've more than once mentioned the special brotherly relations among the SWAT soldiers. Though, as you know, sometimes even brothers can find a good excuse to measure their strength. And should their father walk in to find them fighting, he'll naturally take a whip and teach them a good lesson about what it means to be brothers.

The Vityaz method to teach brothers to love each other dearly was the "bride" game.

* * *

The entire 3rd SWAT team was up on the roof of the detachment's headquarters. Yegor was the last to enter through the attic door, concluding the line of soldiers, and he stopped at the edge of the roof.

"Now, guys!" he called for the soldiers' attention. "Follow my lead!"

And Yegor sat down, throwing his legs over the roof edge.

Exchanging glances, the soldiers started moving toward the edge slowly.

"Come on, guys!" Yegor was commanding buoyantly. "To the right and to the left of me, at an arm's distance! Watch your neighbours!"

The soldiers, fear obvious in their eyes, were taking their seats, very slowly and very carefully.

"It's fine, it's fine," the commander cheered them up. "Take your time! Don't look down; only to the sides!"

He was watching everyone carefully. Someone might get dizzy, then he'd need to arrange for help. He could tell that the guys were scared. Yegor totally understood their feelings. He felt no different from them when he was starting the psychological drill — all by himself. The drill was meant to let the soldiers overcome the fear of heights and improve their psychological condition. Yegor had suffered from this fear for rather a long time, so before he got his soldiers on the roof he actually coped with the fear himself.

"Dima!" he called out to Phil.

"Here!" Phil replied, and Yegor felt some restraint in his voice.

"How are you?" Yegor asked, watching Phil with a considerate smile.

"I'm fine," Phil answered, through it looked like he was far from being fine.

"How much is seven by eight?" Yegor knocked him off with an unexpected question.

It took a little longer than usual for Phil to give him the answer, because of the fear. "Fifty six!" he finally spoke up after a long pause.

"Good," Yegor commented approvingly and then called out to Kirei. "Sanya!"

"Here!" Kirei's voice also sounded constrained.

"What is the danger range for a Kalashnikov machine gun when shooting at a chest-high figure?"

There was a small pause before the answer. "Four hundred forty metres!" Kirei remembered at last.

"Right!" Yegor replied with satisfaction.

Gradually, the soldiers were overcoming their fear. Some even began smiling and joking.

"At times, our fear strikes us numb, and we can't do what we are supposed to," Yegor explained to his soldiers. "So, guys, we need to know how to fight our fears." He examined his soldiers carefully and decided that would be it for that day. "All right," he summed up. "Now, we're going down to prepare for duty assignment."

The soldiers got up and headed down the stairs, sharing their impressions with excited smiles on their lips and making fun of each other.

Here's what I used to do. In summer, whenever I took over as the team's duty attendant, I used to run cross-country with my team on my days off. Once we were done with the running, we would stop at Mu-Mu Lake to have a swim. There was a tree we used as a diving board. We jumped from a platform that was about seven to eight metres above the ground. And if one is standing at their full height, it would be about ten. I would shout, "Follow me!" and then climb up the tree to jump. My soldiers followed me. Some, of course, couldn't do it at their first try, but I would then help them out. "I'm counting to three — and you should be in the water! One!" As I was shouting "Two!" the soldier would already be flying down toward the water. Then I'd make him do it once more, just to nail it down. And the next weekend, he'd be jumping all on his own.

Naturally, we observed all the necessary precautions. I always had three guys standing on guard in the water who would rush to the splash area right after the jump.

Talanych and Malysh had already exchanged their parts and now, though considerably tired, kept on running, crying out their confessions.

"I love you!" one of them would cry out.

"Love you, too!" the other one would echo back.

"Come up here!" Kisel finally commanded, coming out of the bay.

Malysh, Talanych still comfortably cradled in his arms, turned around and rushed to the sergeant.

"Drop him!" Kisel put an end to the wedding dance of the couple.

Relieved, Malysh let Talanych jump down onto the floor. Then, the bride-couple, all red and sweaty, froze in front of the sergeant, who was now staring at them with the same stern expression on his face.

"And God forbid I should ever see or hear you're tangling with each other," Kisel gave them a harsh warning and, keeping his stern gaze on them for some more seconds, let them go. "Dismissed!"

And the bride-couple sprinted off to the washing room.

---

1. As I've mentioned before, SWAT procurement left much to be desired. Almost all the materials and equipment were self-made, such as the sports facilities

(bags, dumbbells, barbells) for the gym. So, the detachment had to actually do these side jobs to get some extra money for those purposes.

2. *Near the division's premises, there's a lake. Some say it's where the famous Mu-Mu movie was filmed, hence, the name of the lake and the adjacent area. It was a terrific ground for training, by the way, the field and the forest. So, Vityaz used it for tactical training.*

CHAPTER 21

Next day, all the detachment's units were away from the premises, training. Some teams headed for the villie, and while the 4th and the 1st SWAT teams were shooting at the shooting range, the 2nd and the 3rd were having altitude training. Yegor lined up his team to remind them of safety measures.

"I need you to remember altitude safety measures. At the top," and he raised his hand, showing the direction, "we have the releaser, who controls the descent. At the bottom," and he showed it with his hand again, "we have the spotter, who ensures the safety of the one who's descending. Next." He picked up a rope from the ground to show it to his soldiers. "If a rope has some splits, fractures, thin places, or such, you can't use it! No way! However, the rule has nothing to do with us. Why? Because the ones we have are all like that."

This explanation of Yegor's made the soldiers smile.

"And one more thing," Yegor continued, demonstrating carabineers and descenders. "If those have chips, cracks, or indents, we are supposed to throw them away because they are unusable. However, we can't do that, for the same reason. Any questions?"

The soldiers were silent, waiting for the start command.

"If you have no questions, let's secure the ropes and start the training."

The soldiers took their climbing equipment and scattered about the location.

Makei had left the Assault Forces a while ago and joined Vityaz as a contract soldier, succeeding in his second test try. He was in Artur's team. And now it was his first experience of descending from a building. His suspension was on and the rope connected to it. He was standing at the window as Artur was giving him instructions, his machine gun hanging at his neck.

As an Assault Forces soldier, Makei had made over a dozen parachute jumps. Despite this, he was nervous, as it was his first experience of the kind.

I was actually surprised at the fact that people who'd parachuted more than once were afraid to go through the fifth-floor window, just like anyone else. They said it was a totally different experience. Of course, I'm generalizing here a bit. Other people might well have had some other feelings about this.

"Got me, Lekha?" Artur asked Makei before letting him go.

"Yes," Makei choked out.

Artur nodded.

"Onto the windowsills, everyone!"

Makei, Artur assisting him, climbed onto the windowsill.

"All rightie. Now, you hold the rope tight and just go through the window. Go!" Artur commanded and saw Makei standing on the same spot.

"Go, I said! What's the problem?"

"Just a sec," the soldier was begging, out of breath.

The second was gone, but the soldier was still there and Artur was still waiting for him to jump. "Makei!" Artur was running out of patience. "What's up with you?"

Artur finally realized what the problem was and decided to help Makei out. "Holding the rope?"

"Yes."

"Tight?"

"Yes."

Then, Artur, taking a step back, booted Makei out. Makei shot out through the window, grabbing the rope with both hands, and was now hovering in front of the window opening.

"That's it! Release one hand now and just move slowly down!"

However, Makei kept on holding tight to the rope with both hands, not even attempting to move. The basic descent principle is that, as long as one holds on tight to the rope, they just stay where they are, but as soon as one opens their hand, they start moving down the rope.

Artur was about to lose his temper, so he put the barrel of his machine gun up to the back of Makei's hand. "I have blank bullets only," he informed Makei. "Let the strap go or I'll shoot your hand through." A moment later he cried out, "Let go!"

Makei snatched his hand off the rope and started sliding down the rope slowly.

"That's it, you see?" Artur shouted after him.

Hit or miss, Makei finally made it to the ground.

"Now get back here!" the team's commander cried out. "You'll be doing it until you stop shaking all over!"

In the meantime, Lis was getting ready to go through the window with the rest of the 3rd team.

"Go!" Yegor commanded, and Lis was soon in the fifth-floor window opening.

"Good," Yegor was directing him. "Push off and go through the window!"

Lis pushed off the windowsill, slid down the rope, and landed on the fourth-floor windowsill.

"Good! Turn over!"

Lis swayed his leg awkwardly and turned over, his head down.

"Good!" Yegor cried out approvingly. "Now, push off and slide down!"

However, Lis remained hovering by the window, his position unchanged. In fact, it was not the first time he was descending from a building, but he still lacked experience. And with your head down, the descent is even scarier.

"Push off and release the rope!" Yegor pitched his voice. "Go ahead!"

"Dddd-amn it!" Lis stuttered. "Ddddd-amn ssscaary!"

He let go of the rope a bit, but then, having barely slid down another half a window, he caught hold of the rope again, hovering in the window opening. His legs moving awkwardly up in the air, he tried to reach out for the windowsill.

The way Lis was twisting and squirming made Yegor laugh. "Go! Go!" Yegor encouraged him. "Go, spiderman!"

At first, when you're descending with your head down, it's even scarier. To slide a floor down, one needs just to suddenly open one's hands for a few seconds and let the strap go. In this way, the descending person finds himself approaching the ground at the speed of free fall, so, naturally, his instincts interfere and he snatches at the rope tightly. He slows down, coming to a sudden halt in a window opening, his legs doing a strange dance in the air to find some support. And it really looks funny.

* * *

A phone burst out ringing in the office of the detachment's commander. Nenashev picked up the receiver. "Nenashev speaking."

"It's Colonel Taburetkin!" and Nenashev recognized the voice of the division's logistics deputy.

"My greetings, comrade colonel!"

"Greetings! And where are your guys?"

"Training, in Novaya village. Why?"

"The trench — that's why!" Taburetkin seemed to be both outraged and taken aback by the question.

"What trench?" Nenashev switched on the "what are you talking about" voice.

"I told you yesterday we needed fifty people from you to dig a trench!"

"Oh! That!" the commander exclaimed, as through remembering. "Yes, the trench. Exactly! You called me yesterday. My bad, comrade colonel! It just escaped my mind completely! I'll contact my guys via the radio; they'll be here in an hour!"

"You!" Taburetkin was shouting now. "Damn!" He was lost for words. "Damn you all — SWATs! You've all got your brains knocked out! Belay!"

And then the colonel's voice faded, leaving the short dials only.

"No problem, we'll belay that!" Nenashev finished to the peeping sounds and hung up, smiling.

Special training is the basis of any Special Forces activity. It comprises a number of sections, such as special tactics, special weapons practise, and special physical training, plus the practise that the regular motorized rifle units don't have, such as altitude, assault, and diving training.

However, Vityaz special training is not limited to the above activities; it's about everything. These are the trifles Vityaz incorporated in regular, all-arms tactical courses. While everyone would move one particular way, SWAT soldiers would do it a bit different. The same applies to the way SWAT soldiers would hold their arms or shoot and so on. Everything's a bit different. However, the small differences made us faster and more efficient. Moreover, Vityaz practise included battle formation training in various situations, such as military advance, defense, retreat, breaking out of encirclement, actions while marching, etc. At first sight, it may seem quite the same as written in the Land Forces Charter, but in fact it's essentially different.

All the trifles making up the tactics were developed by Vityaz proper, in most cases, at least. And this is another thing that makes Vityaz stand out. It's constantly looking for new ways and new opportunities to improve its efficiency. Back in 1977, when the Special Designation Training Company (which gave rise to Vityaz) was formed, the SWAT soldiers decided to take the best of what the

Main Intelligence Directorate, the Assault Forces, and Alpha team had developed. So they borrowed and improved their best developments. In fact, their tactics are in the process of continuous improvement, new elements introduced after every battle or special mission. It usually happens that, when Vityaz participates in a battle, teams have a joint discussion, and, based on the discussion, they conclude what their strength and weaknesses were, what they should add, and what they should eliminate. First theory, then practise; and if things go smoothly, they introduce the changes, and then improve them over and over again. This is how special training techniques are developed.

Back then, in the very beginning, we had no instructional aids and no opportunity to communicate with our more experienced foreign colleagues. We actually studied by photos. Say, we saw a photo of a SAS soldier as he's practising and we would wonder, "What is the stance for? Why is he holding his arms that way?" Then we tried doing the same and concluded, "Oh! It's a lot easier to move and shoot like that." And so on.

And it's not the special training programme that contributes most to the Special Forces' efficiency, though it sure makes a difference. The reason we are more often successful than not is our continuous training!

If the rest of the army were training as hard as we were or at least as hard as they were supposed to, that'd be enough for them to catch up on us!

At present, there's a huge variety of documentary films, instructional videos, and training aids available, featuring the way our special trainings are arranged. Apart from the documentary films, the Hollywood blockbusters are sometimes no worse than training aids, especially for freshers, as the actors in such films are usually well trained and the consultants they use are some of the most experienced professionals in the world.

So, why don't the regular troops use it? What is the problem with their training? I believe I've already dealt with it in the chapter about the Hans and the Hans stuff.

There's also this problem that commanders of our regiments, brigades, and divisions are sometimes more worried about the curb painting, the lawn mowing, and the cleaning than training. So, naturally, their soldiers would be doing fatigues, mostly.

Personally, I know some stories of when a SWAT officer (including from Vityaz) would be transferred, for any reason whatsoever (a wound, some family circumstances, etc.), to some Hans troop, sometimes even to the escort guard, and then put in charge of a unit where the military uniform was the only reminder of their being part of the army. It would take him only a couple of months to sort out the mess, getting soldiers up to speed.

You might wonder if such officers had some special secret. But it was actually nothing special. They simply planned things properly and got their contingent to train. And it was nothing like special training — just as prescribed by the combat training programme: physical workouts, tactical and weapons practise, marching, etc., but the training took up the entire free time of the contingent. Both the soldiers and the officers were sweating blood. And the officers treated their soldiers in the way usual for the Special Forces.

So in just a few months' time, those would, indeed, turn into mission-capable units!

I'd like to add a few more words for those officers who complain about someone preventing them from training properly.

Once we had a new officer appointed to be the commander of our detachment. The officer came from a Hans unit, so naturally, at first, he was totally opposed to all our traditions and tried to stick to his old Hans methods. All of a sudden, we found ourselves forced to do all the Hans stuff we hated so much. However, our officers were strong enough (spiritually strong, I mean) to break him down. A few months later, he was into our traditions and proved himself to be a good leader, though, at first, the picture was really sad and we had a lot of conflicts. Once, on a field day, I was planning to practise shooting with my soldiers. It was supposed to be an all-day practise, and I was going to give my team a hell of a shooting run. After the wake-up, the detachment's commander gathered us all to get the details of our plans. Everyone told him what they were up to, and everything seemed to be fine. However, at the formation, the commander suddenly changed his mind and started giving us new instructions. I answered: "Aye!" just as I was supposed to, and stuck to my own shooting plan. An hour later, the commander gathered us all again and changed his plan. Again! Well, he was the boss. And I told him, "Aye!" and went on with the shooting. The commander changed his plans two times more on that day. I always agreed to whatever he said and just went on with my plans. And that's what most of the other teams' senior officers did.

And the story I told you was not a one-time experience. Whenever some commander would give us a useless assignment, I'd ignore it, pretending to agree with the order, and went on training my team as I thought best. So, as they say, those who are willing look for opportunities, whereas those who are not look for reasons.

CHAPTER 22

The 2nd and the 3rd teams were now practising shooting at the shooting range, taking the place of the 4th and the 1st teams. While one part of the 2nd team was shooting, the rest were having tactical training near the shooting range, practising battlefield movements, casualty evacuation, and retreat actions.

Kot was assisting a grenadier, dragging along his bag with RPG-7 grenades. He stopped to rest, put the bag down, and started kneading his shoulders. Then an idea struck him and he looked around.

"Talanych! Come up here!"

And the young soldier rushed to Kot. Kot handed the bag to him, commenting, "Take it."

Talanych did as the old-timer asked him to.

"Hey, Kot!" Kisel approached them. "I don't get your point here. Why does the fresher have to carry the bag instead of you? No one forced you to assist the grenadier; that was your wish. So, just do it!" Then he turned around to Talanych, saying, "Give it back to him."

Just as before, asking no further questions, Talanych gave the bag back to Kot.

"Sanya, can't anyone else be the assistant?" Kot was disgruntled. "Why can't some of the freshers carry it along? Why me?"

"Fine," Kisel agreed impassively. "We'll choose someone else, but for now, you're the assistant."

Pouting, Kot slung the bag over his shoulder and started walking away, looking around. Suddenly, his eyes caught on a bus that had brought them there. He had another quick look around to make sure no one was watching and then headed for the bus. Inside, he took off the bag and put it under a passenger seat.

In the evening, the APCs of the 2nd SWAT team and the bus arrived at the detachment's premises, unloaded the soldiers and all the equipment: the targets, the climbing facilities, and the ramps. As soon as the last soldier was out, the bus and the APCs left, the bag with RPG-7 unnoticed, lying under the same seat.

After the evening roll call, Artur decided to fill in the combat training log, but was distracted by the phone ringing. He picked up the receiver, saying, "Senior Lieutenant Kovalev speaking. Good evening! Right."

As he was listening to the voice in the receiver, his face was growing darker.

"Inside the bus? All right. Got you!"

He hung up and went out of the orderly room. "Team Two, line up!"

"Team Two!" the orderly shouted. "Line up at the line-up site!"

"Duty attendant, come up here!" Artur commanded.

The duty attendant approached him.

"Is there anything missing from the AS?"

"No, nothing," the duty attendant was positive.

Artur gave him a freezing look and beckoned toward the AS. "You go, count!"

The duty attendant headed for the AS, while Artur turned around to face the lined-up team. "Don't you have anything to tell me?"

There was no answer to follow.

"Fine. Then we'll just wait for the duty attendant."

Artur, his head down, started pacing along the line.

Half an hour later, done with checking the weapons, the duty attendant reported, "Comrade senior lieutenant! The bag with RPG grenades is missing!"

Kisel, startled, cast a glance at Kot.

"Team, assembly!" Artur cried out. "Line up on the training ground!"

The soldiers scattered to prepare for the assembly, while Artur turned around to the duty attendant and commanded, "Put on the armour vest and the helmet!" and then he added a promise, which sounded more like a threat. "I'll make sure you'll remember the duty."

The soldiers dropped in at the AS, took their weapons, and hurried down to the training ground. It was 21:50.

When the same soldiers were back running in the building, dirty, wet, and exhausted, it was already 02:15.

Artur was the last to come in. "Now, I want to know who left the bag."

Everyone was silent.

"You may keep silent, but then, tomorrow, we'll have to continue."

Still no response.

"Fine," Artur concluded serenely. "Then lights out!"

Artur went back to the orderly room while the soldiers headed for their bays.

As soon as they were in their bay, Kisel approached Kot. "Kot! What's up with you? Son of a bitch."

"What?" Kot retorted.

"Those were your grenades!"

Kot kept silent, undressing.

"It's because of you we had to run all night long!"

Kot didn't say a word.

"You are a jerk, Kot, you know?" Kisel added calmly, realizing Kot didn't care much about what he was saying.

So, he stepped aside and Kot, lying down on the bed, heaved a sigh.

Five minutes later, Kot was standing in front of Artur.

"In fact, I'm not surprised at all," Artur spoke calmly and paused to add, "Well, the very fact that you, soldier, left the ammunitions unattended — it's unacceptable! But you also forgot them! And what's more upsetting is that you didn't admit your fault and set up your team! And it was not your first time!" Artur emphasized, staring intently at Kot. "Well, I'm fed up, I tell you."

The commander made up his mind. "Tomorrow, we'll have to summon the Crimson Beret Board to deprive you of the beret. And if I ever catch you in a situation like this one more time — forget about the detached service, my dearest comrade!"

Kot cast a sharp glance at Artur. He didn't expect such a harsh punishment!

"You'll be clearing dung till retirement, I promise!"

Kot heaved a sigh, looking down.

To be excluded from the team going on a detached service or on a battle mission was another serious punishment for a SWAT soldier.

Next morning, Kot, having changed into a regular cotton outfit, soldiers' knee-high boots, and a cap, was standing at the orderly post. "Team, lights out!" Kot cried out.

Kisel, who took over that day, was standing beside Kot at the orderly post. On hearing some strange sounds, he looked through the unlocked doors to see what was going on at the stairs, but the stairs seemed to be empty.

In the meantime, the Detachment's Logistics Deputy, Lieutenant Colonel Artsybashev, was tiptoeing up the stairs, his back pressed against the wall. As he reached the door, he stopped, speculating on how he could catch the duty attendants off guard. And his prying mind prompted him to what he believed was a super brilliant idea. Artsybashev got down on his hands and knees and set out to sneak in through the door.

Hardly had Artsybashev crawled over the threshold when he

bumped into Kisel, who was also on his hands and knees, saluting with one hand.

"Comrade lieutenant colonel," Kisel reported in conspiratorial whisper, "I've had no incidents while on duty. The team is having a rest. Duty Attendant Sergeant Kiselev reporting!"

Abashed, Artsybashev sprang up to his feet only after the sergeant was done with reporting. Shaking dirt off his clothes, he was casting glances now at Kisel and then at Kot, who was about to burst out with laughter.

"Well, you know ..." Artsybashev struggled for words. "And how are you? Everything fine?"

"Yes, comrade lieutenant colonel!" Kisel replied loudly, giving full value to each word, his face wearing what was supposed to be an earnest expression.

"Okay, then," Artsybashev murmured. "And ... you know. No, it's fine."

Artsybashev had nothing to do but turn around and leave. Kisel and Kot exchanged glances and laughed out loud.

The next venue Artsybashev meant to check was the 3rd SWAT team. As he entered the bay, accompanied by Yegor, he saw Sieda sleeping with a grip.

"Why is the soldier sleeping with a grip?" Artsybashev pointed at the machine gunner.

"He's a big sports fan, comrade lieutenant colonel."

Artsybashev turned around to look at Yegor. "Really?"

"Yes, a huge fan!"

Artsybashev dropped an unhappy sigh and left the bay.

In the passage, he saw the orderly practising hand-to-hand techniques — blocks, kicks, and punches.

"Soldier!" he snapped at the orderly. "What are you doing here? Is it your private gym or the orderly post?"

"Comrade lieutenant!" the soldier said and turned to Yegor at once. "What is that all about?"

"Comrade lieutenant colonel," Yegor explained in a calm voice. "It's late. Everyone's asleep; the doors are closed. I don't think it'll hurt anyone if the soldier uses this time for extra practise."

"But, lieutenant, we have the charter!" Artsybashev launched his usual record. "And the charter has certain instructions as to what an orderly can and can't do! I really wish you paid more attention to the rules! It's a hell of a mess you have here!"

Yegor just nodded, realizing it was useless arguing.

"Yes, comrade lieutenant colonel! I'll keep it in mind!" he agreed humbly. "But you should know, the detachment's commander doesn't mind the practise."

Abashed, Artsybashev just stared blankly at Yegor for a few seconds and then, finally, reacted. "I'll sure ask him about it," he promised, giving the orderly a disgruntled look, and marched out toward the exit.

Yegor, watching him go, sighed and shook his head slightly.

"Hans," he stated and turned to the orderly. "Just continue," and then he went back to the bay.

The duty attendant closed the door, while the orderly took the stance again.

Chapter 23

Vityaz soldiers and officers in the first turn worked themselves to death. So, every one or two months we let ourselves go and work off steam.

As I've already mentioned before, the detachment actually was short of officers, so all the duties were distributed evenly among those few officers who chose to stay with Vityaz, and those were the responsibilities of the senior officer of the on-duty unit, the detachment's duty attendant, and the team's duty attendant. During my first year of service, for instance, I had about fifteen twenty-four hour duties a month, plus daily special training sessions, including while I was on duty.

Nenashev, Artur, Yegor, Oyama, Rostigayev, and Fomin, a field engineer instructor, were approaching the entrance of Izmaylovo Hotel, which housed the Bingo night club.

Artur turned around to look at Nenashev, who was following close behind him, and, bending over, announced in a conspiratorial whisper, "Working the left one today. Those who'll use the right one are suckers."

The SWAT gang passed by the security, entered the hall, and seated themselves at a table.

"Now, then!" Nenashev gave his instructions. "No punch fests today! Behave yourselves, guys! Do you hear me?"

"Sure! No prob!" the gang hummed in response.

Nenashev told their order to the waiter. "A couple of vodka

bottles and Coke!"

The waiter wrote it all down carefully and left, while Nenashev looked over his companions, clapping his eyes on the field engineer:

"Sanya! And where's your accessory?"

The field engineer was taken aback by the question.

"Comrade lieutenant colonel, but I've left it at the premises!"

Nenashev glanced at his watch and said, "You've got an hour and a half to be back here with it!"

Fomin got up and sprinted off toward the exit, while Rostigayev bent over Artur, asking, "So you, guys; come here to have a fight?"

"Come on!" Artur seemed to be genuinely offended by the question. "You know SWAT soldiers can't fight!"

"Why?"

"Because fighting with a SWAT soldier is impossible," Artur explained. "You can't have the red and the blue corners in a fight, right? So, it's like one, maximum two, blows — and the problem's gone. No sparring, you see. Just a knockdown and then another one. We have specially trained detachments to clean the corpses."

Rostigayev smiled at Artur's explanation.

Just then, the waiter appeared with their order and filled their glasses with vodka. Yegor was drinking Coke only, as usual.

"Well, happy birthday, Artur! Wish you the best!"

The glasses clinked and everyone took their drinks.

And the fun part began: the talking, the joking, and the dancing. Everyone was having a good time, working steam off in his own way. Oyama was fooling around, performing boxing sets to the accompaniment of music, while Artur and Yegor were doing the acrobatic tricks. Soon, the field engineer joined the crowd, his fitting accessory with him.

Later, as Artur was getting back to the table, he walked into a guy, about twenty-five years old, a cap on his head.

"Hey!" the guy turned around, calling out to Artur. "What's up with you, man? Think you're too broad for the place?"

"So what!"

"So nothing!"

And the guy made a menacing move toward Artur. Yegor stepped in between them, trying to calm the guy down. "Easy, easy! We were just leaving."

Holding Artur by the shoulders, Yegor accompanied him to the table.

As they were at the table, they heard Nenashev having a heated discussion with Oyama.

"Valera, I tell you, the height and the weight — it's nothing! All you need is the right spirit. Do you know what a real SWAT soldier looks like? It's a guy, slight in build, about this high," and he showed how tall the guy should be, "who, with his small fists, will knock any gorilla down and, with his small dick, will fuck any chick's brains out! That's the SWAT soldier!" and he turned to Yegor. "Am I right, Yegor?"

"Absolutely!"

And then Nenashev turned back to Oyama. "The SWAT spirit — that's major! So! To the SWAT spirit!"

And, once again, glasses clinked over the table.

Even when the officers were on a night out, they always talked about their job. It was a powerful brainstorming with lively discussions on how best to arrange this or that practise, how to improve the tactics, on what they'd seen in movies or in magazines and on how to best use the things for training, on what were the results of last training, etc. It was the time when ideas to be later implemented in practise and training seemed to strike their minds in packs. Alcohol was, indeed, working miracles, slowing down the brain, but bringing out what was hidden in the subconscious — the most powerful of computer in the entire universe. That's how the greatest discoveries are made; a scientific fact, by the way. Of course, for the subconscious to bring something about, one needs to really live for it!

An hour later, as Artur was on the dance floor, he noticed the guy in the cap making a pass at some girl. The guy reached out to grab her hand, but the girl somehow managed to wrench herself free and pushed him away. The guy, gesturing in her direction, shouted something at her back and headed for the exit, to where the WC was. Artur followed close behind him.

As Artur entered the WC, he saw the guy at a urinal. He stopped right behind him, hiding his right hand behind his back, waiting. The guy zipped up his pants and turned around, his face growing angry and disdainful as he saw Artur looking at him. He stepped toward Artur with decision and, holding out his arm, made his statement, "Hey, you! You make me sick!"

Artur ducked slightly to the left and threw a left punch into the guy's head. The man flew off toward the wall and crashed down. As he was falling, he dropped his wallet. Artur bent over to pick up the wallet and then stuck it behind the collar of the guy's shirt. Straightening up, he gave him a glance and then bent over to snatch off his cap — a good enough prize for the winner.

He was wearing the cap as he came back to his companions.

"Artur," Nenshev said reproachfully, "Haven't I asked you to behave yourself?"

"But, Alexander Ivanovich, he was too rude to women," Artur defended his point.

Nenashev shook his head, glancing at his watch, "Retreat!"

He got up, heading for the exit, the rest of the gang following him. Artur turned around toward the dance floor and cried out, "Yegor!"

Then he raised his hand, making a circle in the air with his index finger, as though spinning a ring. Yegor nodded, understanding what he meant, and followed him out.

Chapter 24

The entire detachment gathered to see off those who left military service. After the morning roll call, Nenashev commanded, "Demobilized soldiers, come up here!"

Four soldiers fell out of the line, joining Nenashev from the right side. Two of them were in their military outfits, while the other two were wearing civilian dress. But all four had crimson berets on their heads and medals on their chests.

"Soldiers!" Nenashev began his speech. "You've learnt a lot over these two years. You know how to fight now, what a genuine men's friendship is, and how to survive in extreme situations. And, what's more important, you have learnt to be the winners. I hope you'll never need your skills, living your peaceful lives out of the army, and I hope you find a place where you truly belong." Finished with the farewell speech, Nenashev motioned the demobees to the training ground, inviting them to play their last military cord. "If you please."

Traditionally, the demobees were to carry out the third hand-to-hand set as their farewell gift to those they were leaving behind. The soldiers lined up in the box pattern. Kisel fell out of the line, facing them, his legs shoulder-wide and hands behind his back.

"Take up the waiting stance! TA!" Kisel piped the command.

The demobees snorted out, taking the waiting stance.

"Begin the third set!" Kisel gave them a preliminary order and, a second later, barked out, "TA!"

The demobees started moving at once. Done with the third set, they froze up, waiting. It was not the end — they had yet the battle cry to shout.

"SWAT!" Kisel started.

"TA!" the demobees thundered in unison.

"SWAT!"

"TA!"

"TA!" This time Kisel and the demobees had to change their replies.

"SWAT!" the demobees roared in response.

And the entire detachment burst into loud applause. Kisel fell in, while the demobees remained by Nenashev's side.

"Thanks once again, guys!" the detachment's commander concluded. "Wish you the best!"

Then Nenashev, in a fatherly, warm manner, gave each one of them a hug, turned around to face the detachment and commanded, "To the right! Single line column! March, forward!"

And the soldiers, moving in a single line column, set off to say good-bye to the demobees. They each hugged them and wished them the best.

Half an hour later, at the entrance to the detachment's premises, the demobees were talking to Kisel, Chef, Kot, and Kirei.

"So, you've chosen the contract, huh?" asked one of the demobees.

"Yeah," Kisel answered for all of them. "We're staying."

"I see," the demobee nodded. "Well, then, we're off to the gym now, and later we'll come back to say good-bye."

It was another Vityaz tradition to say farewell at the gym. The gym has always been sort of a sanctuary for SWAT soldiers, where men got to become warriors.

The demobees took their time walking around the gym, hitting the apparatuses one time each. At the exit, each bowed to the gym, thanking it. Some were even close to tears.

A Ural vehicle, the four demobees in it, was leaving the detachment's premises, accompanied by joyful cries of their fellows shouting their last wishes after them.

"Glory to the SWAT!" Kirei cried out.

"Death to terrorists!" A demobee gave the traditional response and everyone raised their hands, waving each other good-bye.

CHAPTER 25

Yegor, fully dressed and covered with a jacket, was lying on the bed. It was so cold in the bay he could see vapour coming out of his mouth — apparently, there were heating problems again. To get warm, Yegor set up an old electric stove by his bed, but though the stove was red hot, it was not enough to heat up the air in the room. Yegor was staring wistfully at the ceiling, his thoughts coming back to his last date with Kira.

* * *

Kira, a light dressing gown on, entered the room. Yegor was sitting on the sofa watching TV. She came up and landed onto his lap, as gracious as a cat. Putting her arms around his neck, she looked into his eyes and said, "Yegor, I'm leaving for France, on a business trip." Kira's voice was quiet and sad. "For three months."

Yegor, meeting her gaze, nodded wordlessly. Kira ran her palm over his face, soothing him. "Don't be sad," she reassured him softly. "I'll be back in February." Then, remembering the good news, she exclaimed joyfully, "Besides! We still have two weeks!"

Yegor heaved a sigh. He had nothing to say to that. He knew they had this night only because they were leaving in two days. But he didn't want to talk about it right now. He wanted her to be happy, at least till the morning.

Kira kissed him tenderly and Yegor, cradling her in his arms, laid her down gently onto the sofa.

In the morning, Yegor was drinking tea in the kitchen as he heard Kira's soft footsteps. She approached him from the back, twining her arms round his neck and pressing her cheek against his. She closed her eyes and purred, "Why are you up so early?"

Gosh! He really hated to tell her he was leaving! Hated to make her sad! "Kira, honey," he said gently, "I have to leave, too."

Kira's eyes flew open, and she turned her face to look into Yegor's eyes, worried. "When?"

Yegor met her gaze, hesitating. "Tomorrow," he dared at last.

Kira's brows went up. "Tomorrow?"

Yegor just sighed and nodded sullenly, keeping his eyes on Kira.

* * *

Yegor opened his eyes, recovering from the reverie, and turned his head to the door, toward the sounds of laughter and music coming through it. He had to get up to see what all the noise was about.

He headed for the bay where the noise seemed to come from. Coming in, he saw his soldiers lying on their beds, laughing and talking loudly. The tape recorder was playing some whiny song from a woman with a sweet voice. As soon as the soldiers noticed him entering, they sprang up to their feet.

"Team, stand up!" Sieda, who was the first to see the commander, cried out. "Ready, front!"

Someone switched off the recorder and silence filled the room, the soldiers looking at the commander expectantly. Yegor looked over his soldiers serenely, shifted his gaze to the mask he noticed on the chair, and picked up a rucksack from the floor. He examined it quietly and then, in a low voice, almost a whisper, said, "Team, assemble. Form four. Line up on the training ground."

The soldiers rushed out of the bay, running, repeating the command.

"Team Three, assemble! Form four! Line up on the training ground!"

It was snowing, the snowflakes very small. Holding the "happiness tree" high above their heads, the soldiers were squatting.

"Log on the right shoulder!" Yegor gave the next order. "On the left! On the right! On the left …"

The soldiers could hardly keep up with his orders, shifting the log from one shoulder onto the other and back. Soon, their arms seemed to be as heavy as lead.

"Now shift it into your arms!" Yegor commanded.

And the soldiers shifted the log from the shoulders into the arms.

"Be delicate, like to a woman!" Yegor commanded curtly. "I said, delicate! So, now put it carefully down! Careful!"

The soldiers, exhausted, their faces red with tension and sweat, fought to keep the log in their arms. They lowered it to the ground, carefully, gently, as if it were really a woman.

"Now pick it up and raise it, carefully!" Yegor gave them no time to catch their breath.

As a human being, he was really sorry for the guys, but he also understood perfectly that to survive at war they needed to be disciplined and alert. However, the lads didn't know where they were going in a few hours. For them, it was just another game — no fear, no sense of danger that would keep them alert and focused. So for now, let them be afraid of their commander, at least.

The soldiers were later grateful to him for that attitude.

An hour later, all the soldiers, sweaty and panting, were standing in front of Yegor in the team's quarters, arranged in two lines.

"I don't get it, guys," Yegor was speaking to them. "What's the party about?" He gave the soldiers, almost dying from exhaustion, a severe look. "We're leaving at nine in the morning and, as far as I know, we're leaving to wage war." He paused and looked at the soldiers. "I can tell you're all ready. Right?" he enquired, sarcasm thick in his voice. "Shooters! What about the rifle cases? Done with them yet?"

"Not yet," Lis replied guiltily.

"Not yet!" Yegor repeated, nodding. "Phil! Bring me the rucksack and the mask!"

Phil went to the bay to fetch the rucksack and the helmet and handed them to Yegor. Yegor threw the rucksack onto the floor and raised the mask higher up for everyone to see.

"Where are the covers?[1]" He was waiting for the answer, staring intently at the soldier. "I believe there's no one here who has them!"[2]

Putting the mask down, he picked up the rucksack and pointed at the lacing attached to it. "What are these? Straps?"

Yegor snatched at the lacing with his other hand and tore it off. "That's how you'll lose them at your first outing!" He showed them the damaged remnants of the lacing. "You could have found some spare belts, at least, to have the straps for the entire team." And he put down the rucksack beside the mask.

"What's with the discharge vests? Given it a brush?[2] Or you're going to run with just four magazines? How long can you survive on those, then? Like ten minutes?" He gave his soldiers a stern look and they just looked down, feeling guilty.

"But here you are, having fun!" Yegor made a helpless gesture. "Good job!"

Yegor turned around and made two steps, slowly, thoughtfully, and then suddenly stopped, casting his eyes down. He stared at the floor for some two or three seconds as if he were going to add something more, but then, apparently changed his mind he just said, in a low, tired voice, "Team, lights out!" and left, without looking back at his soldiers.

The soldiers, evading each other, went their own way each, slowly and sullenly.

Yegor entered the bay and went back to bed at once, covered himself with the jacket and closed his eyes, his mind returning to Kira's kitchen.

Kira was sitting beside him, trying to talk him out of the trip.

"Just explain to me, please, will you? Why do you need to

go there?"

Yegor answered, staring through the window, "You know, Kira, honey, it's a vocation," he said matter-of-factly, "to protect the motherland."

Kira was taken aback.

"Motherland? Motherland, you say? So, what's the use of your motherland? Think about it. Where has your motherland sent you?"

Yegor kept quiet as he listened to Kira and then started explaining his point, patiently, slowly, as if he were talking to a toddler. "Kira, a motherland is something you can't choose. You're just born to it."

There was nothing pathetic in his words. He was only saying what he meant — the obvious things he took for granted.

"And it's not the motherland you're talking about; it's the state. And there's a big difference."

He heaved a sigh and continued. "If it were not for the people like us, who believe in words like motherland, Russia, honour, our country would have long ago become history. Nowadays, most of us are ashamed of the words somehow. Even in our detachment, they try to evade those, saying they fight for SWAT ideas. But If we save people, defend them against all the cruds causing them trouble, if we are ready to risk and sacrifice our lives for those people, we're doing it all for the motherland? Right?"

He glanced at Kira, shrugging his shoulders as though to say, "Well, that's how I see it."

"Besides! Who else is gonna do that for us? Today, there are a lot of people who blame their country for all their misfortunes. Sometimes I really want to ask them, 'And what have you done to make your country better?' Unlike them, we are ready to take the responsibility and do something to improve the situation." He paused again and, dropping a sigh, went on, "Well, I don't know; I guess I was brought up this way, Kira. In fact, it all comes down to this: I'm going there to protect the things I treasure. Got my idea?"

He took her hand in his and pressed his lips against it. Feeling helpless, Kira sat down on his lap and, twining her arms tightly around his neck, pressed her cheek against his and closed her eyes. Yegor embraced her tenderly and saw tears in the corners of her eyes.

"At least call me, will you?"

"I don't think we'll have a post office there," Yegor sighed.

* * *

Again, Yegor was woken up by some noise. He got up and went to see what was going on in the passage.

He saw guys walking about the floor, talking to each other.

"Orderly! What's the time?"

"Ten minutes past four!"

"So why aren't you sleeping?"

Lis, passing by with a small case in his arms, replied for the orderly. "Well, comrade lieutenant, you see, we were just working on the faults. Look! It's for the rifles." He opened the case, showing it to Yegor. The inside was finished with foam rubber. "It's enough for two rifles. We've got one for the optics, too."

Yegor looked at the case, then glanced at Lis, and pleased with what he saw, went back to the bay. At last! He got them to under-stand!

---

1. *The masks were painted green. Soldiers sewed special masking covers they pulled over the helmets in either camouflage or white, depending on the season.*

2. *Manufactured discharge vests could hold four machine gun magazines only. So, soldiers had to have two more regular cartridge-pouches sewn on those.*

Chapter 26

At eight o'clock in the morning, the entire detachment was lined up on the training ground, fully armed and equipped. A train of Ural vehicles was waiting in the central valley.

Yegor was completing his last checks. All the faults he pointed out at night were eliminated — the masks lined with a masking cover, new straps sewn to the rucksacks, all the soldiers fitted out with self-made "bra bags" (discharge vests made of two magazine bags sewn together).

On the detachment's commander's order, the soldiers opened bullet cases. Everyone got their ammunition supplies, and having signed off in the weapons and ammunition register, loaded their magazines.

"To the vehicles!" Nenashev commanded. "Take your places!"

It took them only a few minutes to get into the vehicles, and soon the train set off to Chkalovskiy Airport. Two hours later, Vityaz soldiers got onto an IL-76, and the plane took off, heading for Mozdok. About two more hours later, the IL-76 chassis, squealing and producing clouds of smoke, touched upon the concrete of Mozdok Airport runway.

"Yegor, Artur!" Nenashev called out to them as the plane, already braking, was taxiing out to the destination. "Three people for cover, each!"

The officers nodded and gave their instructions at once. A few seconds later, six soldiers approached the exit, took their magazines out of their discharge vests, and attached them to the machine guns.

The plane finally stopped, and a few seconds later, they heard the characteristic bellowing sounds of the ramp lowering. As the ramp touched upon the concrete platform, the soldiers rushed toward the exit. Outside, they scattered around the plane to observe the location, providing for unloading.

No one could ever come close either to a Vityaz camp or its machinery and equipment. Wherever Vityaz was, whether in the action area, at its permanent location, or at any other place, its soldiers were always meticulous about security. Whenever an APC had to make a stop, soldiers would jump down, providing for circular defense. It was a rule to be followed no matter what, eventually growing into a subconscious instinct.

As our army was assaulting Grozniy during the first campaign, one of the regiments was ordered to seize a transport station. Slowly, without any fight, they reached the building and settled to drink tea! They might have thought, "Well, that's it! We are here! Done with the assignment!" Can you believe it? It turned out there was no sensible officer in the entire regiment to give them a good dressing down! It might well be that the regiment's commander and his deputies had lost their sense of reality, but what about all the companies, platoons, and their commanders? However, it occurred to no one that they should arrange some people to watch the perimeter through the windows. As a result, they found themselves besieged by a gang of insurgents at a grenade-throwing distance (fifty metres away)! The regiment was then eliminated to the last soldier. Of course, it never would have happened to Vityaz, and in fact, to any of the Internal Troops' Special Forces units.

Vityaz was to set up at one of the abandoned barracks: no lighting, no beds. Nenashev was the first to enter the room where the officers and contracted soldiers were supposed to live.

"I'm sleeping here." He threw his sleeping bag into the corner to stake the place. A Vityaz commander never had a trailer of his own, living together with his subordinates.

On the same evening, once everyone found a place for their sleeping bag, the detachment's commander summoned his officers for a meeting. "Now, then, guys," Nenashev looked over his fellows, "while we're here, in Mozdok, we're going to patrol the area in helicopters. Those who're not patrolling are to practise the special and combat training, full scope. Taken the situation, we should prepare to celebrate New Year's Eve in Grozniy."

Vityaz arrived at Mozdok in mid-autumn, when it was still hot there. Unlike other units, where soldiers used the relatively peaceful time and good weather to swim and sunbathe, Vityaz soldiers had been sweating their guts out, day and night, day in day out, with field races, tactical practise, plus the helicopter raids to assault high grounds and attack abandoned farms.

By evening, soldiers could hardly feel the ground under their feet. Some, of course, felt jealous of other units, where soldiers were just having fun, enjoying the sun and the water, as they couldn't understand why their officers were giving them such a hard time. However, later, they were all really grateful for them.

Vityaz had its first serious fight in late December 1994, at the station of Ischerkaya. The detachment was ordered to eliminate an insurgents' roadblock. All the access ways, except for the road, were mine-studded. The roadblock itself was made up of reinforced concrete plates, half a metre thick. The train of Vityaz vehicles stopped half a kilometre away from the roadblock, realizing a head-on attack would be unreasonable. So, Yegor offered the following:

The 3rd SWAT team, which was the first one in the train, started turning back, as though retreating, while the 4th SWAT team, which followed close behind, dashed off toward the roadblock, reaching it in a blink of an eye. Meantime, the 3rd SWAT, supported by the rest, covered the 4th team with massed intense fire, including the eight "Shmel" mine-throwers, which virtually razed everything to the ground.[1] Once the 4th SWAT came close enough to start the fight, the 3rd SWAT team popped up there as well. As a result, the insurgents were completely defeated.

As the soldiers entered the roadblock they found only one injured insurgent and one woman. Some of the insurgents had obviously fled to the neighbouring village. Vityaz soldiers took away their weapons and ammunition and gave the injured insurgent a dressing, leaving both the man and the woman intact at the roadblock.[2] By that time, reinforcement was on its way, approaching from the village side. The SWAT soldiers got onto their APCs and returned to their starting position. Yegor asked the driver to record, with his speed metre, the distance from the roadblock to the location of AGS-17[3] platoon, which was assigned to their detachment. As they approached the location, he passed the speed metre readings on to the grenadiers' commander and they, having adjusted the shooting range as appropriate, met the fresh party of insurgents with a rain of fire.

The whole performance took about half an hour, and all Vityaz soldiers remained intact!

For the assault of Grozniy on the night of December 31/January 1, our sapient military leaders decided that Vityaz should go ahead of all the troops, clearing the access ways (I've already mentioned about the way our senior commanders didn't know how to use the Special Forces).

And once again, it was the Internal Troops' commander-in-chief, Anatoliy Kulikov, who, ignoring all the high ranks, refused to let his detachments be used in such an outrageous way. He insisted, "The Special Forces have been formed for other purposes! And I need Vityaz for other purposes!" He saved Vityaz from the useless and merciless bloodbath, which was actually against all the laws of military tactics. Unfortunately, not all the forces were so lucky with their commanders-in-chief. A great many guys were killed because of the worthless generals who didn't care a twopence about whether the soldiers were alive or dead.

---

1. *RFT "Shmel": rocket flame-thrower*

2. *Indeed, in the beginning of the war, before the insurgents started torturing our captives, Vityaz fought to a code of honour, something like Tolstoy described in War and Peace.*

3 *AGS-17 "Plamya": a 30mm repeat fire grenade launcher*

Chapter 27

Chechnya
March 1995

An engineer battalion train was moving slowly along a field road. The soft sunshine, the light spring breeze, and the odors of nature coming alive — everything seemed so peaceful, sleepy, and colourful, as if it weren't war. The soldiers were napping quietly, some on the APCs, leaning against its tower, others on the ICV armour.[1] The machine guns were put aside, not to disturb their sleep.

Drivers were squinting at the bright sunshine, also drowsy. Senior vehicle officers sat sleeping beside them, their heads against the windshields.

Those who were not sleeping were either playing cards or enjoying their travel rations.

One of the soldiers took a condensed milk can his fellow was passing on to him and, throwing back his head, put it to his lips.

Bullets went through his chest before he even heard the sounds of shooting.

In a moment, the forward ICV blazed up, the grenade dispenser hitting the target. And the train came to a halt. The next shot destroyed the trailing vehicle.

Piercing glass and the tarpaulin, bullets cut into flesh. Soldiers were injured and killed, and weapons were falling out of the armoured vehicles every which way. Some never got a chance to wake up.

Out of the entire train, only a few people were shooting back, but the insurgents' shooters were gradually taking those down, too.

The insurgents set an ambush in a ruined building and nearby trenches, about a hundred metres away from the road. They surrounded the train, and as no one was fighting back, they were just eliminating the ones who survived.

Another RPG shot, and one more vehicle exploded.

At one of the APCs, an officer was kneeling at a radio set, shouting, "Typhoon! Typhoon! Seven three two speaking! Seven three two speaking! We've been ambushed and lost many people! We need help! Once more, we need help!"

The commanding general of the group alignment forces and one of his staff officers were studying a map on the table as the duty attendant came into their tent.

"May I come in, comrade general?" he asked in an anxious voice.

"Yes." The commanding general turned around to him.

"An engineer battalion has been ambushed," the attendant reported, "as they were approaching the group alignment position. They've lost a lot of people and ask for help."

The commander heard out the report and turned back to his interlocutor.

"And who do we have nearby?" the commander asked, anxious.

The headquarters' officer looked down, trying hard to remember. "What about the 6th Detachment?" he remembered at last.

The commander nodded at once. "Get me through to them."

A few minutes later, Nenashev, his detachment on the other edge of the group alignment position, was already climbing into the CV to pick up the TA-57[2] receiver.

"It's Baikal," Nenashev introduced himself, taking care to observe wireless communication rules, "speaking."

And then he heard out what the other party had to say.

"I've only one team now," he told the commander. "It's less than ten people; the rest are on a raid."

"I understand," the commander insisted, "but it's not like we have any other options. If you could only help them for a while, till I get someone else to support them."

Nenashev realized one team was not enough and was doing his best to make the commander understand. However, he was obliged to obey orders. "Got you," he concluded calmly and hung up. "Team Three, to assemble!" he told the operator at once.

At that time, Vityaz soldiers were all engaged in various missions. Some were accompanying transportation trains, some were executing reconnaissance and search missions, while others were patrolling the area in helicopters. There was only one reserve team left, for emergency tasks. It was the 3rd SWAT team.

Some soldiers were practicing with hook and jab pad, while others were pumping up their muscles. Yegor was throwing a knife into the board he put up aboard an APC.

Kirei and Phil were simply enjoying the sun, only their underwear on.

"Hey, Dima!" Kirei called out lazily to his friend. "They say the spring sun is dangerous."

"You know, Sanya," Phil made a short pause and then continued in the same lazy manner, "war is dangerous, anyway."

"Sure," Kirei agreed and, hearing battle sounds coming from a distance, added, "Some might have gotten in trouble already."

"Yeah, and quite close, I tell you."

"Aha, I'm worried they might send us up there."

And the next moment they all heard the command. "Team Three, assemble!"

Kirei swore a profane oath, sprang up to his feet, and together with the rest of the team, sprinted off to the dugout.

About three minutes later, the entire 3rd SWAT team was up on its APCs, fully armed and equipped. Nenashev, also fully armed, came up to Yegor and beckoned to where the sounds of shooting were coming from.

"Can you hear it, Yegor?"

"Sure," Yegor nodded, guessing what they had to do.

"We are to go there." The detachment's commander confirmed his guess. "We'll see what we can do on the spot."

And then they both rushed to the APCs and started off, leaving behind clouds of black smoke.

Meantime, the group alignment's commanding general was looking for other solutions. "Get in touch with the helimen," he instructed his assistant. "Ask them to help us with a twenty-four flight, at least."

The assistant picked up the receiver while the general started pacing around the tent, rubbing his chin nervously.

A minute later, the assistant reported to the general, hanging up. "The helicopters will arrive in forty minutes, at the earliest!" He resumed the phone negotiations.

"Forty minutes, you say?" the general was taken aback. "In forty minutes, there'll be no one to save!"

Some of the vehicles in the train were still on fire, and the insurgents kept on shooting, without a break, getting almost no shooting in response.

The one officer who called for help was trying to shoot back. From time to time, he would stick his machine gun out from behind the APC wheel and give a squirt. As he leaned out another time, he saw tracer bullets flying toward the ambush, kicking up dust fountains at the insurgents' position. Switching his head round, he caught sight of two Vityaz APCs rushing full speed toward the train, clouds of dust trailing behind them. The APCs were firing from all of their guns, which made the insurgents hunker down and cease fire.

Their noses dipping, APCs came to a sudden halt right beside the train of vehicles. The soldiers jumped down from the APCs, scattered quickly along the train, hid behind the vehicles, and opened fire.

Down on the ground, Yegor rushed to the nearest engineers' APC, choosing it as a shelter. He swung his body a little to the right, leaned out, raised his machine gun, and gave a squirt, aiming at the insurgents' position. Out of the corner of his eye, he also noticed some soldiers lying across the road. They got there as they were falling off the APCs at the onset of the attack. Some were killed, others were injured. It took Yegor only a moment to make his decision, and he rushed to their APC. Opening the hatch, he cried something out to the driver and the direction layer. As the hatch went back down, the APC set out across the road.

"Phil!" he called out to Filatov, who was shooting from behind a wheel of the nearest vehicle.

Phil turned around and Yegor motioned him to follow.

"Follow me!" he added aloud.

And Yegor, crouching, followed the APC across the road, using its armour to protect him against the fire. Phil sprang up to his feet and hurried after his commander.

Yegor's APC stopped between the ambush and the train, shielding the soldiers lying across the road. Yegor sat down beside two of them, shoving them in their backs.

"Pick up the injured, quick! Hide them behind the APC!" he cried out, showing the APC he had hid behind a few minutes ago.

The soldiers were struggling up to their feet, scared and awkward.

"Quick!" Yegor barked out.

His shouting worked all right, and the soldiers, picking up their injured fellow, took him inside the APC. Yegor took another injured soldier by the arm.

"Run up here!" he cried out to Phil.

Phil was there in no time, taking the soldier by his other arm, and they dragged him, barely alive, toward the engineers' APC.

As Yegor and Phil were transporting the soldier across the road, other SWAT soldiers were covering them. Nenashev gave short squirts from the cabin of the Ural vehicle, while Sieda, realizing the insurgents had adjusted the shooting range, rushed to change his position. Throwing himself down behind a small hill, he opened fire again, covering Phil and Yegor.

The APC of the 3rd SWAT team was also unceasingly firing from all of its guns, crashing down what remained of the walls and raising soil into the air. Once, an insurgent got up for a moment to throw a RPG-7. The grenade exploded a little away from the APC.

As they reached the engineers' APC and hid the wounded soldier behind it, Yegor looked inside through the open APC hatch. "Who's the driver?" he turned around, speaking to the soldiers they brought across the road.

One of them raised his hand. "Here!"

"Take your place, quick! The rest of you, everyone, pick up the injured and the killed and get them inside the APC! Move!"

The soldiers started getting up slowly.

"Quick, I said!" Phil yelled at them, and to make his words more convincing, booted one of the soldiers.

It worked, and the soldiers were now faster.

"Phil!"

He heard Yegor calling out to him and turned around.

"Go to that one!" and Yegor motioned to the APC standing a little further away. "Use that one, too!"

Phil glanced in the direction Yegor was showing and nodded. "Got you!" he answered and hurried to the vehicle, crouching.

"Three two!" Yegor commanded via radio. "Back off, but make it slow!"

The APC backed off onto the road, its nose facing the enemy.

Approaching another engineers' APC, Phil saw a soldier hiding behind it, weaponless, his hands over his head. Phil grabbed him by the collar of his camouflage outfit and shook up a bit. "Hey, soldier, where's your machine gun?"

The soldier looked up at Phil, fear in his eyes, and shrugged his shoulders, "Don't know."

"Yeah, that's why they kill you like moths!" Phil pushed him away, annoyed, then turned around to the other engineers who were lying nearby and snapped at them, "Get the injured inside and find the driver!"

The engineers began picking up the injured and the killed, laying them inside the APC and leaving those killed soldiers who remained on the armour where they were — it didn't matter much to them now. In just a few minutes, they were done with the loading, and the APCs took off, the SWATs covering their retreat.

Nenashev was changing his magazine, hiding behind the Ural's cabin as Yegor approached him.

"Comrade lieutenant colonel," Yegor sat down beside the detachment's commander to share his plan. "I'll take an APC and some assaulters and try to outflank them from the left. If everything is fine, we can attack them with grenades. Then we'll decide what to do next, depending on the situation."

"All right, Yegor," Nenashev agreed. "Let's take a try."

Yegor nodded and got in touch with Kirei via the radio, "Kirei, nine zero three calling!"

"Kirei speaking!" Kirei's voice spoke up on the radio.

"Tell all the assaulters to come up here!" Yegor gave his order.

"Got you!" Kirei replied.

Yegor turned back to where he came from and cried out, "Phil!" He motioned to him and then picked up the radio again. "Six three two!" he got through to the APC crew. "Drive up here!"

As soon as Yegor saw the APC moving in his direction, he turned around to Lis, who was lying beside him, behind a wheel.

"Lis!" he began his instructions to the shooter. "Find a proper position and make sure none of those bastards can get us with their grenade launchers!"

"Got you!"

As soon as the APC arrived, Yegor, Naum, Phil, Kirei, and Miron hid together behind one of its sides.

"Ready?" Yegor asked, looking over his soldiers.

They nodded with confidence and Yegor commanded via the radio, "Three two! Start moving! Slowly!"

The APC started off, the soldiers following it. Then it took a turn, heading across the road, toward the ambush, simultaneously firing from all of its guns. The rest of the SWAT soldiers were covering the assaulters with dense precision fire.

An insurgent with a machine gun noticed the APC moving and turned around, bringing his fire on it. Bullets kicked up fountains of soil in front of the APC, clattering against its armour.

Sieda got sight of the opponent through the optics and pressed the trigger, bringing a long string of bullets onto him. The ground around the machine gunner started boiling and then he jerked, suddenly sagging onto the trench bottom.

The insurgents' shooter found Sieda through his optics, but Lis was a bit faster. Breathing out to calm down, he pressed the trigger smoothly, and the bullet he sent smashed through the insurgent's head.

Lis, observing the directions, noticed an insurgent pointing his RPG-7 at the assaulters' APC. Keeping Yegor's words in mind, he pressed the trigger with one quick movement. The bullet went through the grenadier's chest. He twitched, the RPG jerking up higher, and the grenade flew past the APC, exploding further away.

The SWAT soldiers moved on, crouching, toward the insurgents' position.

All of a sudden, the APC guns fell silent, the barrels raised high up in the air to the maximum.[3]

The direction layers inserted quickly a new PKT[4] feed and closed the barrel extension cover. Having armed the PKT, he took another case with KPWT[5] bullets and hung it up in one rapid movement.

The barrels of the machine guns moved quickly down, and the tower shifted first to the right, then to the left, and then the machine guns were shooting again.

The APC stopped about thirty metres away from the ruins. Yegor peeped out cautiously from behind the APC to evaluate the situation and turned back round to his guys.

"Get the Fs!" He told the guys to get their F-1 grenades ready.

Yegor made a quick movement, reaching out for a grenade, and pulled out its safety ring, then he took two steps away from the APC. The soldiers did the same. Yegor showed the direction with his other hand.

"Attention!" he shouted over the thundering shots.

The soldiers got ready for the assault and Yegor commanded, "TA!" and the soldiers threw the grenades over the APC. "One more!" Yegor's order followed immediately.

Three seconds later, five explosions sounded in the ruins. Some of the insurgents fell onto the ground, while two of them sprang up to their feet and dashed off in the opposite direction, away from the APC.

The soldiers took one more grenade each, getting ready to throw them.

"TA!" and the soldiers threw five more grenades, pressing themselves against the APC.

Five more explosions followed. A second later, Yegor pointed the barrel of his machine gun at the enemy's side and peeped out cautiously.

"Come on!" he cried out, emerging full height from behind the APC, the APC ceasing fire at once.

Nenashev saw the guys set out and shouted via the radio, "Six three one! Don't shoot!"

The second APC fell silent, too.

All the five SWAT soldiers, dispersing in width, set off running toward the ruins, holding their guns pointed at the enemy, ready to shoot.

At the trenches near the ruins, Yegor slowed down. Passing by, he saw some corpses of insurgents lying here and there. "Phil, Kirei, you follow me! The rest — clear the ground here!"

Three of them moved on, while two stayed back to make sure the insurgents they saw were dead and no one would be shooting after them.

As the soldiers approached the ruins, Yegor, going first, fired two double shots to kill an insurgent who suddenly emerged out of the ruins.

Slowly and cautiously, they moved on along the insurgents' position, killing the rest of the gang. Done with clearing and having checked the corpses, the soldiers kneeled down, observing the area.

"Baikal, nine zero three calling!" Yegor got in touch with Nenashev, using his radio.

"Speaking," Nenashev responded.

"Clear," Yegor reported.

"Got you, nine zero three!"

A few minutes later, the duty attendant reported the same to the commanding general on the phone.

"Fine, then." The general sounded a bit perplexed. "Tell the helimen to stand down!" He hung up and stared thoughtfully at the phone for some seconds, then turned around to his assistant, and added, "What the hell is going on?" he began, surprise obvious on his face. "They took down the entire battalion; an engineer battalion, of course, but still. At least seventeen people were killed!" He raised his index finger. "And then there arrive some ten Vityaz soldiers with two APCs and eliminate the enemy in less than an hour." He raised his finger again. "An enemy exceeding them in numbers! Without casualties!" The general fell into surprised silence, making a helpless gesture. "Can it be true?"

The assistant was listening to the general with a thoughtful expression.

"Well, maybe that's why they are believed to be the best," he commented, shrugging his shoulders as though suggesting it was the only plausible explanation.

After 1995, the government declared a truce (which I believe to be treachery on the part of the government). After the declaration of the truce, our soldiers had to meet with insurgents from time to time for confidential talks. The insurgents told them, "We have learnt to recognize you guys by the way your APCs move, by the way the soldiers are positioned on the vehicles, by the way they hold their weapons. So we just let you pass by, as we knew perfectly well that attacking you would do us no good. We'd rather attack a train of twenty vehicles than two APCs with ten SWAT soldiers."

---

1. ICV: infantry combat vehicle

2. CV: command vehicle; TA-57: a field telephone set

3. To load the APC guns with bullets, one needs to raise them up.

4. Kalashnikov tank machine gun

5. Vladimirov heavy machine gun for tanks

Chapter 28

Soldiers were cleaning their weapons as Artur entered the dugout. "Lebed!"

"Here!"

"Lekha, get ready! A truck is leaving soon to bring food. You and your section are escorting it."

"Okay," Lebed replied. "Section Three, get ready!"

The soldiers stripped their guns quickly and went to change their dress.

"Comrade senior lieutenant!" Kot approached Artur. "May I join them?"

Artur glanced at Kot and nodded. "Go ahead!"

The weather was disgusting; it was drizzling. The APC of the 2nd SWAT team and a Ural vehicle were slowly moving along a village street. There were no people to be seen, either in the streets or inside the yards. From time to time, the soldiers came across a ruined house. Each of the soldiers on the APC was watching carefully its observation range, everyone alert and ready to open fire immediately. The soldiers held their weapons with both hands, the stock at the shoulder and the barrel tilted slightly down. Suddenly, Lebed seemed to notice something.

"Stop!" he cried out to the driver.

With a squeal of braking shoes, the APC came to a halt and the soldiers jumped immediately down, scattering on either sides of the street to provide for perimeter defense. Only Kot remained sitting on the armour, looking around with caution. Down on the ground, Lebed headed along the road, keeping his eyes on what caught his attention. From time to time, he cast glances to the right and to the left while approaching his target, and then stopped, looking down. On the ground, at his feet, he saw a kitten, wet and shivering with fear and cold. Picking it up, Lebed looked into its eyes and the kitten, as though realizing it was time to seize the chance, squealed a meow. Lebed smiled at it and touched its pink nose with his finger, then cuddled the kitten and headed back toward the APC. Back at the APC, he opened its hatch to let the regiment's adoptee into the personnel compartment.

"Take your places!"

The soldiers went immediately back to their positions on the APC. Lebed took his place as well, checked the soldiers, and then went back to what his was doing before, observing the area.

"Go!"

It was getting dark as the APC and the Ural vehicle arrived at the base, which was actually a former school building. As soon as the APC stopped at the building, Lebed jumped down and headed toward the entrance, where two soldiers from the procurement team were smoking. The soldiers never left the place and, unlike the 2nd SWAT team, they were clean and dry, their faces showing they had regular meals. Lebed approached them and dropped, without even looking at them. "Where's the chief of staff?"

He decided not to wait for their answer and just entered the building. One of the soldiers finally obliged him by shouting at his back: "To the left! Enter the quarters!"

A few minutes later, Lebed was back. Coming up to the APC, he commanded, "To the vehicle! Arms inspection!"

The soldiers, leaving their positions, formed a single line by Lebed's side, holding up their weapons at sixty to seventy degrees. Then they detached the magazines and thrust the bolt carrier assemblies back, unloading the barrels. Lebed was examining soldiers' weapons, walking behind their backs. Done with the inspection, he tapped a soldier on the shoulder and proceeded to another one, saying, "Inspection over!"

Having released the carrier bolt assembly and done with control triggering, the soldiers safetied their weapons. Then they picked up the bullets that fell off when unloading and loaded them back into the magazine, putting the magazines in their discharge vests.

"Now change, wash yourselves, and have your supper," the sergeant gave further instructions. "After the supper, we're cleaning the weapons. And don't forget to feed the kitten!"

The soldiers picked up their rucksacks and headed for the building at a leisurely pace. Having looked around, Lebed noticed a local squeezing through a hole in the fence.

"And what's that?" Lebed came up to the Chechen and enquired aggressively, "You! Who are you?"

The Chechen didn't expect such a meeting and was obviously scared, "I live here, not far off."

"And why are you here?"

"Well, hmm, I've come for food."

Abashed, Lebed had to ask for more details. "What food?"

"Well, canned meat, sausage, cereals; you know."

Lebed, still unable to make out what the man was getting at, cast glances now at the Chechen and then at Kot, who also joined their company.

"We come here every day," the Chechen explained.

"We?" Lebed was shocked.

Peeking through the hole in the fence, he saw like fifteen more people, then finally realized what was going on.

"Son of a bitch!" he almost hissed and, turning around to the Chechen, snapped out, "Now then! Look here and pass it on to the others. The shop is closed! If I ever see one of you here again, don't blame me! Got my idea?"

The Chechen started nodding violently, scared as hell, "Yeah,

yeah! I got it!"

"Dismissed!" Lebed resumed and the Chechen was gone.

"And you, Andrey; got the idea?" Lebed turned around to Kot.

Kot replied to him with a silent nod. He got the idea.

Having changed their clothes and had a wash, Kot and Lebed came to the canteen. The 2nd SWAT team was already there, nibbling listlessly on what looked like barley groats.

"Now then!" Kot had a look inside the pot. "What do we have here?" and then he turned around to the cooks, indignant at the sight of barley. "Hey, you! I don't get it! You're doing it on purpose, huh? Barley there and barley here. What are we, horses or something? Can't you guys bring us some edible food?"

"Well, that's the only food we have," the cook said.

"You're trying my patience, huh?" Kot approached the cook. "You! Follow me!"

And Kot, together with Lebed and the cook, went out of the canteen, moving along the passage, and stopped at one of the doors, a padlock on it.

"Is this the storage?" Kot asked the cook.

"Yes."

"Open it!"

"Only Artsybashev has the keys," the cook replied. "I don't have them."

Then Kot found his own key, smashing the door open with a kick.

When inside, Kot and Lebed couldn't believe their eyes. The room, from floor to ceiling, was packed with humanitarian aid: smoked sausages, cheese, chocolate, biscuits, fruits, juices, Coca-Cola, mineral water, cigarettes, and brand-new outfits.[1]

Boiling with anger, Kot turned around to Lebed:

"Check this out, Lekha! We've been eating barley for a whole month, and Artsybashev is doing his business here. The stinking bastard!" Then Kot turned back to the cook and, his tone authoritarian, declared, "Now then! Tomorrow," and Kot pointed around the storage room, "you're to load it onto our truck. Are we clear on that?"

The cook had nothing to do but agree. "Sure," he said, dropping his head.

"But, for now, we'll take some of these for our guys in the canteen." And the three of them started picking up the foodstuffs.

As the soldiers were all in their beds, Kot, Lebed and the chief of staff arranged a meeting to have a discussion. They had a table set with some simple food on it — sausages, canned meat, onions, and bread. On the floor, right beside Lebed, the kitten was lapping condensed milk.

Kot was unburdening his mind to the chief of staff. "You know, comrade lieutenant colonel, some people risk their ass every day, swimming in mud and shit, while there are some who're just enjoying the warmth, the drinks, and the meals, and sell what belongs to soldiers! And, surprisingly, those people even manage to get medals and orders somehow, and then they beat their breasts about how bullets were whizzing above their heads!"

Right then, Artsybashev burst into the room. Outraged, he rushed to the table and started yelling at Kot, who was sitting across the table from him. "Don't you think you've crossed the limit, soldier? Who's given you the right to break into the storage? You—"

Kot gave Artsybashev no chance to finish the sentence, snatching his APS out of his holster and pointing it at him. He chambered the bullet, and the gun banged. Fortunately, the chief of staff managed to grip his arm somehow, and the bullet flew past Artsybashev, some millimetres over his head. Artsybashev had to bend down and, yawping, hurried out of the room. Lebed and the chief of staff were both pulling Kot away, while Kot was trying to escape, shouting after Artsybashev, "You son of a bitch! Sucker!"

Finally, the chief of staff wrenched the APS out of Kot's hand and they let him go. "Andrey, what's up with you, man?" Lebed was staring at his friend in horrified shock.

Kot was literally shaking with anger.

"So, now, guys, time to go to bed!" The chief of staff declared their meeting closed.

Lebed and Kot got up and, taking the kitten with them, went to bed.

Next morning, watching soldiers load bags and boxes with food, Kot noticed the chief of staff appearing on the porch and approached him, asking, "Comrade lieutenant colonel, will you give me my APS back?"

"No stupid things, you promise?"

"I promise," Kot returned him a guilty smile.

"Fine then. Let's go."

And they entered the building.

An hour later, as the loading was over and the soldiers took their places on the APC, Kot and Lebed were saying good-bye to the chief of staff.

"Well, guys, take care!" the chief of staff said.

They hugged and Kot and Lebed headed for their APC. Lebed jumped onto the footboard, checked the soldiers carefully to make sure everyone was in their proper places, then he breeched the gun and took his place. The soldiers followed his example, breeching their weapons.

"Go!" he commanded to the driver, and the train of the APC and the Ural vehicle started off, moving out of the yard.

---

1. *Humanitarian aid includes the things various charity foundations and private sponsors donated to those participating in battle actions.*

Chapter 29

The spring sun was bright and pleasantly warm. Music was flowing through the camp. Done with their battle missions, SWAT soldiers got a chance to brush up their arms and equipment, to train, and to have some rest. The APCs were parked in trenches, and the drivers, their backs up, were pottering about the engines. Some were cleaning their weapons, some were pumping up their bodies, and some were practicing with hook and jab pads, while others were simply enjoying the good weather, sunbathing.

Artur, wearing pants, a T-shirt, and boots, had his eyes closed and was lying on a bunk bed in the dugout. Nenashev left for a meeting at the group alignment position, appointing Artur as senior officer. He first heard footsteps and then saw Kisel entering the dugout.

"Comrade senior lieutenant! There's some general over there, asking for the senior officer."

Unwillingly, Artur got up and they both headed for the exit.

At the edge of the camp, they saw a UAZ and two APCs with an infantry escort. A general was pacing leisurely, his posture dignified, in front of the sentry, who, of course, was not going to let anyone in without permission. The general had a new, well-ironed camouflage outfit (without shoulder straps) and shiny boots on, which made a sharp contrast to the way the SWAT and infantry soldiers looked in their everyday uniforms. He seemed to have just emerged from an office with polished parquet.

241

Artur was approaching the general leisurely, buttoning up on the way.

"Senior Lieutenant Kovalev, acting for the commander of the 6th Detachment," Artur introduced himself politely, keeping his tone impassive.

The general cast a disdainful Napoleon glance at Artur, out of humor with such a welcome. For a general, of course, talking to a senior lieutenant was sort of an insult. Artur could easily guess it, so he explained calmly, "The detachment's commander is away at a meeting, at the group alignment position."

Before the general finally introduced himself, he made a theatrical pause for everyone to understand how much of a big shot he was and how he was obliging them all by talking.

"Lieutenant General Gundosov, the Deputy Commander-in-Chief of the Group Alignment Forces!" he spoke up in a scornful manner, dead serious about his importance, and giving Artur a discontent look, commented, "And what's that look you have, senior lieutenant?"

Absolutely unaffected, Artur retorted, "I believe that of a commander, enjoying his rest."

Apparently, the answer got to the general, but he chose to skip it and, after another dignified pause, he went on, "What is your contingent doing?"

"The drivers are repairing vehicles," Artur began his report, speaking quietly, "while the rest are training."

It was obvious the general was completely uninterested in whatever Artur was saying and was listening inattentively. "Fine!" he concluded with discontent. "Just fooling around."

The disdainful tone could not leave Artur unaffected. "Comrade lieutenant general!" He pitched his voice a tone higher and repeated, emphasizing each word, so that the deaf general could hear him. "Once again, the drivers are servicing vehicles, the rest of the contingent are training!"

The general just gave Artur another frown. "Report on the situation, senior lieutenant!" he said, changing the subject abruptly.

Artur paused for a second to cool down and then reported, "At the forest fringe, insurgents have set up dummies," he went on in a calm tone. "Their base camp must be about two hundred metres away, deeper into the forest. We've seen smoke over there."

Avoiding looking straight at Artur, the general was just nodding, as if saying, "Yeah, yeah, things are the way I suspected."

"Give you a 'bad' for your awareness!" the general said, pulling another trick.

Artur was genuinely taken aback! "What do you mean, bad?" he asked, sneering. "I'm reporting to you our observations; we're not supposed to conduct any detailed reconnaissance."

The general ignored Yegor and turned around to show him a map he had ready on the UAZ hood. "Now then!" the general continued his solo performance. "Take two teams and go over here," he traced a pencil about the map. "Outflank the forest from the left and move on over there," he explained, gesticulating violently.

"You can read the map, right?" His abrupt, sweeping movements looked as if he were cutting a piece of paper with scissors — one, two, three! No big deal!

"Then proceed through the forest, going out on its other side. Got me, right? Four hundred metres deep into the forest, okay?"

Artur was watching the general without enthusiasm. He already got it all. The man was one of those warlords who thought it was possible to occupy Grozniy in two days, having one Assault Forces battalion only.

"I got you," Artur answered, just as unenthusiastically. "But what is it all for?"

The general gave Artur a harsh look, "For reconnaissance."

"I got you," Artur nodded, with emphasis on the "got" part. "But what's the purpose? What are we gonna find there?"

Apparently the general didn't expect such a question, so he made another dignified pause and finally asked, "Patrolled with helicopters yesterday?"

Artur was silent for some moments, remembering who, when, and where. "Yes, we have," Artur answered, his answer rather meaning, "So what?"

"So, take a closer look at it!" The general formulated the task.

"Take a look at what? How leaves have all fallen down?" He beckoned toward the mountain. "There they are, the trees; you can see them all right from here."

Losing his temper, the general decided to bring the impudent senior lieutenant to his bearings.

"You're way too talkative, senior lieutenant!" He switched his tone to formal, which was the traditional trick for such ignorant honchos. "Get your contingent going! Now!"

Artur, meeting the general's infuriated gaze with the same peace and calm, announced his final decision. "I'm not going anywhere!" he stated confidently. "I'm not going to risk my soldiers for something like that."

His statement flared the general up. "What?" He simply flew off the handle. "Don't you realize? Arrest him!" he finally cried out. His command, however, had no effect.

Artur was looking at the general, impassive. "All right," he paused for a moment. "And who's gonna arrest me?"

He had Kisel and the sentry standing behind his back. Kot, Chef, and Lebed also joined them. Grinning, Kot was practising leisurely with his shadow. Chef was scratching his bristle, while Lebed and Kisel were just standing there staring at the general, their faces sullen and stern. The sentry, watching the situation with caution, got his machine gun ready. He was perfectly sure he would be faster than any of the infantry soldiers.

The general, of course, had enough time to evaluate the situation. The way the eyes of SWAT soldiers were blazing with animal fire froze him out a bit. He was smart enough to understand it was war and war allowed lots of things that otherwise would be unacceptable.

"Your surname, senior lieutenant?" the general asked, or rather commanded, in a calmer voice, though still disdainful.

"I've introduced myself before," Artur answered calmly, and uninterested in any further discussion, turned around and headed back for the camp.

"Don't move!" the general cried out, but remained where he was. "Come up here!"

"Go to hell!" Artur dropped under his breath, without even turning his head.

Then the general, glancing at the stern, determined faces of the soldiers in front of him, snatched at his map and got into his UAZ, murmuring swears and threats. The UAZ started off, while the infantry escort went back to its APCs. One of the infantry soldiers, apparently an old-timer, made a dry comment as he was passing Kot, "A pretty cool rascal you have here. Bold!"

And then the soldier was down on the ground, wincing with pain from Kot's sudden blow. His face smeared with blood, he tried to get up, but his feet failed him. The rest of the infantry soldiers remained seated on the APCs, staring blankly at them. Kot bent over the soldier and explained to him his mistake, in quite a harsh manner, "Look here, you freak! Your officers might be rascals — call them anything you want! Our officers are real men, and the guy, the senior lieutenant, is like a father to us all! So, don't you ever try this subject again — or don't blame me if anything happens. Got me?"

"Got you," the infantry soldier choked out.

"Now get out!" Kot commanded.

The soldier rose to his feet and climbed up onto the APC, not without difficulty. The APCs then started off and the SWAT soldiers, their faces wearing happy expressions, scattered about the premises.

When Nenashev came back, Artur reported to him in detail on what had happened. Nenashev heard him out impassively and said, "You did it right. Just forget it now."

Artur nodded, breathing a sigh of relief, and turned around to call the sergeant major. "Chef! Get the team to line up, fully armed!"

Artur told me once, "A SWAT officer must be bold!" And I agreed with him, absolutely, adding, "But his being bold must be based on professionalism. With a basis like this, it's gonna be a true officer's spirit. Without it, it's just cheap showing off." Artur said I was right.

As for me, I believe it's not about SWAT officers exclusively, but rather about Russian officers in general. Back in the early twentieth century, Russian General Krymov said, "Officers must be brave both facing their enemy and their commanders. It's a quality that is essential for an officer."

The Russian Officer's Code of Honour reads: "The honorable status of a Russian Officer is not something one gets together with shoulder straps. One has to prove they deserve the status throughout their lives, holding their own no matter what. Being a Russian by origin and wearing a military uniform can't make one a Russian Officer. Any person, even those who weren't born Russian, can become a Russian Officer, if they've devoted their lives to serving their motherland — Russia."

Two minutes later, Artur was checking the ammunition of his soldiers. "Magazines!" he commanded, approaching Talanych.

Talanych had the magazines ready and held them out to the commander. Artur examined the magazines, one by one, and the bullets inside.

"Grenades!" Artur requested once done with the last magazine.

Talanych put the magazines down at his feet and took four grenades out of his pockets. One of the RGNs[1] caught Artur's eye. As he took it in his hands, he saw its fuse had burnt off.[2] The damage was so serious that the safety pin was hanging on by the tips of the feelers. It made Artur's hair stand on end. "What's that, soldier?"

"Well, it's just …" the soldier stuttered, frightened. "I fell asleep at a fire. It burnt off."

"Are you out of your mind, soldier?" Artur was both shocked and enraged. "Sergeants, come up here!" he cried out, looking sideways, and gave the grenade back to Talanych. "Unscrew the fuse! Careful!"

As Kisel, Lebed, and Chef came up to him, he asked, "Who's his commander?"

"Here," Kisel answered humbly, apprehending a punishment.

"Have you checked the grenades?"

"Yes!"

"And have you seen the fuse?" Artur pointed at the damaged fuse.

Kisel had no decent answer to that, so he was silent.

"What the hell is going here?" Artur hissed angrily. "Huh? You want this jerk to blow himself up? Anyone willing to keep him company?"

Sergeants were looking down, silent. Artur took a deep breath, breathed out, and continued, in a calmer voice. "Now then, take shovels and go dig a pit." He gave them a level look. "One and a half by one and a half. Let's bury your silly brain here! Move!"

The sergeants turned around and left. Artur turned toward Talanych, who was sniffing and looking down, feeling guilty and scared.

"Give me the fuse!"

Talanych handed him the fuse. Taking it, Artur commanded, "And you, go to the dugout and do press-ups until I say stop!" and then added, "Double march!"

Talanych picked up the magazines hastily and sprinted off to the dugout.

Thirty minutes later, Artur was examining the square pit the sergeants had dug. The sergeants were standing right beside him, shovels in their hands.

"No," Artur made a whimsical face and shook his head. "No, it's no good. I don't really like it."

Then he just turned around and left, while the sergeants, sighing, got down to dig another grave for a silly brain. Half an hour later, Artur was back to examine the newly dug grave.

"I don't really like the place. The place should be like 'Wow!' you know," and he shook his fist in the air to make it more emotional. "It's for the trash in your head; you see my point?" he added, accenting the trash part.

It was getting dark as Artur and the team of diggers, dirty and tired, were standing by another — the seventh — pit.

"Well, that one is all right," and Artur handed over the ill-fated fuse. "Bury it!"

Kisel jumped down and put the fuse down at the bottom. Lebed and Chef helped him out, and then their team, working vigorously, buried it under a layer of soil.

"So, done with the funerals," Artur commented, looking at the sergeants. "Whenever you pass it by, it will remind you of the silly brain you buried here." He stared at his sergeants for some more time and then nodded, saying, "That's it. Go back to your contingent!"

He turned around and headed for the dugout, the sergeants dragging slowly along.

"Get up!" Artur commanded, approaching the dugout.

Talanych struggled to his feet. His face was red and sweaty, his hands were shaking — for all this time he'd been pressing up in the leaning rest position on his fists.

"Soldier!" Artur sounded calm, but reproachful. "Use your head! It's not for eating only. Understand?"

"Yes!" the soldier swallowed down, his throat feeling sore.

"Dismissed." Artur let him go, and Talanych, panting, stumbled into the dugout.

---

1. *An offensive hand grenade explodes when it touches the ground.*

2. *The RGN fuse, unlike in conventional design grenades, is made from plastic.*

Chapter 30

Kira and a friend of hers were enjoying their coffee, comfortably seated in a café.

"I was shocked!" Kira was sharing her impressions. I love Russia but I see how it is being torn apart now… Everyone is trying to tear off a piece…And I come across these people who talk about such things as motherland, serving." Kira glanced wistfully through the window, remembering her argument with Yegor. "And, you know," she recovered from her reverie, "they do believe in those things, in the SWAT idea, which I didn't quite get!" She shook her head and shrugged her shoulders. "They don't have anything, anything at all, and I mean it, but they are ready to risk their lives for others!" She glanced at her friend, her eyes questioning. "Can you believe it? I'm going on a business trip to France, and they are going to war, and they call it a trip, too." She sighed and continued. "People are just making money from that, and they don't even care; they don't, really. They believe they are doing something important." She glanced away through the window and resumed. "Seems they've come from some other planet."

Her friend smiled sadly.

"In a sense, yes… Only not from another planet but from another time… Roughly from the nineteenth century…"

She noticed that Kira didn`t understand and explained:

"Russia has always rested on Russian officers. And listening to you I see these Russian officers still exist… which means Russia will definitely be reborn…"

She smiled again but this smile was joyful.

"But are you sure you're ready for more? Now, you see, Russian officers are going through hard times… Neither flats nor money… Constantly in hotspots…"

For a couple of seconds Kira looked away.

"You know… Like any woman, I always dreamed of meeting a real man… Strong, courageous, noble… With whom it`s calm… And I don't have to seem strong, but can just be a woman…" And Kira shrugged as if saying: "Like that".

The friend smiled once again and squeezed her hand gently.

"Then, he is that one you were looking for… Because the Russian officer is exactly like that".

CHAPTER 31

Yegor was standing at the dugout, staring wistfully at the starry sky. He only glimpsed at Nenashev as he approached him and went back to staring at the stars. Nenashev, guessing how Yegor felt, was just standing there by his side, staring silently at the stars.

"Alexander Ivanovich?" Yegor broke the silence. "When's the relief?"

"As scheduled; you know it yourself, Yegor. On the eighteenth."

"Yeah, I know," Yegor nodded. "I was just hoping you'd say the relief is already here."

The way Yegor's voice sounded, the strange intonations confirmed Nenashev's suspicions that something was wrong with Yegor. "What's the matter with you, Yegor?"

Yegor sighed and replied, his voice sounding muffled and hoarse, "I'm tired."

"I understand it, Yegor," the commander tried to cheer Yegor up. "Just wait a little more."

Yegor nodded, as though to confirm he, of course, would wait. "Good night, Alexander Ivanovich!"

"Good night, Yegor!"

Yegor turned around and went down into the dugout. Nenashev stared after him for some seconds, then sighed and followed him in.

Of course, some might say, "Big deal, he's tired! I've been there, too. For three, six, nine months I've stayed put there — and nothing happened!"

When one finds oneself at war, one is naturally scared. If one insists one is not afraid, it means that person is either stupid or lying. To feel scared is pretty normal for a mentally healthy person. Fear is a protective instinct, which makes one more attentive, alert, and focused. It means a person is under constant mental strain. Naturally, our mind must have an integrated switch that would prevent us from exhausting our mental resources to madness. So, fear fades away — in just a month or a month and half. And that's it! We're no longer afraid, no longer focused, hence the stupid casualties in our army.

So, it's one of the qualities of a real professional to stay always focused, which means a person has to deliberately keep himself alert, almost every single minute. And this kind of mental strain is more exhausting than physical loads. One should also remember that war might sometimes not even look like war. It's not like we have battles every day when at war — it's mostly peaceful days, without shooting. And add the spring and the sun, the birds singing, the scent of grass and field flowers — does it really look like war?

This is the weapon insurgents kill the Hans with.

As for Yegor, he had always been the highest-grade professional! So, he never let himself nor his soldiers relax for a moment.

CHAPTER 32

Vityaz train, back from marching, was now approaching a field where they could see APCs of the 7th SWAT detachment "Rosich."

"Here are the brothers from the 7th Detachment," Yegor thought aloud.

Indeed, it was a brotherhood one rarely comes across. Well, in fact, all the detachments of the Internal Troops' Special Forces considered each other brothers. Whenever they happened to meet, walking in the streets, or on a detached service, crimson berets would act like they'd known each other for ages, even if it were their first meeting.

Once, on a vacation, my schoolmates and I were walking around Pyatigorsk, the city where I was born and grew up. At the local railway station, I came across a soldier in a crimson beret who was waiting for his commuter train. I came up to greet him, "Hi, brother!" We shook hands and I asked him, "Where're you from?"

He replied, "The 17th Detachment."

"I'm from the 6th," I said. We talked for a couple of minutes, having found we knew some common acquaintances. When it was time for him to get on his train, we hugged, wished each other luck, and he left. My friends had been standing there for as long as we had been talking. So they heard our conversation.

When my brother from the 17th Detachment was gone, they asked me, "Is he your friend?"

"No, it's the first time I've seen him," I replied.

They were surprised. "But you were talking to him as if you'd been friends for ages."

Then I had to explain. "Well, for us, it's pretty normal to come up like that, no matter where you are at the moment, and to start a conversation, offer help if needed. That's the way our SWAT brotherhood is."

My friends were amazed, in a good sense of the word, of course. Yes, this is the way we are, the Special Forces soldiers. All crimson beret soldiers call each other "blood brothers."

However, the brotherhood between Rosych and Vityaz was special, unprecedented, which is quite understandable. Rosych was the second SWAT detachment of the Internal Troops, inheriting its traditions directly from Vityaz. So, the SWAT spirit was especially strong there, making up for all the faults in their special training. Vityaz wasn't able to teach them how to use all of their developments because regular training assemblies were a problem. Video recording was also a problem, as they were rare back then. So, whenever a Rosych soldier happened to visit Vityaz for whatever reason, he'd try to absorb the maximum he could to share this knowledge with his fellows on coming back to the detachment's quarters. It was one more quality the two detachments shared — thirst for knowledge and self-improvement.

Jumping down from their vehicles, the detachments lined up facing each other, and Rosych started the traditional greeting. Rosych's greeting is its calling card they present to whatever unit they meet.

First, all the soldiers of the 7th Special Designation Detachment start stamping and clapping to the tune of the famous Queen song, "We Will Rock You." One of the soldiers, standing in front of the line, begins the war chant:

Hi, guys!
How do you do?

SWAT Division is greeting you!

Special Forces are here, before you!

And then the entire detachment joins him: "We are Special Forces!"

It goes the same as the refrain in the Queen song: "We-e-e will, we-e-e will, rock you!"

And, finally, "Hey, brother, quit smoking and drinks! Go, brother, for the beret, take risks!"

There's no one who'd stay indifferent to a greeting like that.

So, Vityaz awarded their brothers with hearty applause. Then the Vityaz commander fell out of the line and made a ceremonial statement. "And now let's give each other a hug, brothers, and wish each other luck and whatever happiness a soldier could dream of!"

He approached the commander of the 7th SWAT team, Semyonov, and gave him a hug. The rest of the SWAT soldiers from both detachments followed their example.

"Glory to the SWAT!" Yegor approached one of the Rosich soldiers.

"Death to terrorists!" Tsymovskiy echoed. "Yegor! Brother!"

"Hi, Tsyma!"

And they hugged.

At one of the training sessions, they managed to arrange in Moscow, several Rosich officers had to take the exam. Yegor was their instructor during the march and the hand-to-hand fight. So all Rosich officers had developed genuine respect for the young Vityaz officer. This was when their friendship began.

"Where's your position?" Tsyma asked Yegor.

"Not far away."

"So why haven't you dropped at our place yet?" Tsymovskiy asked in a wounded tone. "Come visit us today then, at least."

"No problem," Yegor shrugged his shoulder. "Now we'll have to make out heads and tails. And then, sure, we'll come."

"You promised!" Tsyma said in a tone that meant he wouldn't take no for an answer. "So, we'll be looking forward to your visit."

Vityaz set up its camp not far from Bamut. Having settled all the urgent issues, Artur, Yegor, Chef, Kot, and some other soldiers got onto their Ural to pay the duty visit. As Yegor sat down on a bench, he noticed Chef carrying a case with GP-25[1] grenades.

"Why do you need the grenades?" Yegor turned around to Artur.

"The 7th Detachment got the new bounding ones. We have a deal with them — case for case."

"Don't forget about me, then, all right?"

"No prob."

"What took you so long, guys?" Semyonov came out to welcome the dear guests. "Everything is cold now."

They shook hands and hugged once again, for the second time on that day.

"Igor," Artur said, "What's with the GP exchange? Are we good?"

"Sure, Sanya will take care of you," and Semyonov pointed at one of the officers in the welcoming party.

"Come on, Dima," Artur beckoned to Chef and they followed the Rosich officer.

"I'd say our soldiers are hungry," Artur said.

"Of course, Artur. We'll get things right now. Come on!"

They headed for the dugout, Semyonov letting the guests lead. Near the dugout, Yegor saw a pull-up with a boxing bag hanging from it, and, passing it by, Yegor threw a kick in it.

Once the rest of Rosich officers had welcomed the guests, everyone took their places at the table, where they saw fried meat, potatoes, sausages, greenery, vodka, mineral water, and condensed milk. Vodka was immediately used to fill the cups. Tsyma, who was sitting beside Yegor, moved the condensed milk closer to him.

"I know, Yegor, you don't drink, so here's your treat."

"Thanks, Tsyma."

Semyonov, being the host of the evening, raised his cup to give the first toast. "So, well, to the meeting!"

The cups clinked, and the soldiers took their drinks. By this time, Chef and the officer he was assigned to were back.

"Commander!" Chef reported to Artur at once. "We're done with the grenades."

"Good, Dima," Artur nodded and Chef joined them at the table.

"So, what's your assignment for tomorrow?" Yegor asked Tsymovskiy.

"Well, the Sofrins[2] are taking away their corpses to Lysaya Mountain, so we're to consolidate there and to cover them."

On hearing that, Artur turned around to Semyonov at once.

"Hey, I've been there, on a fighting reconnaissance. Look, Igor," Artur advised, "you'd better arrange some covering force before going there — some people on the right and some on the left, 'cause you won't get out of there should anything happen." He gave Semyonov a serious look. "Set up some cover block and then proceed. If you don't have enough people, you'd better stay away from the place. Covering force is a must!"

"You guys need to be careful, too," Zoza joined the conversation. "I say you'd better watch your ass."

Then it was time for another round of vodka.

"To SWAT!" Artur toasted.

The cups clinked again, the soldiers taking their drinks.

"The only good thing about it," Yegor was thinking aloud rather than talking to anyone in particular, "is that Romanov is in charge of the mission."

His fellows agreed, nodding.

"Which means, they won't leave you all on your own," Yegor finished.

"Yeah," Artur confirmed, "our luck is still with us when it comes to commanders-in-chief."

General-Colonel Anatoliy Alexandrovich Romanov was a legendary commander-in-chief of the Internal Troops.[3] He was a skilled commander (a real professional!) — that's for one thing, plus he was a good person! He knew every Vityaz officer (and, in fact, whomever he happened to work with) by name, greeted them all with a handshake, treating all as equals.[4] On October 6, 1995, his car exploded on a landmine. No one survived except for Romanov, who's been in a coma ever since.

"Terekha!" Artur called out. "Let's have a smoke."

They rose to their feet and went out. Terekha had been serving his regular term in Vityaz and then was contracted by Rosich. So he sort of belonged to both detachments. They had a smoke, talking and joking, and, after a playful fight, hugged each other joyfully and, laughing out loud, went back to the rest.

Sometime later, when everyone was tipsy enough and divided into clubs of interests, Semyonov told Artur about his discovery.

"It's a cool method, Artur," Semyonov was persuading him. "You slip off a cane and give it to a soldier. He walks ahead, carrying the cane in front of him. So, if the cane bends — there's your trip wire."

"Syoma, are you nuts?" Artur gave Semyonov a bewildered look. "If he is walking like that, he won't see a thing. There could be a mine right under his nose, and he'll notice it only as it hits his forehead. All you need is to pick a fresh soldier to walk ahead every fifteen minutes."

Tsyma bent over Yegor.

"We're really sick of this cane thing, you know," he said in a low voice. "We even had a special training. The entire detachment had to walk holding out the canes, all day long."

Yegor laughed at Tsyma's story, Tsyma confirming it was nothing but the truth with a nod. "I swear to you, Artur!" Semyonov insisted. "That's the real stuff! I read it in some military journal."

"As you wish, Igor," Artur gave up on the argument and raised his cup. "So, brothers, to our luck! Let bullets fly past us!"

The entire Rosich detachment gathered to see off the guests from Vityaz.

"Igor," Artur called out to Semyonov, already up in the Ural, "I've got your frequency, so I'll keep in touch."

"Right, Artur," Rosich commander replied. "So, good luck to you all, guys. Go!"

One of the Vityaz soldiers tapped on the cabin cover, and the vehicle took off.

"Glory to the SWAT!" Yegor cried out.

"SWAT is the best!" Tsyma echoed, raising his fist up.

Vityaz and Rosich soldiers put their hands up, in this way saying farewell to each other. The vehicle soon disappeared in the darkness, leaving only clouds of dust behind.

---

1. GP-25: 25mm rifle attached grenade launcher

2. The Sofrins are soldiers from Internal Troops' Sofrinskaya Brigade. Shortly before, they'd had an engagement at Lysaya Mountain.

3. There's an annual All-Russia Hand-to-Hand Fighting Tournament held to honour Hero of Russia General-Colonel A. A. Romanov. In 2000, I was lucky to be awarded the champion's title in my weight category.

4. When I was a first-year student at the military school, Romanov, back then General-Lieutenant, Deputy Commander-in-Chief of the Internal Troops of the RF Ministry of Internal Affairs, visited us once. Right at that time, we were practising shooting at our training center. I remember him (though back then I didn't even know who he was) talking to a friend of mine, an ordinary first-year military student, in a very casual, genuine manner, with a smile on his face.

Chapter 33

Preparations for Bamut military action were in full swing as the sun rose above the mountains. Drivers were warming up engines of their APCs, the radio sets were hissing and peeping, the weapons were rattling.

The detachment's commander gathered the teams' commanders to give them his last instruction.

"The brigade leads," Nenashev was detailing the plan. "We're following close behind them; the 8th Detachment is the reserve unit."

Back from the instructional meeting, teams' commanders, just as they were supposed to, lined up their teams to assign combat duties and instruct them on their tasks.

Yegor lined up his team as well, checking that everything was ready for action. At that moment, the 3rd SWAT team comprised twelve people only. "Got spare batteries for the radio?" Yegor asked Kirei.

"Yes!" the soldier gave him a precise answer.

"And what about you, Andrey?"

"All's fine, commander," Naum replied.

"All right," Yegor nodded.

"Make a semicircle," Artur commanded to his team.

The soldiers of the 2nd SWAT team surrounded their commander.

261

"Kuzya, give me the map!" Artur gave his next order.

"Aye!" Kuzya replied and sprinted off out of the line to clear the ground in front of Artur.

Artur, taking down his AK-74, knocked out its rod and began drawing a scheme on the ground.

"We're the second serial ..."

Simultaneously, Yegor was also instructing his team. As both commanders had about the same expertise in tactics and used similar logic, their words were almost the same.

"Our task is as follows," Yegor was giving his instructions. "If the brigade bumps into an obstacle, we'll have to eliminate it. As for those who've just arrived," and he glanced at the five young soldiers who had arrived some days ago and were totally new to war, "you'd better look carefully around and watch me — follow my lead, repeating all the commands I give. And stick together, covering each other."

Artur was tracing his scheme with the rod, showing how they should proceed.

"Everyone, watch the rest, on the right and on the left," he continued with explanations, "and don't you dare to go ahead without cover." Then he looked up and gave his soldiers a meaningful look. "Collect all your belongings — the record books, the photos, tapes, and so on. Kuzya!"

"Here!" Kuzya reacted immediately.

"Secrecy order."

"Aye!"

Kuzya jumped out of the line to wipe out the drawing on the ground. Even in such a situation, Vityaz have always found ways to crack a joke.

Artur inserted the rod back into his AK-74 and looked back at the soldiers. "And one last thing," Artur began.

"And the most important thing," Yegor emphasized.

"Don't leave your fellows," Artur started.

"It's either everyone or no one," Yegor finished the basic SWAT principle.

"Any questions?" both the commanders asked in unison.

The soldiers from the 2nd and the 3rd teams were only silently staring at their commanders.

"Take your positions!" sounded another order, the commanders giving it simultaneously.

The detachment's train stopped not far from Bamut entrance way. All the SWAT soldiers were focused to the utmost, glancing now at Bamut, which lay in front of them, and then at Lysaya Mountain, to the left of the settlement. No one talked, the silence broken only by the growling of APCs where the infantry brigade was seated. Unlike Vityaz soldiers, almost all infantry soldiers were drowsy. Yegor, having glanced at them, heaved a sigh and shook his head in disapproval.

Falling asleep right where they're sitting, Artur thought. *Either they don't realize where they are going or they have seen so many things they just don't give a damn about their lives.*

Yegor glanced at Lysaya Mountain. "We're so plainly visible here," he said to himself. "Put a landmine at the entrance — and who needs watchers then? An explosion — and we can say we've arrived."

In the meantime, an ACV[1] surveillance patrol set out toward Bamut. About one hundred metres away from the settlement, a land mine, which had been set up on the road, exploded, tearing the vehicle to tatters, a huge, fiery mushroom rising into the sky.

The SWAT soldiers, all at once, switched their heads round to watch the mushroom expand above the trees.

"Here we go," Yegor said, heaving a sigh.

The brigade soldiers, however, weren't going to wake up, apparently ignoring the sounds of the explosion completely. Only a few people looked up to glance at the mushroom and then closed their eyes, disinterested.

Some minutes later, the brigade moved on, and the detachment followed it cautiously.

Passing by the explosion site, they could see what was left from the ACV, though actually, there was nothing to see except for pieces of bodies hanging on the bushes and the trees.

What the hell have the engineers been doing? Yegor thought to himself.

Once they entered their street, Yegor looked carefully around and parted his arms. After he voiced his command, "To the vehicle!" his soldiers jumped down from the APCs immediately to quickly scatter on either side of the street, clearing after the brigade.

Meanwhile, the APCs of the 2nd SWAT team were slowly moving along the neighbouring street, Artur and all his soldiers looking around intently. Occasionally an infantry soldier would appear, running out of a yard with a hen, a jar, or a bag. A dirty soldier emerged from the nearest yard, stumbled over something and dropped his bag, walnuts falling onto the road.

"Soldier!" Artur called out to him harshly. "Where's your company?"

"Well, I'm, you know," the soldier was embarrassed. "They sent me."

Artur lipped a curse quietly and then, glancing over the houses, cried out to the driver, "Kochetok, stop!"

With a squeal of brakes, the APCs came to a halt.

"Team, to the vehicle!" Artur commanded, and the soldiers, repeating his command, jumped down and scattered on either side of the street.

"Watch it carefully, guys!" Artur told them. "I've got a feeling, you know, the warriors have made some balls!"

Kisel and Lebed were working together, inspecting cellars. Coming across one, they'd clear it with grenades, Kisel opening the cover and Lebed throwing a grenade. Done with the exploding part, they gave a squirt down the cellar with their machine guns.

At the next cellar, Kisel pulled the cover while Lebed was preparing to throw a grenade, the guard ring already off. Just as Lebed held out his hand to throw the grenade, Kisel suddenly stepped toward him, making a warning sign with his hand.

"Stop!" he cried out.

Holding the safety pin, Lebed lowered his hand while Kisel bent over the cellar.

"Hey!" he shouted, looking inside. "Anyone? Come out!"

And soon some Chechens — an old man, an old woman, and two middle-aged women — emerged at the entrance, shaking with fear.

"Is there anyone else there?" Kisel asked.

"No," sounded the old man's scared answer.

"Do it, Lekha!" He gave his permission to Lebed then.

Lebed threw a grenade and they both added a squirt with their machine guns.

"I tell you what, Sanya," Lebed commented with a note of annoyance in his voice as they were leaving the house, "they are cutting our guys' heads off."

"Lekha," Kisel looked quietly at his friend, "you have to be human even at war."

Lebed glanced back at Kisel, sighed wordlessly, and they moved on to the next house.

In the middle of the settlement, all the streets ran into one and then separated again. From above, the layout resembled a sand clock. All the units were almost simultaneously at the narrow neck of the clock. Yegor stopped and gave the way to the brigade, the 1st and the 2nd SWAT teams.

At that moment, Artur's radio came alive, Semyonov's voice barely recognizable over all the shooting. "Nine zero two, it's Seven calling! We're in trouble! There are casualties! Request your help!"

"Seven is in trouble!" Artur reported to Yegor loudly. "They've casualties!"

Yegor turned suddenly to Artur, as though stung by some insect. "Kremen's in trouble?"

Sanya Kremnyov, the commander of the CSG,[2] had the nine zero seven calling signal — Seven for short, so Yegor mistook Semyonov for Kremen.

Artur didn't manage to reply as Yegor was already shouting to the driver, "Turn around! We're coming back!"

The APCs turned around and kicked a start back along another street. Meantime, Artur got in touch with Semyonov. "Seven, where are you?"

"At the mountain!"

Artur switched his head round toward Lysaya Mountain, where he could hear the sounds of shooting.

Executing its assignment, the 7th SWAT Detachment Rosich bumped into an ambush at Lysaya Mountain. The fight had only been going on for a few minutes, and the detachment was already suffering considerable losses.

The APCs of the 3rd SWAT team were riding full tilt through the settlement as Yegor saw Kremen standing amidst the street.

"Stop!" Yegor shouted to the driver.

The APC braked at Kremen, raising a cloud of dust.

"Artur told me you were in trouble!" Yegor said, anxiety in his voice.

"It's not me, it's the 7th Detachment!"

Yegor realized his mistake at once. And as soon as he looked up at Lysaya Mountain, sounds of a fierce battle wafting from there, he hesitated no more.

"I'm going there!" he voiced his decision to Kremen and turned around to the driver. "Grab the wheel! At the turn, go to the right! Move!"

And the APCs took off.

Artur kept on listening to the radio.

"It's Seven," Semyonov reported. "We're in big trouble here!

We've two-zero-zero. Once again! We've some two-zero-zeros!"[3]

"Seven, it's nine zero two! We need a reference! Once again! Shoot a signal cartridge!"

Artur turned around to look at the mountain, waiting for a signal. A few minutes later, he saw a signal cartridge flying across the sky.

"I can see you, Seven!" Artur assured Semyonov.

The APCs of the 3rd SWAT team gunned into a bridge.

"Stop!" Yegor cried out.

The driver hit the brakes, but as the speed was considerable, the APC went wide, its nose smashing down a small tree. Thank God, no one was injured!

"To the vehicle!" Yegor commanded and then started instructing, his instructions quick, precise, and short. "Secure the munitions! Take only the essentials! Leave all the rest in the APCs!"

The team jumped to the ground, preparing for the march. While the team was getting ready, Yegor approached Naum.

"We can't use the bridge; it must have been mined. We should find some ford, I think."

Ready for marching, the soldiers lined up in front of Yegor and Yegor told them his strategy.

"The 7th Detachment needs our help. We've got no order to help them, so those who don't want to go may fall out — won't blame you for that," and then he stared intently at his soldiers for some moments. Indeed, he wouldn't blame them — the soldiers knew it, but stayed as they were. "Follow me," Yegor commanded in a calm voice and, turning around, he ran back toward the settlement, his team close behind him.

Despite the insurgents being more numerous than SWAT soldiers[4] and despite Vityaz being assigned to follow the brigade into the settlement, they decided to help their brothers out. For them, it was the only possible decision. The 1st and the 4th teams remained in the settlement, supporting the brigade, while the 3rd and the 2nd teams plus the combat support group rushed to Rusich's help. In total, the three teams numbered about fifty people.

For all this time, Artur remained in the centre of the settlement, communicating with the 7th Detachment via radio.

"Baikal," he called the detachment's commander. "It's nine zero two. The Seven got two-zero-zeros. They need our help."

"Nine zero two," Nenashev answered after a short pause. "I've got no order." Then he paused. "You understand that, right?" he concluded.

Sure, Artur realized that, but he was going to stick to his decision, whatever happened. "Kochetok, we're turning around!" he cried out to the driver.

There was only one thing left to do — to inform Nenashev of his decision. "Baikal! It's nine zero two! I'm heading for the Seven!"

The radio was silent for some moments, and then Nenashev's calm voice sounded, "Go ahead, nine zero two! God bless you!"

"Get us out of here, brothers," the radio spoke with Semyonov's strangely quiet voice. "We can't make it on our own," he added just as calmly.

The APCs of the 2nd SWAT team turned around and started off after the 3rd SWAT team.

Meanwhile, the 4th SWAT team moved on through the settlement, stopped, circled the perimeter, and settled to wait for further events. Soon they heard shooting somewhere within the settlement and, a few minutes later, a brigade's APC flew past them, coming from that direction. They could see its hatches open, the soldiers sitting on the armour, their eyes completely insane, along with the injured and the killed. As soon as the APC passed the 4th SWAT team, someone started firing at them from somewhere within the settlement. Bullets were whizzing above their heads, hitting the ground and the walls of the houses with dull thuds, clattering against the armour and striking sparks on the metal fence.

"Got you!" Oleg Rostigayev shouted via radio.

"Valera!" he called out to Oyama at once. "They have a machine gun in the mosque! Tell the direction layer to work it!"

"I'll do it myself!" Oyama cried out in response and rushed to the APC. As he reached the vehicle, he opened the hatch and shouted at the direction layer, "Get out! I'm getting in!"

And soon he was inside.

The 3rd SWAT team was now down at the river and Yegor saw some people coming out of the shrubs across the river. He leapt to the side to hide behind a hill. The soldiers, driven by an instinct, followed their commander's example. Yegor checked his guys and said, "Upon command, we all get up and give a squirt. Ready. TA!"

And the entire team sprang up, emerging full height out of their shelter, each of the soldiers gave a long squirt and was back down hiding just as quickly. The other bank of the river responded with choice swearwords — in Russian.

"Who're you?" Yegor cried out, raising himself a bit above their hiding hill.

"Sofrins!" he heard the answer.

Those were the very Sofrins whom Rosich soldiers were to escort.

"Shit!" Yegor cursed. "Are you okay?"[5]

"Yeah!" the soldiers responded and Yegor breathed a sigh of relief.

The 3rd SWAT team left its hideout and rushed to the river. At that moment, Kremen, with his CSG, joined them. Yegor made a decided step forward, going into the water, and was at once knocked off his feet by the flow. He went under entirely and his Panama hat slipped off his head. Someone gripped him by the hand, and as Yegor emerged on the surface, he saw it was Kirei, who was following close behind him. Yegor made another two steps, and a wave knocked him off once again, his body back underwater. And again Kirei was there to help him out. The rest of the soldiers were crossing the river a little further upstream, where the water was shallower.

The machine guns of the 4th SWAT APC were still silent, so the machine gunner in the mosque was spraying with dense fire.

"Valera!" Rostigayev called out to Oyama, approaching the APC. "Why aren't you shooting?"

"The optics is dirty!" Oyama's voice sounded from inside the APC. "Can't see a thing!"

Rostigayev looked up at the mosque, then glanced at the APC machine gun and an idea struck him.

"Give a squirt!" he cried out to Oyama.

Oyama pushed the launch button, and the KPWT snorted fire.

"To the right and higher!" Rostigayev started correcting when he saw where the bullets hit.

Oyama gave another squirt with the machine gun.

Right then, some bullets hit the APC, one of them nicking Rostigayev's arm. He ducked and examined his arm.

"Damn it!" he swore and was then back to correcting the fire. "A little to the left!"

He was perfectly aware that the machine gunner in the mosque wouldn't leave them alone unless APC machine guns were shooting properly. So, remaining by the APC, he kept shouting directions to Oyama, "A little more to the left!"

At last, the 3rd SWAT team managed to cross the river.

"Team!" Yegor commanded at once. "On your backs!"

Both he and his soldiers threw themselves on the ground, backs down.

"Legs — TA!" he gave his next order and everyone raised their legs up, shaking off the water.

"Stand up!" sounded Yegor's harsh cry. "Follow me!"

They sprang up to their feet and rushed to the trees where the Sofrins were waiting.

"Where's the 7th Detachment?" Yegor asked as he approached them.

"This way." One of the soldiers showed them the direction.

Yegor picked up the radio set to call the 7th Detachment, but the device was all wet. "Damn it! The radio is wet!" Yegor swore at the *force majeure*.

However, the radio operator from the BSG, who was also there, handed him another radio set, a dry one.

"Thanks, brother!" Yegor said and switched on the radio.

"Seven! Six is calling!" He attempted to connect to Rosich, but there was no reply.

"Follow me!" Yegor commanded, not to waste time when every second was precious.

The team passed through the shrubs and started climbing up the mountain.

"Check it out, Andrey!" Yegor complained to Naum. "I've lost my Panama! It's a shame!"

"I got it, commander!" Kirei, who always seemed to be in the right place at the right time, cried out.

"Good job, Sanya!" Yegor thanked the sergeant, taking back the Panama. "Thanks!"

Another party of Vityaz soldiers — Chef and Kot — approached the river. They could hear someone occasionally firing shots from the shrubs on the other bank.

"So, what's the plan?" Kot enquired in an offhanded manner.

"Let's go and see who's shooting," Chef replied.

"Why go? Let's shoot some, too."

"And what if those are our soldiers?" Chef objected, then commanded, "Run!" and kicked a start.

Kot had to follow behind him. Once across the river, which didn't take them long, they had to duck and sprint off to the shrubs. As they reached the shrubs, they kneeled on one leg and had a look around.

"Chef, let's shoot some!" Kot persisted.

"Get off!" Chef hushed him down, a little annoyed.

And they rose slowly to their feet, looking around cautiously.

Meanwhile, Rostigayev was correcting the APC's range. Finally, bullets hit the target.

"Got them! Now make it nonstop!"

Oyama pressed the electric trigger, launching both machine guns, and bullets immediately hit the mosque, crushing the place where the shooter was hiding to shreds of rubbish and dust.

Right then, a brigade's truck, its driver scared as hell, gunned into the street. As it reached Rostigayev's APC, a landmine exploded beside it. The truck's driver, scared enough before the explosion, went completely mad with fear and swerved the wheel toward the APC. The truck bumped into the APC board, right where Rostigayev was standing. A doctor, who happened to be nearby, ran out from behind the APC as soon as he heard the sounds of clashing and saw Rostigayev pressed down with a car. He rushed to the truck's cabin and banged on its door with the stock of his machine gun. The door finally opened and he saw the scared driver.

"Get the truck away!"

The truck drove away, and Rostigayev's body sagged down to the ground. It was almost impossible to recognize Rostigayev in what was left of his body. The doctor hurried to make a two-dose promedol injection[6] and then tried the heart massage. But as he pressed his hands against the officer's chest, it fell in at once.

"Damn it!" the doctor swore, realizing he could do nothing about it. "Load him up!"

The soldiers ran up and picked up Oleg, loading his body carefully into the APC.

"Who's he, anyway?" the doctor asked Oyama.

"Oleg Rostigayev!" Oyama replied sullenly.

"Rostigayev?" The doctor was taken aback. "Can it be Oleg, really?"

There was no time for shock. Another mortar bomb exploded, knocking down a soldier from the 4th SWAT team. The doctor rushed to help him. One of the fragments got stuck in the magazine, while the other one pierced the stomach.

"Cover us!" the doctor cried out and began his medical procedures.

First he made a promedol injection and then proceeded to the dressing, while Oyama was pulling magazines out of the discharge vest of the injured soldier. He wouldn't need them anymore, whereas for others, the battle was not going to be over soon.

As Kremen and his team crossed the river, they headed for the shrubs and were welcomed with fire. The soldiers reacted fast, throwing themselves down to hide behind the trees. To evaluate the situation, Kremen peeped out cautiously from behind the tree — and some bullets whizzed, scratching against the tree. It all happened so fast he didn't have time to duck. He felt a sting of pain as something hit his throat. Kremen reached out for it and sagged, croaking and gasping for air. He grabbed the radio, choking out, "Nine zero three! I'm finished!" Yegor heard Kremen's croaking voice. "It hit the throat!"

Overwhelmed with anxiety, Yegor stopped short on hearing the message. However, he realized he could do nothing about it, at least at the time. So he just pushed the talk–listen button and ordered, "Nine zero seven, just don't move! We'll get you out later!"

Releasing the button, he clenched his teeth, an animal roar coming out of his throat — he had to let it out somehow, the helplessness and the anger.

Kot and Chef chose their own direction and were now climbing up. Occasionally, bullets coming from somewhere up ahead would whiz above their heads, cutting down branches and leaves of the trees.

"Chef!" Kot called out to his friend again. "Are we going to shoot today at all?"

"Kot, will you calm down, please? Whom are you going to shoot here, huh? Can you see anyone around?"

"But someone is shooting up there."

"Well, it could be anyone. Just move!"

Kremen had finally come to his senses, catching his breath. He took his hand from his throat, lifting it to his eyes, and saw no blood on it. He brushed his hand lightly against the throat and caught something in between his fingers. He raised it to his eyes to see it was just a splinter. It was the splinter that caused him pain as it hit the throat. Kremen breathed out a sigh of relief and put the radio up to his mouth. "Nine zero three," he called Yegor to calm him down. "I'm fine; it's just a splinter."

Now it was Yegor's turn to breathe out a sigh of relief.

Having crossed the river, Artur, Frants, and Siziy had to hide as the fire coming down on them from the shrubs was pretty dense. Actually, the fire was so dense they had to press into the ground.

"Where's the shooting coming from?" Artur couldn't make out the direction.

The 3rd SWAT team was climbing on up. Hearing helicopters humming, they looked up. Two MI-24s flew past them very low, almost touching the tops of the trees, and fired some rockets.

Kot emerged from the bushes on the right.

"Kot!" Yegor called out to him. "Slow down!"

Yegor was down on one knee now, the rest of the team doing the same, scattering about the perimeter. Yegor and the radio operator, an R-159 behind his back, remained in the center of the circle that the soldiers formed.

"Kutkin!" Yegor glanced at the operator. "Do whatever you want, use any frequencies, but get me through to the 7th Detachment! Just do it openly — Vityaz, Rosich, I don't really care! Get me through to the Seven! Now!"

"Look here, commander!" Yegor heard Naum calling him.

Three steps and Yegor was right beside him. Naum beckoned to four soldiers with an injured fellow on a stretcher going down the mountain.

"It's the Sevens!" Yegor exclaimed, excited. Then he rose to his feet, full height, and headed toward them, swinging his arms in the air. "Rosich! Vityaz!" he cried out the words that were supposed to calm the soldiers down and let them know they were their friends. "Moscow! Novocherkassk!"

The soldiers ducked at once, bristling up their barrels. Yegor could see they were wound up, so he went on shouting familiar words as he came closer. When Yegor was close enough, one of the soldiers rose to his feet, pointing his gun at him.

"Where's Semyonov?" Yegor asked.

Only then did the soldier recognize Yegor and, relieved, lower his AK.

"Comrade lieutenant," he said with relief. "That way," and showed Yegor the direction.

Yegor glanced at the injured soldier and caught his breath. He saw his old friend Terekha lying on the stretcher, smeared with blood, and unconscious.

"Terekha!"

But then he had to pull himself together. For now, he had to focus on helping those who remained up on the mountain.

"You're going the wrong way, brother," he turned to the Rosich soldier. "You should go there," he added, showing them the right direction, and called out to his team at once, "Everyone, up here!"

Here the soldiers separated. The 3rd SWAT team moved on up the mountain, while the soldiers from the 7th Detachment moved on down.

Artur, Frants, and Siziy had to remain on the ground, the insurgents' fire giving them no chance to move on. The fire was so dense they had to lie with their faces down, the bullets ploughing the soil around them. Pressing his face against the ground, Artur managed to somehow turn it toward the shrubs and saw what was causing them inconvenience. Two big, bearded, and well-equipped insurgents had positioned themselves at the edge of the shrubs and were fearlessly bringing down fire on SWATs. One of them had an AK, the other one a PK. Artur pulled his machine gun close, attaching a new magazine to it, pointed it at the insurgents, and pressed the trigger. Giving a jolt, the machine gun fired, and one of the insurgents fell down. Wasting no time, Artur pointed his gun at the second insurgent, who was changing the magazine right then. Another shot and the gangster sank to his knees beside his fellow, as if broken down.

Once Rostigayev and the other injured soldier were inside the APC, the doctor got into it, too, and shouted to the driver, "Go!"

The APC started off and the doctor picked up his radio to call Nenashev. "Baikal, it's the doctor! Can you hear me?"

"It's Baikal! I can hear you!" Nenashev's voice sounded.

"I'm with the fourth one! We've got a three-zero-zero and a two-zero-zero!"

"Who is it?" The doctor heard Nenashev's voice change.

Yegor was listening to the doctor's radio report, too.

"It's Rostigayev."

He couldn't stifle a moan as he heard the doctor's reply.

At once, Kremen connected to Yegor over the radio, shouting, in shock, "Nine zero three! Have you heard? Oleg Rostigayev is dead!"

Yegor, looking up at the mountain, said through his clenched teeth, "Yes, I did, nine zero seven! We're moving on!"

The news of Rostigayev's death made Artur roar with rage and his body jerked up from the ground.

"Follow me!" he cried out to his guys. "Double, march!"

He sprang to his feet and, ducking his head, sprinted off toward the shrubs, his soldiers following him. Bullets clattered, bouncing off the ground around them and whizzing over their heads, searching for a place to sting. One of the bullets hit Artur's boots, smashing the heel and almost knocking Artur off his feet.

Having reached the forest, they stopped and kneeled, on the defensive.

"So? Where do we go now?" Artur asked himself.

The soldiers started looking around, remembering the scout lessons.

"Comrade senior lieutenant," Frants called out to Artur. "Someone has been passing here. The grass is stamped flat."

Concluding it was their only option, they chose that direction and set out up the mountain.

Artur immediately called everyone else from his team. "Kot! It's nine zero two!" he called Kot.

"Kot speaking!" Artur heard Kot's cheerful intonation.

"How're you doing?"

Kot and Chef were moving on at a cracking pace. So Kot, his voice bright and vivacious, responded to Artur, "We're fine! Birds are singing! Someone's shooting at us!"

"Got you," Artur replied and thought to himself, *Well, if Kot is so peppy, I have nothing to worry about.*

At last, Yegor reached the position of the 7th Detachment and found Semyonov lying at the bottom of a crater, surrounded by some soldiers.

"Tsyma is killed," Semyonov told Yegor. "Zoza, too. They're over there," he beckoned to where the shooting was coming from.

It took some time for Yegor to recover from another shock. For a few seconds, he just stared blankly at Semyonov. "So, what're we going to do now?" he asked when he finally came to his senses.

"Get them out."

"And where are they?"

Semyonov showed the direction. "Over there, about eighty metres away."

Yegor glanced in the direction, analyzed the situation, and made his decision. "Now then!" he looked at Semyonov. "All the weapons are to work the right flank! And work it properly!" he emphasized. "I'll take my guys and head straight to the left!" He paused for a second and, staring into Semyonov's eyes, concluded, "You can't know your fate, but we have to get the guys out of there, no matter what."

In return, Semyonov detached the magazine and showed it to

Yegor. There were only three or four bullets left in it. "That's all we've got," he reported on the ammunition.

Yegor looked first at the magazine and then at Semyonov and said, "Then we'll wait for Artur and his team."

Just then, Artur, Frants, and Siziy were climbing up the mountain. As they noticed two people going down, they hurried to prepare for action. They also saw the people were carrying an injured man on a stretcher.

"Freeze!" Artur cried out. "Who are you?"

The people reacted immediately, hiding behind the trees and pointing their guns at Artur's soldiers.

"And who are you?" they asked the same question.

"Friends! Vityaz!"

"Show me your face!"

"So you could shoot it off? I'm telling you — we're friends!"

"Who do you know from the 7th Detachment?"

"Tsyma, Terekha!" Artur cried out, and the soldiers stepped out of the trees, lowering their guns.

"Where are your people?" Artur asked as they approached them.

"Go up there, this way," the soldier showed the direction.

Grenadier Siziy took the RPG-7 ammunition from the injured soldier.

"Don't think you'll need them," he explained.

Lis, positioned not far from Yegor, was searching for targets within the shrubs through his optics. Having identified a machine gunner, he breathed out to calm down, aiming. Just then, a few bullets raised the soil beside him, but Lis paid no attention and, unaffected, pressed the trigger.

The bullet hit the machine gunner in the head, his body thrown onto the ground, face down.

The next target Lis identified through his optics was a shooter who was running over from tree to tree. The SWD recoiled against Lis's shoulder — and the shooter didn't manage it to the next shelter, stumbling to the ground.

Kot and Chef were already shooting as the other soldiers from the 2nd SWAT team joined them. Kot turned around to Kisel and, motioning up the mountain, said, "Sanya! Up there, on the right, there are still some guys from the 7th Detachment; we need to get them out!"

Kisel looked up the mountain, turned around to Kot, and nodded. "Let's go!"

And the soldiers of the 2nd SWAT team moved on in pairs up the mountain, covering each other.

Lebed ran up to the tree, kneeled on one leg, and gave a squirt with his AK. Then he turned around to check Sychev, who was moving behind him, at five o'clock. Sychev was shooting in the opposite direction. In addition to his SWD, Sychev had two flame-throwers behind his back.

Lebed turned round back to where the enemy was hiding and saw an RPG-7 grenade approaching him. A second later, the grenade hit the tree, about one and a half metres above Lebed's head. The blast wave knocked him off his feet. As the smoke cleared, Lebed sat up, shaking his head. Then he looked up and saw the tail section of the grenade stuck in between the branches of the tree.

"Good lord!" he exclaimed, amazed. "And they'd write the safe distance is at least a hundred metres." He sprang up to his feet and engaged back in the battle.

Down on one knee, Talanych was looking around. The tension of the battle made it all look like a film in slow motion. Makei was running right beside him, and there was Kisel shooting, down on his knee.

Running over, Talanych turned his head round to notice fountains of soil rising in his direction and, all of a sudden, Kisel's voice sounded in his head: "Down! Roll over! Attention!"

Talanych threw himself down, rolled over, and raised his machine gun up, simultaneously noticing an insurgent shooting at him.

Talanych fired two double shots and the insurgent fell down.

"Thanks, Sanya!" He was now grateful to Kisel for all the terrible training he made him go though.

An insurgent shooter sighted through his optics a soldier from the 2nd SWAT team and fired a shot. The bullet wounded the soldier in the leg and he fell down. One of his fellow soldiers came to his rescue immediately and, kneeling on one leg, took out a first aid dressing package. Now, the shooter was aiming at the other SWAT soldier. A shot sounded —and the other soldier, already done with the dressing, fell down beside his fellow, the bullet wounding him in the stomach.

Talanych was next to run up to do the dressing.

Down on one knee, Lebed began checking the shrubs for the shooter. Throwing his AK up, he gave a squirt at the shooter's probable position.

Lebed's insight was dead on — some bullets hit the tree where the shooter was hiding. The shooter had to crouch over to another tree.

"Sych!" Lebed called out to Sychev. "Give me the flamethrower!"

Sychev headed toward Lebed, taking down the flamethrowers. Then he held out one of them quickly to the sergeant and ran some distance away from him. Lebed placed the tube over his shoulder, aimed, and pressed the trigger. However, for some unknown reason, the flamethrower refused to throw any flames, and Lebed had to throw it aside, taking the other one.

The shooter changed his position and settled to search for a new target through the SWD optics. He noticed a shadow slipping past him, but as he returned the sight, he only managed to realize someone was pointing a flamethrower at him. The next thing he saw was the flash of the shot and the approaching capsule. The capsule engulfed the forest in fire, together with the shooter and some other insurgents.

Lebed threw the empty tube aside and, kneeling on one leg,

began changing his magazine.

Talanych was done with dressing the other injured soldier and some soldiers ran up to him to drag away both casualties.

Talanych ran over to join two Rosich soldiers lying on the ground some distance away. "Is there anyone of our soldiers up there?" Talanych cried out.

"Not alive!" one of the Rosich soldiers replied, glancing at Talanych.

Talanych stared at the soldier for a few seconds, his mind grasping the essence of his words.

"Talanych!" he heard Chef calling out to him.

He turned his head and saw Kot and Chef motioning him to come up to them. He sprang up to his feet and, ducking his head, headed to where the master sergeant was lying.

"GP across sectors!" Chef instructed him.

Talanych nodded, understanding the task, and charged a GP-25 grenade. All three of them raised their machine guns at forty-five degrees and fired a shot, then recharged their arms quickly and, making a slight lateral shift, fired a second shot, and a few seconds later, another one.

Then the mine throwers were launched. At first, mines were hitting the insurgents' position only, but then the explosions moved closer to the SWAT side, and the hot metal was now showering over the SWAT soldiers.

"What the hell are you doing?" The artillery direction layer was cursing at the mortar gunners. "Make it a hundred further!"

"It's not us!" someone replied to him in an annoyed tone. "We've got no mines! We haven't brought them over yet!"

The direction layer looked up at Semyonov and Yegor. "The insurgents," he commented impassively.

Mines were exploding all along the SWAT position, but somehow they hit the 7th Detachment soldiers only. Another shot — and another one of them would be injured. Then two more soldiers would run up to take him away down to the shrubs.

Something heavy hit the ground right in front of Mironov, so he screwed up his eyes instinctively. When he finally managed to open his eyes, he saw a tail of a mine sticking out of the soil. The mine hadn't exploded!

As another mine exploded, it blew three Rosich soldiers apart. Sieda was also there, but remained intact. He glanced at the injured soldiers and crawled over closer to Yegor. "You guys seem safer," he commented.

Yegor looked at him, grinning. "Sieda! You've been some five metres away from me!"

"Still," the machine gunner insisted.

Lis, unaffected by all the mine throwing, kept reducing the insurgents' numbers. As his rifle gave a jolt, another rascal fell down.

Running over, Kot heard a strange whizzing and saw a mine landing at his feet. For some seconds, Kot disappeared in smoke, and as the smoke cleared, Kot got up and hid behind a tree. Chef, who was lying some metres away in a crater, stared at him, incredulous.

"Kot!" he called out to his friend anxiously. "Are you alive?"

Kot examined his legs carefully.

"Chef! Come up here!"

"Why?"

"Come up here! You need to check this out!" Kot insisted.

"Later, Kot!"

"Chef! It'll only take a minute!"

Chef gave a squirt and sprinted off, ducking, to where Kot was standing with an annoyed expression on his face. They heard another mine whizzing and ducked. A second later, they understood it was a blunt lie that a bomb never lands in the same place twice as the bomb landed right where Chef had been lying before! One could read it in Chef's eyes as he turned to the grinning Kot.

"And you didn't want to come."

"So, what's the rush?" asked Chef as he came to his senses.

"Check this out, Dima! The pants are chopped up all over!" and Kot demonstrated his pants, which were indeed, severely damaged, "but the legs are fine!"

"And the balls?" Chef asked jokingly.

Kot checked his apparatus and replied with confidence, a smile on his lips, "Fine, too."

The rifle fire was no denser than the mortar fire. It was almost impossible to keep one's head up. The soil was infested with lead, while the air was filled with tracers, their buzzing and whizzing unceasing.

A little to the left and above Yegor, a soldier from the 7th Detachment positioned himself, his legs at about the level of Yegor's head. When another mine exploded near them, Yegor could see clearly how its fragments cut through the soldier's calves.

"Legs again!" soldier exclaimed, annoyed, his intonations a silent rebuke to the ill fate. "Why me?"

One more explosion followed and Yegor cried out in pain, gripping the back of his hips. "A-a-ah!" he cried as his pain became intolerable. "I can't feel my legs!"

"Someone, give promedol to the commander!" Naum shouted.

"Wait, Naum!"

Yegor got really scared. The blow was so powerful and the pain was so strong he thought his legs were torn off. He was afraid to look down. However, overcoming the fear, he raised his hands to his face and — saw no blood on them. Breathing out a sigh of relief, he looked down. His legs were right there, where they were supposed to be!

"Commander!" he heard Naum call out to him again.

Yegor turned to Naum's voice. "Here!"

Naum held out a bomb fragment to Yegor. "It was just below you!"

Yegor took the fragment in his hands. It felt still warm. He stared at it for a few moments and then remembered the guy from the 7th Detachment.

"Andrey! Promedol!"

He turned his back on Naum while Naum was taking out his first aid kit from his back pocket. He found the promedol tube and handed it over to Yegor. Yegor took the promedol and turned to the injured soldier. "Just a sec, brother," he calmed him down. "Just a sec."

Yegor gave the tube cap a twist and ...[7]

An explosion ... Then darkness ... And quiet ...

He heard some muffled noise from somewhere far off. It seemed like Naum's voice, "Take his vest off!"

Yegor, all dabbled in soil, was crawling around on his knees, searching the ground.

"The machine gun!" he was shouting, while Naum was trying to press him against the ground and Miron was cleaning Yegor's machine gun, stuffed with soil the explosion had raised.

"The machine gun!" Yegor went on, screaming wildly and squirming on the ground.

Miron tucked his gun into Yegor's hands. Yegor relaxed down on the ground.

Some metres away from where Yegor was lying, Kremen was struggling with another soldier from the 7th Detachment. A mine exploded nearby, and the contused soldier, holding his head in his hands, was now making attempts to get up. Kremen had to leave the insurgents alone for some time to calm the soldier down. He pressed him against the ground, but another mine sent Kremen flying away. So, he was now struggling up to his feet, contused by the explosion.

Yegor was gradually recovering his senses. First the picture appeared, then the sound. And the first thing he saw was Kremen standing up, full height, and staggering down with a zombie face. The soil around him as he walked on was swarming with bullets, tracers cutting through the air some centimetres from him with shrill whizzing.

"Kremen!" Yegor was trying to get through to him, horrified at the sight. "Kremen, get down!"

However, Kremen couldn't hear him. In fact, he could hear and see nothing, nothing at all. So he just kept staggering down, further and further away till, completely intact, he disappeared in the shrubs. Indeed, miracles happen sometimes!

Yegor looked around. Over the time they'd been on the mountain, their numbers had been halved. He saw another explosion and some soldiers dragging away their injured fellow. Yegor shook his head. "That's it," he said to himself quietly. "No chance to break through now." Then he turned to Semyonov, calling to him over the noise of the battle, "Syoma!"

Semyonov turned to Yegor.

"Retreat!" Yegor was shouting. "If you're not leaving, no one is leaving at all! We're just gonna all stay here! So, retreat!" and added, "We're the last!"

Artur ran up and, lying down beside Semyonov, produced his arguments. "Why are you still here? How long has it been now?" he insisted, firm but friendly. "These are mountains, Igor! No light — and we're done![8] Get away! Why else would we be here?"

Semyonov hesitated, as this decision was too hard to make; they hadn't got their dead guys out of there. However, he realized it was next to impossible in the circumstances. So, Yegor had to help him a bit, too.

"Retreat, Syoma," he said, his voice calm and cold. "Retreat!"

Semyonov glanced at him, and however hard it was, he finally announced the decision that was most sensible in the situation. "Retreat!" he shouted to his guys.

All the soldiers from the 7th SWAT Detachment, less than ten now, got closer to Semyonov, surrounding him in a semicircle.

"Fire!" Semyonov cried out.

And they fired their last bullets, funneling all their rage in the fire. Then, having divided into pairs, they began to retreat, while Vityaz soldiers were doing their best to cover their brothers.

Sieda was passionately giving long squirts with his PK, cutting the insurgents down in packs. Yegor had to change his magazine and then continued giving short squirts. The grenadier found his target through the optics and was about to press the trigger, his finger already on it, when one of his fellows suddenly appeared right in front of him.

"From the rear!" the grenadier cried out.

The soldier's instinct he obtained through all the hard training made him throw himself onto the ground, face down. Immediately, he heard the RPG-7 fire a shot, and a grenade flew right above his head.

In the meantime, Lis took another gangster down.

Yegor looked back to see how the 7th Detachment was retreating and, just then, he heard Naum exclaim, "Look, commander! Those bastards!"

Yegor switched his head round to see insurgents trying to out-flank them on the left. "Sieda! Go to the flank! Quick!"

Sieda sprang up to his feet and, ducking, sprinted off to the specified position while Yegor ran over to position himself in the center of the team.

Phil ran out of bullets. So he kneeled on one leg, quickly detached the empty magazine and put it into his vest, but didn't manage to change the magazine. Ten metres away, a gangster jumped out of the shrubs, bringing down fire onto the soldier. Phil somersaulted and began rolling over, miraculously evading the bullets. Fortunately, it's only in the movies that magazines can last endlessly. In real life, one magazine lasts for about three to four seconds. So, soon, the insurgent ran out of bullets, too.

As Phil noticed the man detaching his magazine, he kneeled down quickly and pulled a full magazine out of his vest. The insurgent did the same. Phil attached the magazine, pulled back the carrier bolt assembly, chambered a bullet, and pressed his machine gun against his shoulder. And, just a moment before the insurgent raised his barrel up, Phil pressed the trigger three times. The first bullet in his magazine was a tracer, so Phil could see how it went through the insurgent's chest. The insurgent sagged awkwardly, but Phil kept his machine gun pointed at him for some more seconds — just in case.

As Miron was running over, he bumped into an insurgent. Ten metres separated them. Fire contacts as close as this one were pretty usual at this stage of the action. They both threw their guns up simultaneously and pressed their triggers. However, neither of the machine guns fired. Miron hurried to change his magazine, but the insurgent snatched out a grenade and threw it at Miron's feet. As Miron saw the grenade, he froze up, waiting for an explosion. The insurgent expected the grenade to explode, too. However, for some unknown reason, the grenade didn't explode. Evidently, it was Miron's lucky day. He snatched out an F-1 of his own, pulled out the guard ring, and threw it at the insurgent, who was changing his magazine. Miron plummeted onto the ground, while the insurgent raised his AK up. Luckily, SWAT had good ammunitions, and the grenade went off, saving Miron's life.

This is where all the hellish toil of Vityaz soldiers was paying off. The soldiers were driven by instinct, their moves were precise and quick — the running, the falling and rolling over, the stripping for action and the shooting, the changing of magazines. This is why their enemy had no opportunity to use precise fire; the bullets were too slow to get them, and their shots were quicker and more precise. This is why their luck was always with them.

Speaking about luck: Luck always comes to those who deserve it, those who've put enough effort and energy into practise and training. This is actually what luck is. And it's a universal law.

The fighting had been going on for hours — down and up the mountain, in the forest, with full ammunition load, always focused and never slowing down. The soldiers had awoken at four in the morning and had eaten just once — at six o'clock.

It was evident the insurgents were also good at action, moving in pairs and threesomes to cover each other, just as the SWAT soldiers did. They used the same sequence, too — run over, fall down and roll over at once. As someone was injured, two other men would pick him up and drag away into the shrubs.

Most people thought Special Forces were actually fighting against peasants, totally untrained and ignorant of military tactics. However, the reality was quite the opposite — our nineteen-year-olds were set against tough Basayev's daredevils, all of them trained in special terrorist camps by highly qualified professional instructors and boasting a pretty extensive experience of military action. Besides, they were well-equipped, armed, and used efficient tactics. It was actually an extremely strong enemy, and victory over such an enemy was of special value.

And one more thing — SWAT soldiers have never fought against the Chechen people; they were eliminating gangsters and those gangsters were of various nationalities.[9] Besides, Chechens often joined our forces to fight the insurgents.

Hidden behind a tree, Kot was shooting, standing on a knee, as another mine tried to get him. A fragment chipped a lump of bark. The chip hit Kot in the forehead, and he passed out.

Coming around a few minutes later, Kot sat up, shook his head, and checked his forehead with his hand. Right then, a string of tracers whizzed above his head (from our side, mind you!) and Kot, still recovering from the previous knockdown, had to throw himself onto the ground, his hands digging hastily into the soil (later, he couldn't explain why he was doing it). He stopped only as he felt someone kicking him in the leg. Looking up, Kot saw Frants, standing full height, a machine gun atilt, and smiling at him.

"Kot!" Frants called out to him cheerfully. "Stretching out, huh? Forgot about the war?"

Kot sat back up and shook his head, trying to come to his senses.

Artur had a look around and, realizing the 7th Detachment had retreated, shouted via the radio, "Attention! Nine zero two, everyone! Retreat!"

Once Kisel heard the command he turned around to Makei. "Lekha!"

Makei gave a squirt and glanced back at Kisel.

"That's it; we're retreating!"

Makei nodded and, turning to the other side, repeated the command for everyone to hear, "Team Two! Retreat!"

The soldiers started retreating in the same manner as they had going up the mountain — in pairs, one of them running and the other one covering.

Talanych and Malysh worked as a pair, covering each other's backs, just as Kisel predicted a couple of months before!

Talanych ran some distance away, threw himself down, and stripped for action. "Malysh! Go!"

Malysh sprang to his feet and ran over, a mine hitting the place where Malysh had been lying just a moment ago.[10]

Kisel and Makei were covering as the rest of the team were retreating. Kisel detached his empty magazine to change it and glanced inside his vest to find all the magazines there were empty. He looked back at the retreating soldiers, then shifted his look to Makei and almost immediately took his decision. He attached the empty magazine back to the machine gun and took a grenade.

"Lekha!" he called out to Makei.

Makei turned around to look at him.

"Retreat!"

"We're going together!" Makei shook his head.

"I'll be the last!" Kisel assured him.

Makei stared at him for a moment and then got up, rushing back, while Kisel unpinned the grenade and, rising up a bit, hurled it forward and, before it exploded, sprinted off to the opposite side from where Makei was lying to sidetrack insurgents, the bullets raising the soil all around him. As soon as he threw himself down behind a tree, he heard some bullets bounce off the trunk, chipping the bark. He glanced back at Makei and saw he was ready to cover him. Kisel scurried over to the nearest tree, reaching it in just one plunge, and hid behind it.

"TA!" he gave another order to move on.

Makei stopped shooting, sprang to his feet, and rushed down, while Kisel darted off in the opposite direction again. Reaching a tree, Kisel glanced back at Makei and saw him still running. So, Kisel just stepped out from behind the tree, raised his gun up, and cried out, "A-a-ah!"

Kisel stepped back at once behind the tree and down on the ground, some dozens of bullets hitting the soil and the tree beside him. Catching his breath, Kisel glanced back at Makei one more time. He could tell his fellow was far enough now and ready to cover him. So, Kisel decided to proceed with retreating and hurled down toward the nearest tree. He was almost there.

A bullet got him in the shoulder, coming out through his throat.

Makei, who was behind a tree covering Kisel, could see Kisel heading down and suddenly falling as he almost reached the tree, as though tripping over something.

"Sannnyaaa!" he cried out instinctively.

Some bullets hit the tree, and Makei had to duck down.

By then the entire 2nd SWAT team was gathered at the 7th Detachment position.

"Kisel and Makei are missing!" Chef reported to Artur.

Everyone looked up and, in a few seconds, saw Makei running out from the trees, his eyes mad.

"Kisel's dead!"

Time seemed to freeze, the soldiers turning to Artur, waiting for the commander's decision. It was hardly likely that Artur could realize at the moment what was happening. Those were pure instincts, subconscious of a commander. So, as he shifted his gaze from Makei to where his subordinate was lying killed, there was only one command that could come to his mind: "Team! We're attacking!"

He was the first to start off toward the trees, his team supporting his counterattack. The soldiers followed their leader with loud shouts, their faces contorted with rage. Each had his own battle cry. Some were shouting "SWAT!" some "Hurray!" some "TA!" and some were just screaming, "A-a-ah!"

Based on tactical norms, an attack can't succeed unless the attacking forces are, at least, three times more numerous than their enemy. In this case, twenty-five Vityaz soldiers attacked (counterattacked, to be precise) six hundred insurgents.

The grenadier kneeled on one leg and put the RPG-7 over his shoulder. He cried out, "Shooting," pressed the trigger, and the grenade launcher spat out a grenade. Reaching the trees, the grenade exploded.

Hundreds of tracers from the shrubs raising fountains of soil into the air met the team.

Down on one knee, Chef fired a string of tracers, aiming at the shrubs. Kot soon joined him and, also down on his knee, raised his machine gun and opened fire to cover Chef, crying out, "TA!"

Frants was giving his hearty welcome to the insurgents in the shrubs with his machine gun, too.

Artur kneeled on one leg, gave a squirt, and looked back at the team. His ego of a commander was infinitely pleased and proud for his guys. They did it right how he taught them. Just like at their trainings, they were moving quickly and swiftly, covering each other. Back to the enemy, Artur only managed to notice an RPG grenade approaching him in the air. Some metres before him, the grenade hit against a small tree.

An explosion ... Then darkness ... And quiet ...

The mist slowly cleared away and he could hear some sounds.

Then Artur saw the insurgents about ten metres away from him. He managed somehow to outflank them, and the insurgents were not expecting him. He stood up full height and began shooting, his teeth bared and his face contorted with rage. He caught the insurgents off guard and they just scattered, running away from him, without even attempting to shoot back. Soon his soldiers joined him, supporting him with fire (just like at the shooting range with moving targets). Now, Artur could see corpses of insurgents as far as his sight could reach.

Down on his knee, Talanych was working the area with his GP-25 as Kot approached him. Wordlessly, he fished a grenade out of Talanych's rucksack and loaded his GP-25. As Talanych, surprised, looked back at him, Kot had already fired the first grenade and was now loading another one.

"I've got none," Kot gave him a brisk explanation, taking a third one out of Talanych's rucksack. Indeed, Kot was as fast as a devil when it came to shooting.

Just then, Lebed and Makei found Kisel. He was lying with his back up and his hands stretched out to the sides. With his left hand, he was gripping his machine gun.

"And what if they've set up a mine?" Makei asked, worried.

"I don't think they had time," Lebed objected. "Otherwise, they'd have taken his machine gun."

And then Lebed raised Kisel's body carefully to check the ground beneath it. As they turned him back down they saw blood spilling from the pockets of his vest and a small scratch on his throat.

"Take him by the legs!" Lebed cried out to Makei.

Makei picked Kisel up by his legs, while Lebed gripped him by the arms. And, suddenly, Kisel threw his head back, moaning. Lebed felt his pulse on the neck.

"He's alive!" Lebed shouted, and they picked Kisel up in their arms and rushed down.

As soon as they got Kisel out, they proceeded with the retreat.

Just then, Talanych heard Nenashev and Artur trying to get through to each other over the radio.

"Nine zero two! It's Baikal calling!" Nenashev was shouting.

"Baikal! It's nine zero two calling!" Artur was also trying to get through to the detachment's commander.

"Nine zero two!" Nenashev's voice sounded again. "It's Baikal calling!"

Realizing neither Artur nor the detachment's commander could hear each other, Talanych stopped.

"Baikal! Baikal! It's nine zero two! Can you hear me?"

So, having glanced back first at the retreating team and then at where the insurgents were supposed to be, the young soldier made a decision worthy of a general. Hiding behind a tree, he pressed the talk–listen button of the radio station and shouted for both parties to hear: "Attention! Baikal and nine zero two! It's me, Talanych! You can't hear each other, but I can hear you both! So speak via me! Once again! It's me, Talanych! Speak via me!"

Talanych peeped out from behind the tree and saw no insurgents nearby.

"Talanych!" Artur's voice sounded over the radio. "Pass it on word for word!"

"Got you, nine zero two!" Talanych replied and almost at once heard the detachment's commander.

"Nine zero two! It's Baikal! Report on the situation!"

"Nine zero two!" Talanych repeated. "It's Talanych! Report on the situation!"

Then he peeped from behind the tree once again and saw some insurgents coming back down. Talanych raised his AK, aimed, and fired some double shots. One of the insurgents fell down, while the rest hid and began shooting back at Talanych. Talanych had to hide back behind the tree. Soon, he heard Artur's voice again: "Baikal! It's nine zero two! The Seven has retreated! I've got three three-zero-zeros!"

"Baikal!" the soldier engaged back into the radio communication. "It's Talanych! The Seven has retreated! I've got three three-zero-zeros!"

Kot heard Talanych speaking over the radio and looked up to where they had just come from.

"Did he really stay there?" Kot was taken aback, a decision formed in his mind at once. "Chef, I'll be right back!" And then he sprinted off back up the mountain.

"Kot! Where're you going?"

Talanych continued providing communication between Nenashev and Artur, simultaneously shooting back at the insurgents. He fired some more double shots, taking down another insurgent, and rolled back down behind the tree, squatting and pressing his back closer to the tree to hide his body to the maximum. Just then, bullets, one after another, hit the tree and the soil near Talanych.

"Nine zero two!" Nenashev's voice sounded again. "It's Baikal! Retreat! Nine zero three will cover you!"

"Nine zero two!" the young soldier put the radio station to his mouth. "It's Talanych! Retreat! Nine zero three will cover you!"

Talanych picked up his machine gun, the barrel up, threw his left leg forward ("pistol squat"), rolling over on the stomach, and stripped for action. Then he fired some double shots, taking down one more insurgent, and rolled back down behind the tree. Having changed the magazine, he cried out via the radio, "It's me, Talanych! Can't stay here anymore! Have to retreat!"

And then Talanych sprang up and, crouching, darted off toward another tree.

"Talanych!" someone called out to him suddenly.

Talanych looked around and saw Kot, who was ready to cover him.

"Come on!" Kot cried out and gave a long squirt.

Talanych ran over and threw himself down beside Kot. Then he opened fire to give Kot a chance to retreat.

Kot jumped to his feet and ran some distance away, fountains of soil following close behind. Passing by a tree, Kot gripped it with his left hand, his legs thrown forward by inertia. His body turned over and, falling, he threw his machine gun up and, barely touching the ground, opened fire.

Nenashev and Putilin were sitting at the table in the command vehicle.

"Guys from the Seven have retreated," Nenashev began thoughtfully. "Artur and Yegor are also retreating." He paused, turning something over in his head. "I think we need to get the APC going," he said, concerned, and stood up.

Then he took his machine gun and turned around to Putilin. "Seryoga, you stay here for me," and jumped out of the vehicle.

Artur was running over as he saw a barbed wire fence appearing right in front of him. He didn't manage to stop, so he just jumped over it and came a smasher down the slope. Out of the corner of his eye, Artur noticed a small tree in his way and held out his hand to grab the tree to make his body stop. Looking up, he saw Siziy, an RPG-7 in his arms, following him down the slope. Holding the tree with one hand, Artur reached out to catch the soldier with his other hand. The soldier first turned over by inertia and then stopped, kneeling on one leg. He cast a quick glance at the RPG and saw it was loaded. So he just threw it over his shoulder.

"Shooting!" the soldier cried out before shooting, just as he was supposed to, and pressed the trigger.

Artur managed to duck to the side and cover his head with his hand right at the supreme moment.

The 3rd SWAT team let the 7th Detachment and the 2nd SWAT team retreated and was now firing in three directions, almost encircled.

"Retreat!" Yegor commanded as he realized the retreat was both necessary and inescapable.

The team began retreating, the soldiers covering each other.

Yegor, Naum, and Miron were the last to leave Lysaya Mountain. As they were the only ones who had stayed behind, the insurgents focused on them. The fire was so dense it was impossible to run over. So, the SWAT soldiers had sometimes to roll back over, bullets haunting them. They'd give a squirt and roll over and the insurgents would, almost at once, plough the place where they used to be just a second ago with bullets. So, rolling over in this way, they finally reached the shrubs, their heads attacked by the branches and the leaves cut down by the enemy's bullets.

(When I was doing my research for the book, one of those soldiers who was there during the battle said the only thing he could remember was that the fire was so dense the air was whizzing and hissing with bullets and it was raining branches.)

Down on one knee, Yegor took a grenade, raised his hand to load it into his GP-25, and, horrified, found out there was no grenade launcher over his shoulder.

"Naum!" he turned around to Naum. "I've lost my GP! Cover me!" And then he was down on his belly, crawling back.

"Commander!" he heard Miron call out to him. "I've got it!"

Yegor switched his head around to look at Miron, who was showing him the AK and the GP.

"I gave you my machine gun!" he explained.

Yegor, relieved, turned around and exchanged machine guns with Mironov.

Frants ran over and, lying down on his back, looked up at the sky. *Damn it! It's so nice to be alive*, he thought.

All of a sudden, shooting ceased, and the world fell silent. One could hear birds singing and see the sun shining bright. Frants rose to his feet slowly, took his machine gun, and headed for the settlement. He could see soldiers running out of the shrubs.

At the river, Frants seated himself behind a small hill. Right then, a hail of bullets came down crashing on him! Frants threw himself down. He had hardly managed to hide behind the hill when bullets rained fountains of soil atop him.

The 2nd SWAT team didn't manage to cross the river so they had to hide out on the riverbank.

"I've got smokes!" Talanych cried out. "I throw and we run!"

Talanych took a smoke grenade out of his rucksack, fired the pot, and threw it at once. As the guys saw the smoke flying, they sprang to their feet and darted off across the river. No one noticed that the grenade didn't explode and that there was no smoke. The pot fell out of the grenade so it could not set it on fire. However, everyone crossed the river without incident and reached the hideout.

The 3rd SWAT team jumped out of the shrubs, running toward the river, and Yegor saw APCs from the 7th Detachment crowding around them. They were loading the injured and settling themselves down on the armour. Their actions were both slow and hasty, as though they were hip.

"Why are they crowding like that?" Yegor exclaimed indignantly and looked around. "Team, follow me!" he cried out to his guys and set out running away from the APCs. As he approached a small hill, Yegor hid behind it, his soldiers soon joining him.

"Sieda!" he glanced at the machine gunner. "You work the open areas — all of them! And make it nonstop!"

Sieda nodded, drawing his PK closer against his shoulder.

"GP!" Yegor gave his next order, and all the soldiers with GP-25s surrounded him quickly. "Repeat after me!" Yegor decided to make it short so as not to waste his time on explanations.

He inserted a GP into the barrel and aimed up the mountain. The soldiers followed his example, making sure the angle and the direction were the same.

"Ready! Fire!"

They fired a volley and then reloaded their weapons. Asking for no more details, the soldiers kept on working the mountain.

Nenashev ran up to them and, throwing himself down beside Yegor, asked, "Yegor, are you all back?"

"All!" Yegor replied, shooting.

"Cover the detachment as we retreat!" Nenashev instructed. "Artur will cover you guys later!"

"Got you!" Yegor kept on shooting without pausing to reply, even without looking at Nenashev.

Nenashev rushed back, running.

Kisel, his face grown blue, was down on the ground now. Lebed was feeling his pulse, his face tense, dirty, and sweaty.

"No pulse," he said, feeling simultaneously dismayed and helpless.

The doctor joined them in a minute and examined Kisel quickly. Then he took a tube out of his bag and inserted it into Kisel's throat, blowing strongly through it. As he raised his head for the next blow, a fountain of blood burst out of the tube, splashing all over his face. He jerked his head instinctively and then wiped the blood slowly off his face.

"It's from his lungs," the doctor concluded. "The end."

Lebed, his eyes wet with tears, looked at Kisel. At first, he cried silently, producing no sounds, but then his lament grew louder and louder, finally turning into sobs. Kot, Makei, and Kuzya felt pretty much the same. Together they had carried Kisel, but now there was nothing these strong big guys could do about it, so they just cried.

Kot looked up the mountain, his face dirty and wet with tears, saw something, got up, and rushed away.

On the right, at the foot of the mountain, three injured Sofrins were walking very slowly, helping each other. Now, as there was no one in the mountains, part of the insurgents followed them down. They got one of the soldiers and he fell down. The other two picked him up and dragged him away, hiding behind the hill.

The 3rd SWAT team was distracting insurgents from the others to cover up their retreat. Sieda gave long squirts up the mountain, almost nonstop. From time to time, however, the feed would go sideways, and then his machine gun would fall silent.

"Fire, Sieda! Fire!" Yegor would shout at once.

And Sieda would adjust the feed and resume fire.

Thanks to Sieda, the insurgents couldn't hold their heads up, let alone open precise fire. So, both Rosich and the 2nd team had a chance to retreat.

Yegor and his three soldiers were like a small-caliber artillery unit now, showering the shrubs with GP-25.

The insurgents realized the 3rd SWAT team was their major threat, so they focused their fire on them, a hail of tracers coming down on them and GP-25 grenades whizzing to explode nearby.

Kot ran up to his APC and looked inside. "Follow me!" he cried out to the direction layer and the guy rushed after him.

Frants had just crossed the river and was approaching Bamut suburbs when he heard Kot's message over the radio: "It's Kot! Cover me!"

Frants stopped short and turned around, facing the mountain. He hid at the fence and, holding up the machine gun at his shoulder, aimed up the mountain and pressed the trigger. However, he found out his barrel was too dirty and too hot to shoot, so the PK just spit out air.

"Damn it!" Frants swore, disappointed.

Realizing there was nothing he could do to help, he took his PK and the feed case and headed for the settlement, dragging his feet slowly. He was exhausted — both mentally and physically.

Down the street, Frants noticed APCs of the 8th SWAT Detachment and infantry soldiers. He was more than shocked as, approaching, he saw soldiers on the APCs smoking leisurely and watching Vityaz fighting. Some were playing cards.

Frants was too exhausted to yell at the spectators. So he just came up to one of the APCs, put the PK and the feed case down, his eye catching an interesting detail. He bent over, picking up the case, and saw it was perforated all over with bullet holes. It was an unexpected surprise — for all this time, the case had been standing at his head, only a little above.

Artur and Nenashev threw themselves down behind a small hill. Looking back at the settlement, Artur saw the same picture Frants observed — the APCs and the 8th Detachment, and the soldiers sitting leisurely on the armour and watching the battle.

"Alexander Ivanovich!" Artur turned around to Nenashev. "Is it like we're the only soldiers here? No other troops around? Or, maybe, it's just a performance here and we're the fucking stars of the show!"

"A good joke," Nenashev praised him, unaffected by the irony. "Funny." Then he glanced back and asked, "Who's the first to run?"

"You go," Artur offered. "I'll cover you." And, raising himself above the hill, he gave a squirt up the mountain while Nenashev darted off running towards the settlement. However, this time the insurgents were faster than usual with shooting, and soon Artur had to duck down. A bullet, passing some inches from his scalp, knocked the cap from his head.

"Damn it!" Artur cursed. "It was a cool cap!"

This was the very cap he took as a trophy at the nightclub. Artur got up and sprinted off after Nenashev. On his way back, he had to cross a small wastewater ditch. At first, Artur wanted to jump over it at once without slowing down. But right when he was about to jump, he tripped over something, plummeting straight into the liquid shit, his head going under the water completely. As he emerged out of the water, spitting out the dirt, he got out of the ditch and headed toward the vehicles, angry and irritated with all the firing and the jumping. Just then, Chef appeared running toward him, motioning to the mountains.

"Kot is over there!" he explained. "Getting the Sofins out!"

"Will it end today at all? No!" Artur growled with anger and turned around, showing the direction to his soldiers. "Everyone," he shouted, "work this way!"

The soldiers scattered, hid, and opened fire.

The injured Sofrins were still behind the same small hill. Kot, accompanied by one more soldier, ran up to them and took out his first aid kit quickly to find promedol tubes. One of the tubes he gave to his improvised assistant, while the other two he used for the most seriously injured soldier. Then he picked the soldier up, placing him on his back, and rushed toward the settlement. The rest of the injured were able to walk on their own. As soon as they left their hideout behind the hill, fire grew still denser. The injured soldier Kot was carrying on his back got four bullets more — all in the same injured leg. Two more bullets hit another Sofrin soldier, while Vityaz soldiers remained intact, not even a scratch on their body!

One of the APCs managed to cross the river somehow and was now approaching the 3rd team. As it reached the team, they got onto its armour. Yegor, his face stern and sullen, walked up to the APC slowly and took its commander's place. Picking up his machine gun by the barrel, he threw it down with anger, onto the seat next to the driver.

"Get it the hell out of here!" the commander growled.

Then he seated himself on the armour and the APC started off. Yegor, enraged, was not even paying attention to what was going on around him, the way bullets were whizzing past him, bouncing off the armour. Suddenly, he felt a sting of pain and raised his palm up to his eyes to see a burn he got from holding the hot barrel of his machine gun. Looking back, he saw young soldiers cringing and shivering with fear.

Yeah, sons of a bitch, you're scared to death, I bet! Yegor thought to himself with an anger he couldn't explain. *Brats!*

It was not like Yegor at all. Later, talking about the battle, he couldn't say what all that anger was about.

Two APCs of the 8th Detachment approached the APC of the 2nd SWAT team, which was firing up the mountains. The first APC had an officer aboard.

"Stop!" the officer cried out to the driver.

The APCs stopped short, and the officer cried out through the hatch, "Fire!"

The APC tower turned around toward the mountain, fire bursting out of its machine guns with a deafening noise. A second later, the other APCs joined in.

Shooting, Artur noticed two APCs approaching the mountain.

"Who the hell are they?" Artur asked, addressing his question to no one in particular.

"I'll find out now!" Talanych, who was lying next to him, cried out and sprang to his feet, heading back for the mountain.

Chef was shooting with APC machine guns, while Kot got an injured Sofrin soldier inside the APC and ran away. Chef seated himself next to the injured man and took a belt to strap his wounded leg.

At the moment, an infantry soldier with an RPG-7 ran up to the APC and stripped for shooting right in front of the hatch, pointing the RPG-7 tube straight at Chef. Turning around, Chef found himself facing a grenade launcher tube and had to duck to the side.

A shot — and Chef, wincing, covered his ears with his hands and closed his eyes. As he opened his eyes, he saw the soldier reloading the RPG and aiming its tube right at where Chef was seated. Chef had to duck to the side again.

And then the soldier fired another shot.

"Mother fucker!" Chef cried out, enraged, and jumped out from behind the APC, hitting the grenadier on his helmet. "What the hell are you doing, sucker?" Chef was yelling at the muddle-headed grenadier. "You want to kill me or what? Huh? Get the hell outta here!"[11]

As he finally got rid of the stupid soldier, he went back to tend to the wound.

Panting, Talanych ran up to the APCs, the soldiers bustling about, looking up the mountain. "Why are you here?" Talanych asked them.

"Our injured people are here!"

Those were evidently the Rosich APCs that had finally made it to the mountain.

"We've got them out already!" Talanych explained.

The soldiers of the 7th SWAT team exchanged confused glances. "So where do we go?" a Roshich soldier, finally, asked Talanych.

"This way!" and Talanych showed them the direction.

"Thank you, brother!" Roshich said. Then the soldiers got on their APCs and left, while Talanych ran some distance away to hide behind the nearest hill. He had to cross the river now.

"Crap!" Talanych said as he turned around, watching the APCs leave. "I should have asked them to give me a ride." And then he sprang to his feet and headed across the river.

The detachment was almost entirely back in the starting area when Yegor's APC arrived. Jumping down, he turned to Naum at once. "Now, Andrey, you eat, load up with ammunition, and wait for orders. We're leaving back soon."

He hurried away, while Naum began instructing soldiers, "Get the bullets off the armour!"

Two soldiers rushed to the APC to take down bullet cases from the APC boards, while Naum turned to the driver, who, standing up atop the APC, was checking the power unit.

"Hey, you, driver! Get your ration out!"

The driver opened the case with SPG-9 (mounted grenade launcher) shells located on the APC and took a can out of it.

An APC with Chef seated on its armour drove up, full speed, to the takeoff ground where a helicopter was waiting. Chef jumped down and opened the hatch to take out an injured soldier. One of the doctors rushed to the APC. Having had a quick examination of the injured man, he took out a promedol tube. And before Chef could say something, he did an injection and ran away to tend to the other injured soldiers. A few seconds later, aidmen with a stretcher ran up to them and tried to lay the injured Sofrin onto it. However, the Sofrin just pushed them away, and rising to his feet, set off on his own, paying no attention to the leg that was wounded in several places. Hardly had he walked some five metres when he fell down, his leg failing him. Another doctor who was close enough to see the whole show came up to them, suspecting there was something wrong with the soldier.

"How much promedol have you injected?" he asked Chef.

"Two doses — me, and one more — the doctor," Chef answered. "Not sure about before."

"Are you out of your mind?" the doctor exclaimed, taken aback.

"Well," Chef shrugged his shoulder. "It just happened somehow."

Finally, they managed to lay the injured soldier down onto the stretcher, then loaded him into the helicopter and the helicopter took off, almost at once.

Yegor approached a group of officers, two of them being their relief.

"Our relief is here, Yegor," Kremen informed him.

Yegor nodded and hugged each one of the officers.

"Commander," Yegor heard Naum's voice and saw him approaching. "Look here."

He showed him a zinc case with bullets he had taken from a box on one of the APC boards and a can with meat from the box atop the APC. Both the zinc case and the can were all perforated and now looked more like a sieve.

"Have no idea how we got away with it," Naum shrugged his shoulders, bewildered.

"Sort bullets," Yegor hurried to give his orders, "eat the good rations and get rid of the bad ones."

Naum nodded and left.

"Let's go see the Seven," Yegor offered and they all headed for the camp of the 7th Detachment.

Vityaz soldiers were walking slowly to where the 7th Detachment was located. They knew Rosich was now mourning its soldiers. The air was thick with despair and sorrow. Some of Rosich soldiers were crying. As they approached, they saw a group of officers at an improvised table — a box with vodka, snacks, and mineral water on it. Not far away, a soldier was opening canned meat, his cheeks wet with tears.

"Here, let's drink to the guys!" one of the Rosich officers offered.

Yegor squatted near the box and filled his cup with mineral water; the rest chose vodka.

As Commander-in-Chief Romanov and detachment commanders emerged out of the headquarters tent, Nenashev was immediately surrounded by his officers.

"That's it," Nenashev informed everyone. "We're not going anywhere. Romanov has talked to Basayev and they've made a deal to exchange killed soldiers. The exchange is tomorrow."

The 3rd SWAT team was sitting on the APC and around it, ready to leave.

"Check and clean your weapons, everyone," Yegor announced, approaching his team. "Have a rest once you finish. That's it."

Yegor came up to the APC, taking off his vest. The soldiers began taking off the ammunition as well, slowly, in no hurry.

Talanych, seated on a small log, was cleaning his machine gun on a ground sheet, stripped.

"Here he is," he heard Artur exclaim, and he looked up.

Artur and Yegor were standing nearby, staring at him. Talanych sprang up to his feet. Yegor made a step forward and held out his hand to Talanych. Talanych, quite perplexed by the situation, shook hands with Yegor.

"Good job, brother," Yegor said, patting him on his shoulder with his other hand.

For a young soldier, it was like a state award to hear an experienced colleague praise him.

It was getting dark. Soldiers, their faces stern and sullen, holding cups in their hands, were standing around improvised tables set up outside. No one spoke a word, their minds returning to the battle. Keeping silent, they drank without clinking their glasses and, just as silently, ate the snacks. They hadn't eaten the whole day and, as tension was easing, they felt hunger.

Artur, wrapped up in his thoughts, the cup with vodka still in his hands, turned to Nenashev, "Alexander Ivanovich. We should give Kot his crimson beret back."

Nenashev nodded in agreement. "No problem, Artur. We can do it tomorrow."

"And one more thing. I'd prepare an application to award him and Kisel as the Heroes of Russia."

Nenashev sighed and looked at Artur. "Well, we can apply, Artur. But …" and he shook his head, wincing as though he just ate a lemon, "you know better than me what stinkers those responsible for the awards are. They've never heard a bullet whizzing. And what Kot has in his personal file are punishments only. So," Nenashev sighed again and shrugged his shoulders, "I'd be glad if we could do it for Kisel, at least."

Artur was perfectly aware of the things Nenashev was talking about, so he just sighed in response, drinking the vodka from his cup, one shot.

As the commemoration was over, Yegor felt like getting away from people. Walking, he came up to a tree and threw a powerful kick, hitting it with anger. The kick, like a catalyst, released all he had kept buried deep inside; his feelings, all the tension of the battle, the deaths, and, moreover, the wild anger and his own help-lessness found a way out in tears. Yegor sank onto the ground, cry-ing his heart out.

---

1. ACV: an airborne combat vehicle

2. Combat support group

3. Two-zero-zero — killed; three-zero-zero — injured

4. Later it was reported that there were over six hundred insurgents at the mountain.

5. This is what Nenashev was trying to explain to the inspector at the shooting range.

6. Promedol is an opiate class anesthetic. It's included in a soldier's individual medical kit.

7. Promedol plastic tubes are sealed. So, before the drug could be used, one needed to twist the cap with the injector down into the tube. The needle on the inside of the cap perforates the tube, and the anesthetic is then injected into the needle. That's why all the tubes are not tightened up originally.

8. The operation began early in the morning, but the fighting was intermittent. It was almost evening as they were talking and, in the Caucasus, it gets dark early and really fast.

9. Back in 1991, one of Vityaz teams encircled Basayev's gang in the mountains, ready to eliminate it completely. The detachment's commander requested permission to open fire from the seniors, but they responded, "Let them go!" But for the political games, Vityaz might have been spared many casualties and terrorist acts!

10. There were indeed two similar instances during that battle.

11. According to RPG-7 safe shooting rules: "no people can be allowed within the 90° range and closer than 20–30 metres to the RPG-7 while loading, shooting and discharging … the distance between the rear face of the tube and the wall of the trench or any other shelter whatsoever must be, at least, 1–2 metres." The grenadier actually violated this rule in a totally unacceptable way. If Chef hadn't noticed him, he would probably be dead by now. And once again — it's about the Hans and their lack of professionalism.

CHAPTER 34

Next day, truce was declared, and some Rosich soldiers and officers were sent to Lysaya Mountain to get their dead brothers out of there. They went without weapons.

When the insurgents brought them to the killed SWAT soldiers, they said something like this: "These are real warriors. It's been an honor to fight against them. And those are totally different," and they pointed at a killed infantry soldier, dead but still squeezing a chicken in his hand.

"This one," and they pointed at one of the killed officers (Tsyma), "was still alive as we came. And he took down three more of our soldiers before we shot him."

All the corpses of the SWAT soldiers, unlike those of infantry ones, remained intact. Insurgents didn't take off their clothes and left their bodies untouched. It's one more example to illustrate how even enemies respected the SWATs.

However, as they say, it's totally another story. The 7th Detachment Rosich deserves a separate book.

When I was in my fifth year of military school, I considered two options only — both Internal Troops' Special Detachments, i.e., Vityaz and Rosich. Naturally, I'm happy I chose Vityaz (the originator and the basis of the entire Special Forces). However, even now, the 7th Detachment is of special importance to me. All the more, I have friends there.

Next morning, Yegor was leaving for Moscow on a plane. He had some spare time before the flight, so he decided to visit the Sevens. As he entered Rosich's dugout, he saw only an orderly there.

The orderly stood up at once to greet him. "Good morning, comrade lieutenant!" The soldier recognized Yegor at once.

"Good morning, brother."

And they gave each other a tight brotherly hug.

"Would you like some tea, maybe?" the soldier offered.

"No, thank you, brother."

As the soldier was a little off his head because of what had happened with his fellows, he didn't even hear what Yegor said and went to bring him some tea. Meantime, Yegor took off his beret and came up to the beds of the dead Rosich soldiers. The beds were carefully done with clean linen, crimson berets against the background of the snow-white pillows reminding him of all the blood the soldiers spilled.

Kneeling on one leg at Tsyma's bed, Yegor set his forehead against the cold metal of the bed arch. "Tsyma," Yegor spoke up in a low voice. "Forgive me, please. I'm so sorry I didn't manage to get you out of there." A tear appeared in the corner of his eye and dropped to the floor. Yegor's shoulders shook with sobs.

Yegor thought he had betrayed the SWAT principles. So, on coming back to Moscow, he was going to quit the Special Forces and never put on a crimson beret again.

Yegor got up and, heaving a sigh, wiped tears off his eyes. Then he came up to the soldier and, patting him on the shoulder, said, "Be strong, brother!"

Then he headed for the exit, putting on his beret as he went.

During the truce period, Vityaz soldiers met with the Chechens who lived in Bamut. And the people asked if they were the soldiers who participated in the battle at their settlement.

"Yes, we are," the SWAT soldiers confirmed.

"So how many people have you lost?" followed their next question.

"One killed, two injured."

The Chechens couldn't believe it. "On the following day," they told the SWAT soldiers, shocked, "insurgents loaded three trucks with their corpses from the mountains!"

And once again — this is the professionalism we've talked about.

CHAPTER 35

Kira, one shoulder against the wall, was staring wistfully through the dark window. Suddenly, her body jerked, and she, recovering her senses, leaned forward to the window and then sprinted off to the door.

The lift opened its doors, letting Yegor out.

He made a step, freezing in place. The door to Kira's apartment was wide open, and she was standing on the landing. For a few seconds, they just stared at each other without speaking a word. At the moment, words seemed odd, as all the conversation was through their eyes. Then Kira made a step toward Yegor and put her arms around his neck, drawing her body closer to his.

Yegor closed his eyes and embraced Kira, both gently and tightly, burying his face in her hair. He made a deep breath, feeling its sweet scent. Kira stepped back, giving him a hungry look, as if her eyes couldn't believe they were looking at him. But yes, it was him; her darling, her love. His skin had grown darker under the Caucasus sun, he'd lost some weight, and had a two-day bristle. As her eyes satiated their thirst for the loved image, she pressed her lips to his for a couple of seconds — just a hasty, quick touch. Memory was slowly coming back to her: first, her eyes, then her lips, and, finally, her hands. So she traced his face with her fingers, her eyes still on him, gleaming with tears. At last, she gripped his hand with decision, leading him inside, the door thumping softly as it closed after them.

Yegor was, indeed, grateful to the detachment's commander who supported him in those difficult times and talked him out of quitting the SWAT. He was like an older brother and a father to him; he gave him strength to carry on and confidence to believe in himself. Also, Yegor was grateful to his wife, who'd gone through all the troubles of that difficult period, holding him by his hand. Indeed, she was a true war bride. This is how Yegor survived through it all, regaining his powers to serve the motherland and the SWAT!

I'd like to express my special admiration of officers' wives. They follow their husbands all over the country, always on the move, living in barracks and miserable hostels, waiting for their husbands to return alive from the war and spending days and nights beside their beds in hospitals. To be an officer's wife and, all the more, a wife of a SWAT officer, is a special responsibility you bear with dignity — and for all of this, I'm so grateful to you.

By the way, the slogan, "Who else but us?" of the Internal Troops' Special Forces is an invention of an officer's wife. At one festive event, as the wife of Vityaz commander was making a speech, a journalist approached her, asking for an interview. During the interview, he asked, "What is your attitude to what your husband does for his job?"

And she responded, "And what can I do about it? Besides, they keep saying, who else is going to do that but them." This is how the officer's wife rendered unconsciously the very essence of what we do in these few words.

CHAPTER 36

Just as Nenashev and Artur expected, Kisel's feats were not enough to get him the title of the Hero of Russia. The rejection had the following wording: "Sergeant Kiselev's courage is obvious, but heroism is another thing." He and Senior Lieutenant Rostigayev were awarded with Orders of Courage (postmortem).

Kot, just as reckless as ever, remained at war till December 1995, but didn't get any state awards.

Detachment's Logistics Deputy Lieutenant Colonel Artsybashev also was awarded an Order of Courage.

Sergey Sieden (otherwise known as Sieda), the machine gunner of the 3rd SWAT team, was killed on June 2, 1995, at Bezymiannaya High Ground.

Artur stayed with Vityaz till March 1999. Then he joined one of Moscow's SOBRs (Special Designation Units of the Ministry of Internal Affairs) and was soon appointed its commander. Together, we survived through the Second Chechen War. After the SOBR, he got a position at the Ministry of Internal Affairs. I have no idea what his position was, exactly, but he was in charge of all of Russia's SWAT units of the Ministry of Internal Affairs. In June 2006, he graduated from the Management Academy and was appointed to a general-level position. However, he never got to become one. In July 2006, he was killed in a car crash.

Yegor stayed with Vityaz till 1997 and then left it for Alpha, which had been his dream. Yegor is a person whose vocation is to serve the motherland. For him, such words as motherland, duty, and "serving the motherland" are of special meaning and value. One can serve the motherland in many different ways, but his way to serve it is in battle.

I remember it clearly how he told me once, "The 3rd team I was fighting with at Lysaya Mountain was no worse than Alpha, even better in some respects."

Yegor, the legend that he was in Vityaz, became one in Alpha, too. He was one of those who were the first to enter Dubrovka Theatrical Center (Nord-Ost), seized by terrorists via its basement. Together with his unit, he fired gas from there. Later, he also participated in the assault of the center proper. Back then, some Alpha and Vympel officers were awarded titles of the Heroes of Russia (and quite deservedly!), whereas Yegor wasn't even included in the application list for the award, though he undoubtedly deserved it no less than those guys.

For the children rescued in Beslan School in 2003, however, for the professionalism and the heroism Yegor evidenced there with his actions, Yegor was included in the award application. Unfortunately, he did never see the Hero star because of all the dirty political games.

It's not only me, but everyone Yegor knows who believes him to have deserved the honor of being a Hero. At the same time, Egor deserved the recognition of the US "green berets". American Special Forces veterans rewarded him with the Purple Heart Medal!

Besides the mentioned tragic events known worldwide, Yegor has been to many hot spots, but he always avoided talking about them. All of the things I included in this book I heard from other people. Yegor is the right kind of person a Hero should be — very decent and very modest. So, writing about how awards always evaded him was purely my initiative. When I gave him my book for editing before it was published, I excluded this chapter on purpose because I knew he would disapprove.

Over the period Yegor was the commander, his team lost not a person. A lot of his subordinates were thankful to him for staying alive. He was always ahead of others, and his wounds, one of them really serious, are evidence to it.

In 2010, having reached the rank of colonel, Yegor quit Alpha for the Federation Council (though he really wanted to stay with his unit!).

"The ones who save their Land they get to be immortal."

September 2012

Crimson Beret
Code of Honour

1. *A crimson beret is the major symbol of the SWATs, who are always at the cutting edge of the Internal Troops.*

   It can be awarded while serving in special designation units and sections based on the results of a professional exam giving the right to wear the beret or for courage and valour in mortal combats.

2. *A crimson beret entails hard work with deep acknowledgement of what it means to serve the motherland, always on the up-front, fighting terror.*

3. *A crimson beret is simultaneously the highest honour and exceptional responsibility of being part of the elite military forces and intelligence agencies, entailing rights to be the leading forces in fighting an enemy.*

4. *A crimson beret is the pride and valour of the SWATs. So, never let oneself or others throw this away!*

5. *A crimson beret is to serve as an example of how one should be loyal to their ideals and celebrate the glory of their predecessors, cherishing military traditions and the combat brotherhood of the Special Forces.*

6. *A crimson beret means professionalism, initiative, and commitment in executing assignments. Remember — there's no one who can do it better than you!*

7. *A crimson beret means strict discipline — and self-discipline, in the first turn. It's an endless struggle against all the shortcomings that might prevent one from reaching the heights of battle mastery. If you can't fight your bad habits then you don't stand a chance against your enemy!*

8. *A crimson beret is strong friendship and fellowship. To help people out of trouble is the ultimate duty of a warrior. To help your fellow is the rule of conscience and honor — either die or save your fellow.*

9. *A crimson beret is respect for your older fellows. They've lived longer than you and have seen more things. Dealing with your younger colleagues, be patient and gracious because you've lived longer and seen more.*

10. *A crimson beret is to be an example of decency and modesty beyond the military community. Remember! By the way you behave, people will judge all of your fellows!*

11. *A crimson beret is of the colour of blood, the blood spilled by your fallen fellows who sacrificed their lives to save others. It's a memory of all those who never came back from the war, who died in battles and special missions.*

12. *A crimson beret must stop short any attempts to mire the memory of the dead and the reputation of their living fellows! Putting on a crimson beret, one should wear it with honour and dignity, obeying the Code of Honour.*

Crimson beret is the fate one cannot escape!

Review Requested:
If you loved this book, would you please provide a review at Amazon.com?